WHEN EGYPT RULED THE EAST

D0878958

FIG. 1.—STATUE OF THUTMOSE III (CAIRO MUSEUM)

WHEN EGYPT RULED THE EAST

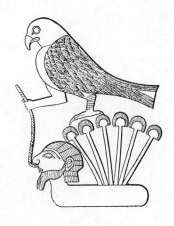

GEORGE STEINDORFF *and* KEITH C. SEELE

Revised by

KEITH C. SEELE

THE UNIVERSITY OF CHICAGO PRESS

CHICAGO & LONDON

To the memory of

JAMES H. BREASTED

and

KURT SETHE

THE UNIVERSITY OF CHICAGO PRESS, CHICAGO 60637

The University of Chicago Press, Ltd., London

Copyright 1942, 1957 by The University of Chicago. All rights reserved. Published 1942. Second Edition 1957 Printed in the United States of America

ISBN: 0-226-77198-9 (clothbound); 0-226-77199-7 (paperbound)

Library of Congress Catalog Card Number: 57-5276
80 79   12 11 10 9

PREFACE TO THE SECOND EDITION

FIFTEEN years are a brief moment in the history of Egypt, but this last "moment" has been filled with significant events in Egypt's modern political life as well as in the archeological investigation of the Nile Valley. There has been a vast amount of excavation and exploration during this time, and many new monuments have come to light. To offset these gains, unfortunately, hundreds, perhaps thousands, of Egyptian antiquities in European museums were destroyed in the recent war. In addition, vandalism has taken a heavy toll from the monuments still *in situ*. And now, as a sort of ironic climax, water conservation in the form of a new high dam at Assuan may soon result in the destruction of all Egyptian antiquities, discovered and undiscovered, between the first and third cataracts of the Nile.

While not all the recent discoveries in Egypt have direct bearing on the period covered by this book, many of the advances in Egyptological knowledge do. No book on ancient Egypt can long stand uncorrected, for the surface of Egypt's soil has even now scarcely been scratched, and the interpretation of known remains is not far past the beginning. Thus, after a decade and a half, this volume, which has enjoyed such wide appeal, most recently in an Arabic translation for Egyptian readers, requires extensive revision and considerable rewriting.

The senior author of *When Egypt Ruled the East* would have been eager to make his own contributions to this new edition. There is no topic introduced in its pages which ceased to hold his keenest interest up to the last day of his long and fruitful life—August 28, 1951, a few weeks before his ninetieth birthday. This great editor, scholar, teacher, and personality is gone; it devolves upon his younger colleague and friend to perform the task alone. He can only hope that his touch of the master's mantle will have enabled him to catch something of his spirit, so that the new may breathe a portion of the charm and genius of the old.

KEITH C. SEELE

CHICAGO, ILLINOIS

PREFACE

A FULL generation has passed since the late James Henry Breasted published his *History of Egypt*. It was the first work of the kind based on an adequate consideration of all the available Egyptian sources. That fact itself, combined with the author's brilliant literary style, made his book a standard in the field; and it not only has held its place at the top in the English language but has been translated into various others as well. Classic though it has become, Egyptologists have nevertheless long recognized the need for a new discussion of ancient Egypt in which consideration would be given to the enormous body of new material which has come to light in the last thirty-five years.

More propitious circumstances would justify a much more exhaustive treatment of the additional knowledge with which a generation of archeological research has rewarded us. At the present time, however, such an ambitious project is out of the question. Even by confining ourselves to a discussion of that golden age of empire when Egypt ruled the East, there is still far too much which we are obliged to leave untold. Perhaps, nevertheless, the present work, with its emphasis upon the greatest period of Egypt's history, will fill at least one conspicuous gap in the literature and supply the student and general reader with a handbook both useful and stimulating to further investigation.

The authors have numerous obligations to acknowledge. Our illustrations have been drawn from various sources, all of which are indicated in the List of Illustrations. We desire, however, to express our special appreciation to Mr. Ambrose Lansing, of the Metropolitan Museum of Art in New York, for permission to publish the photographs reproduced in Figures 9, 13, 33, 47, 69–71, and 95, and to reproduce from plates in several Metropolitan Museum publications the material in Figures 56, 59, and 61; to M. Gustave Jéquier for Figures 15, 19, 41, 42, 44, 45, 54, 100, and 104; to the Trustees of the British Museum for Figures 2, 20, and 25; to the Egypt Exploration Society for Figure 64 and the upper portion of Figure 76; to Dr. Alan H. Gardiner for Figures 12, 35, 39, 50–52, 55, 60, 62, 66, 67, 78, 107, and 108; to Professor John A. Wilson for permission to publish a number of photographs from the files and several of the objects from the collections of the Oriental Institute of the University of Chicago in Figures 23, 101, and 102 and in Figures 17, 36, 77, and 85, respectively; and to the Macmillan Company in New York for permission to adapt to the purpose of this book Map I in Volume II of the *Cambridge Ancient History*. To Professor Wilson, likewise, and to Dr. George R. Hughes, for reading the entire manuscript, and to Drs. Thorkild Jacobsen and A. J. Sachs, for reading portions of it, we wish to express our sincere thanks. Their counsel and criticism have been of great benefit to us, but we alone, or, in a few instances, only the one or the other of us, are responsible for the statements presented in the following pages.

GEORGE STEINDORFF
KEITH C. SEELE

LOS ANGELES AND CHICAGO

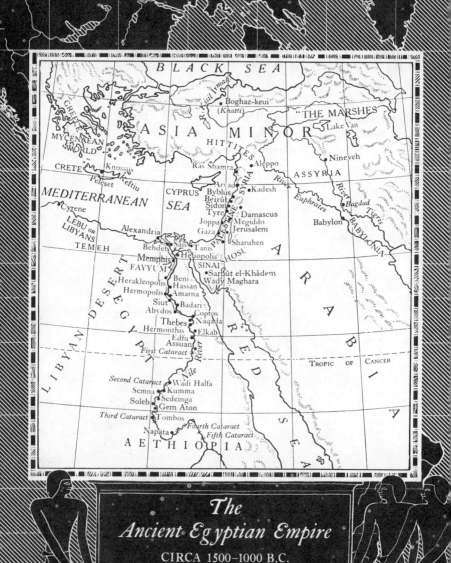

The
Ancient Egyptian Empire
CIRCA 1500–1000 B.C.

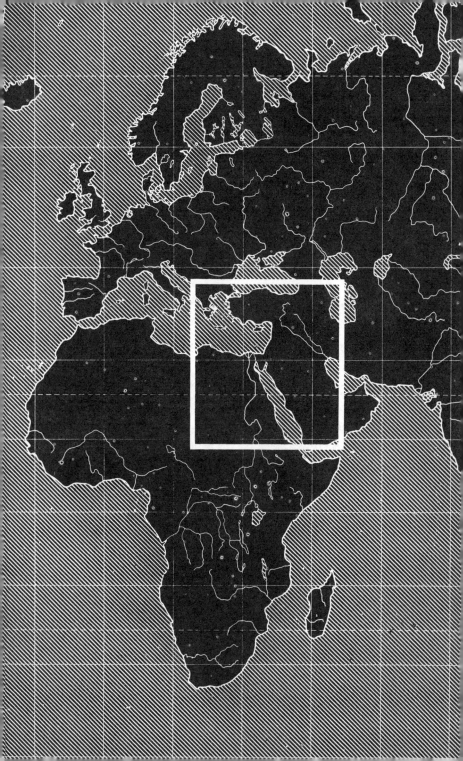

TABLE OF CONTENTS

LIST OF ILLUSTRATIONS

I

HOW THE LOST KEY TO ANCIENT EGYPT
WAS FOUND AGAIN

ON MAY 19, 1798, a French fleet under the command of the young general Napoleon Bonaparte sailed from Toulon in order to challenge the power of England in Egypt. He hoped by the conquest of the Nile to construct a French stronghold in the East from which to threaten British power and wealth in India. While the Nile Valley soon fell into French hands, confused political circumstances at home forced Napoleon to return during the following year, and the possession of Egypt had to be forfeited in 1801.

Though the military conquest of Egypt had failed, yet Napoleon's expedition had a different and an infinitely more significant result. It unlocked to science the door to Egypt's past. For the French fleet had borne from Toulon not only an army of soldiers; an extensive staff of scholars and artists were collected on its decks as well. To this day we stand in awe before the enormous folios and numerous other volumes of materials which they collected during the short life of Bonaparte's campaign. Unending industry had resulted likewise in the garnering of a rich harvest of ancient monuments. Under the terms of the capitulation, most of these were forfeited to the British by General Menou at the surrender of Alexandria. They became the foundation for the magnificent collection of Egyptian antiquities in the British Museum.

In one swift gesture was drawn aside the nebulous veil which had so securely enveloped old Egypt and behind which both the investigators of ancient Greece and the doting writers of modern times had conjured up such a superfluity of profoundest mystery. The educated world was astonished at the magnificent monuments of the land and the primeval culture now first revealed. It was not long until the final barrier was leveled which had prevented an unhindered vista over the long history of Egypt. This came about as the result of a find (Fig. 2) so unusual and significant that the fortunate discoverer immediately ordered an impres-

sion of the inscriptions to be made and forwarded to the Egyptian Institute, which Napoleon had already established in Cairo. The French

FIG. 2.—THE ROSETTA STONE (BRITISH MUSEUM)

savants had no difficulty in reading the Greek text at the bottom of the
stone. It was found to be a decree in honor of the pharaoh Ptolemy V
Epiphanes (205–180 B.C.) composed in the year 196 by an assembly of

Egyptian priests at Memphis. It described numerous benefactions by which the pharaoh had enriched the temples of Egypt, and it extended various honors to the king in return for his generosity. Finally, in order to perpetuate the priestly decree for all time, it was ordered to be engraved on a tablet "in the sacred writing [hieroglyphic], in the native script [demotic], and in Greek letters."

This threefold version of the decree on the Rosetta stone reflected the heterogeneous character of the Egyptian population of the age. Ever since the seventh century B.C., but especially since the conquest of Egypt by Alexander the Great (332 B.C.), numerous Greeks had migrated to and settled in the land, along with the court and the ruling class. It was for this element that the decree was promulgated in the Greek tongue. The native Egyptians were served by two different versions. The "sacred writing" (hieroglyphic) was the time-honored picture script which had been in use for thousands of years but which was understood at this time by the priests alone; the "popular script" (demotic), on the other hand, was universally employed in official and commercial intercourse and in documents and letters. It roughly corresponded to the contemporary spoken language and was familiar to the educated classes, if not to the illiterate masses.

One significant and outstanding fact was unmistakably revealed by the Greek inscription on the "trilingual" Rosetta stone. It was perfectly evident to any intelligent reader that the section at the top composed in the ancient picture symbols, the middle section written in "native" or more accurately in cursive script, and the Greek text at the bottom must include precisely the same content. Thus for the first time the means had come to light by which an Egyptian inscription might be deciphered and the mystery of the hieroglyphic writing might be penetrated.

The key to the understanding of the Egyptian picture script had been lost since the days of imperial Rome. It was evident from the numerous monuments which had been brought to Italy and especially to Rome that this script was composed of a multitude of pictures of concrete objects, but how the signs were to be read was an open question. As a result they had come to be construed as symbols with a definite concept for each character. Such an attack was certain to lead to the most ridiculous results. Thus, for example, the famous Jesuit scholar Athanasius Kircher (1601–80) interpreted the group of signs which represent the Roman imperial title "autocrator" in the following manner: "The creator of fertility and of all vegetation is Osiris, whose engendering power the holy Mophta draws from heaven into his empire."

Under such circumstances what a shock was delivered to the scientific world by the discovery of the Rosetta stone! In 1802 the noted French orientalist Silvestre de Sacy published a pamphlet dealing with the central—the demotic—section of the monument, with an attempt to elucidate the Greek personal names of Ptolemy, Berenike, and Arsinoë which it contains. Basing his efforts on De Sacy's results, a Swedish scholar named Akerblad carried on the work of decipherment so effectively that in the same year he was able to publish a complete alphabet of its cursive Egyptian characters.

No such speedy success attended the efforts of students of the hieroglyphic picture-writing of the trilingual monument. That was destined to come only some twenty years later to reward the ingenuity of the young French scholar Jean François Champollion, who was born in 1790 in southern France. After the English physicist Thomas Young had advanced via the name of the pharaoh Ptolemy to the recognition of numerous Egyptian characters, Champollion independently arrived at the realization of the existence of an Egyptian alphabet. It is not possible to relate here in full detail the devious ways and false leads which Champollion tortuously followed during the decade preceding that fourteenth of September in 1822 when he reached the goal and was able in an ecstasy of joy to announce the triumph of his genius: "Je tiens l'affaire!" A few days later the task was completed. On September 27 he laid before the first scholars of France the results of his long years of labor in an essay in which by a methodical scientific demonstration he proved that the hieroglyphic system of writing consisted fundamentally of alphabetic and other phonetic signs. These had been employed not only to write out the Greco-Roman personal names foreign to the Egyptian language but also to render such purely native proper names as those of the pharaohs Thutmose and Ramesses. Once on this solid ground, Champollion advanced rapidly. In the very next year he published an outline of the Egyptian hieroglyphic system. By 1832, when an untimely death cut short his brilliant career, he had not only succeeded in reading and translating numerous Egyptian texts, some of considerable difficulty, but he bequeathed to posterity a complete Egyptian grammar and a substantial dictionary as well.

The science of Egyptology has at the present time advanced to such a level that it is no longer necessary by a series of more or less inspired guesses to arrive at the approximate meaning of an inscription. The scholar is now able to undertake the interpretation of an Egyptian text much as one of his colleagues would attempt the translation of a passage of Hebrew or Arabic or the reading of a Greek or Latin document.

The successes of the French expedition provided stimulus for a more or less systematic exploitation of ancient Egyptian cemeteries, city mounds, and temple ruins in a series of campaigns which continued throughout the remainder of the nineteenth century and on to our own time. Egyptian museums were founded for the preservation of the finds, and the collections were extensively augmented from time to time by important purchases. Thus in the course of a hundred years collections of scientific materials in the form of inscribed monuments, manuscripts, and works of art grew to enormous proportions and afforded a steadily widening field of investigation. In consequence we are today in a position to survey the history and civilization of the Nile Valley from the fourth millennium before Christ to the seventh century of our era—the period of the Arab conquest—a cultural development spanning nearly five thousand years in an unbroken continuity not elsewhere similarly traceable on this planet. We are able to follow the exploits of a long succession of kings in war and peace. The highly developed constitution of the Egyptian empire and the exemplary political economy of the Greco-Roman period at least have been unfolded to our vision. We have reached an understanding of the religion of the people, of the manifold conceptions which they entertained concerning the life after death, and of the forms of worship which they practiced toward their gods. We have become acquainted with their manners and customs, the pastimes of the wealthy, and the daily life of the rank and file in town and country. Above all, we have acquired familiarity with Egyptian art and technical crafts—the noblest legacy of all—and gained access to a unique world of beauty.

However numerous the surviving Egyptian monuments of stone or the literary works and other records on papyrus, leather, stone, or wood, however enlightening for certain periods of Egyptian history we may find

Bible stories, the reports of the Greeks, or cuneiform documents of the Babylonians, Assyrians, and Hittites—this treasury of material is still insufficient to yield a consistently illuminated picture of ancient Egyptian times and events. Sometimes the stream of tradition flows on and on like a mighty torrent; at others it has shrunk to a mere trickle; on occasions, fortunately very rare, the spring dries up altogether. Thus the intervals of Egyptian history which are well represented by surviving records tend to occupy the foreground of our attention, while those which wholly or partially lack such testimony are undeservedly slighted. For this reason it will be forever impossible to extend to the treatment of Egyptian history the same uniformity which may be applied, for example, to the classical peoples of Greece and Rome or to the peoples of Europe during the Middle Ages. There is, moreover, an additional obstacle to a clear picture. A great majority of the historical monuments were intended as official propaganda with the purpose of transmitting to posterity a "correct" impression of the glory and power of the pharaohs. Crises of revolution and that type of inner strife so common in the Orient, as well as military defeats in foreign wars, were either passed over completely or were interpreted so that the monuments conveyed impressions much distorted and unduly colored to the credit of the Egyptians. In the same manner, darkness must forever continue to "black out" the characters and personalities of most of the heroes of Egyptian history; contemporary chronicles and memoirs concerning them simply do not exist. In compensation for this serious lack of historical data is a vast body of material in the realm of art and culture which embraces practically every branch of material and intellectual existence to a degree scarcely surpassed elsewhere in the world in extent or variety. In consequence, any attempt to portray the history of Egypt in whole or in part must place its emphasis on Egyptian art and culture.

Like the other peoples of antiquity, the Egyptians possessed no fixed system of reckoning time. The events which they desired to record chronologically were associated with certain regnal years of the pharaohs. In the earliest period these were not counted, but, as in ancient Babylonia, they were named for outstanding events which had occurred in them. For example, one year was designated as "the year of fighting and smiting the northerners"; another became perpetuated as "the year of the second enumeration of all large and small cattle of the north and the south." This inconvenient method was gradually superseded by the simpler one of reckoning according to the regnal year, so that an event became dated, for example, to "the fifteenth year of Senwosret [Sesostris] III." Eventually, in order to determine precisely when certain events had taken place, the priests compiled and caused to be recorded in the temples detailed lists of kings in which their names and either the designations or later the numbers of their regnal years were entered. It is quite probable that these archives are the basis both of the king lists carved on the walls of various temples and tombs and of the valuable tables preserved in the historical treatise written by the Egyptian priest Manetho (*ca.* 300 B.C.). In this work Manetho divided all the Egyptian rulers, from the earliest historical king Menes to Alexander the Great, into thirty dynasties, corresponding in general to the various royal houses which successively or even sometimes contemporaneously exercised the royal power. In spite of definite limitations, the convenience of Manetho's scheme has recommended its retention by modern scholars. Certain related dynasties naturally fall together into groups, and these in the course of time have acquired designations of their own. Thus the period covering the Third to the Sixth Dynasty constitutes the "Old Kingdom," that of the Seventh to the Eleventh is the "First Intermediate Period," the Twelfth Dynasty is known as the "Middle Kingdom," while the period of the Thirteenth to the Seventeenth Dynasty is now usually described as the "Second Intermediate Period," and the era of the Eighteenth to the Twentieth is known as the "New Kingdom."

"Egypt is the gift of the Nile." This epigram of Hecataeus, quoted first by Herodotus and frequently since, expresses with admirable brevity and appropriateness the character of the Egyptian country. In the vast almost waterless expanse of the desert plateau which occupies the entire northeast portion of the African continent, the river Nile, descending in two branches from the extensive lake region of equatorial Africa and from the snow-clad mountains of Abyssinia, has painfully through endless ages excavated out of the sandstone and limestone a deep valley the lower end of which—the land of Egypt—it has by its regular annual deposits of alluvium transformed into one of the most fruitful lands on earth. When at length a people settled in this valley in order to pasture its herds and to cultivate the soil, the Nile by strict necessity impelled it to civilization and culture. The abundant flow of water which rushed northward

each summer after the copious rainfall at the sources of both Nile
branches to inundate the land had to be systematically and regularly
conducted over the fields. It was necessary to construct dams and dikes
and to provide canals and sluices. Swamps had to be drained and converted into meadows. Such operations, however, could not possibly be
accomplished by peasants working individually; the inhabitants of the
land were obliged to organize themselves into large communities under a
leader whose guiding hand assisted them to centralize their efforts in the
direction of the common interest. Thus the Nile awakened a demand for
an adequate law code and an ordered commonwealth. For the sake of
reckoning the rise and retreat of the Nile flood and of determining the
season for cultivating the fields, it was imperative to observe the change of
the seasons and the courses of the stars. Whenever, as frequently occurred, an unusually high Nile inundation obliterated the boundaries between neighboring plots of land, the fields had to be remeasured and the
new survey recorded in the official registry. It was the Nile again which
encouraged the development of writing, of reckoning time by a systematic calendar, and the study of astronomy. When later in the historical
period colossal pyramids and mighty temples were constructed, or gigantic statues and obelisks were set up in honor of the gods and the kings,
it was the Nile once more which facilitated or even made possible the
transport of heavy building materials; on its broad bosom the huge granite
blocks were borne northward from the southern border of Egypt all the
way to Memphis or distant Tanis in the extreme northeast corner of the
Delta. The great river always constituted for the country the indispensable
source of life on which the weal or woe of its inhabitants was dependent.
An abnormally high Nile could destroy the villages and rob the people
of their homes; a shortage of water from a low inundation subjected them
to bitter famine; a normal Nile, on the other hand, brought with it a prosperous year. Was it, then, extravagant for the Egyptians to deify the
river as "Hapi" (Fig. 3) and to praise him in inspiring hymns as the one
"who comes to nourish Egypt," or as the one who "bringing sustenance
is rich in food and is the creator of every good thing"?

The oldest traces of human existence in Egypt have been found on the
desert plateaus of the Upper Egyptian valley of the Nile in the form of
crude flint implements similar in appearance to those which have been
discovered in other regions of northern Africa and in western Europe.

They must be assigned to the earliest Paleolithic age, a period far beyond the dawn of history. It was a time in which the Egyptian land as we know it had not yet come into existence, a time when the sea extended as far as Upper Egypt and occupied all the valley as well. What sort of men inhabited the surrounding highlands while they fabricated and made use of those implements utterly escapes our knowledge. By ap-

FIG. 3.—THE NILE IN UPPER EGYPT (LUXOR)

proximately 6000 B.C. Egypt had acquired much the same geographical countenance which it now exhibits. Its inhabitants, to judge by their language, had developed from at least two different strains, the Paleolithic aborigines and the Hamitic tribes. The latter were linguistically closely related to the Semites of the Near East, the Akkadians of Babylonia, the Phoenicians, Hebrews, Aramaeans, and the Arabs. They had dwelt in the North African Mediterranean basin but had gradually drifted into the Nile Valley as the result of changes of climate which rendered their homelands incapable of producing sufficient food to sustain them. It is probable that Nilotic peoples poured in from the south, while from the east, by way of the Sinaitic peninsula or across the Red Sea, came Semitic tribesmen with their gift of agriculture. In the course of a few centuries these diverse elements became mingled until their original identity was wholly lost. The result was a new race—the Egyptians—who were destined to give birth to the culture of the historical period.

The Egyptians of history retained no recollection of their arrival in the land. They considered themselves to be the original inhabitants and designated themselves with vigorous self-consciousness and complacent pride as "men," in contrast to their heterogeneous neighbors, the Libyans in the west, the Asiatics on the east, and the Nubians toward the south.

II

THE OLD AND MIDDLE KINGDOMS

THOUGH speaking similar dialects and possessing a certain community of culture, the Egyptian people nevertheless did not as a matter of course enjoy political unity as well. This was a benefit acquired perhaps only imperceptibly through centuries of development. At first the land consisted of a large number of independent city-states, which were to some extent perpetuated in the historical period in the nomes. But even at an early date efforts toward a closer political unity were rewarded by a certain amount of success. As a result two powerful states came into existence: the northern kingdom, corresponding to the area of the Nile Delta, and its southern rival which extended from the region not far from modern Cairo upstream to the first cataract of the Nile at Assuan and perhaps even farther south into Nubia. The ancient religious capital of the northern kingdom was traditionally located at Behdet, near Tell el Belamun. The principal insigne of its ruler was the "red crown" ⌣. The king of the southern land had his royal residence at Ombos, near the modern town of Naqada, on the left bank of the Nile. He was distinguished in turn by a special type of "white crown" ⌣. In addition, each of the "two lands" possessed its distinctive heraldic plant. The northern kingdom had adopted the papyrus, which was so plentiful in the swamps and marshes of Lower Egypt that it could properly be considered the most characteristic plant of the country. The plant of the southern kingdom has not been identified botanically, but it is popularly if not very accurately referred to as the lily or the lotus (Fig. 44). All these insignia, like numerous other vestiges of the primitive period, can be traced throughout Egyptian history.

In all probability the two Egyptian states flourished for many centuries independently side by side, often clashing with each other in armed strife. At length the northern kingdom asserted its power over its southern neighbor, and the two were united into a single state. Heliopolis (the biblical On), the "city of the sun," in the vicinity of Cairo, was perhaps the political but certainly the religious capital of this united Egyptian kingdom.

How long this political union continued to exist we are unable to discover. After a time, in any case, the southern state reasserted its independence, and two political entities came into being once more, corresponding to the two lands of the earliest period. However, this new political development was attended by the choice of a new capital in each of the two states. The double metropolis of Pe and Dep (Buto) was the seat of the northern king, while the corresponding role in Upper Egypt was played by Nekhen and Nekheb, on opposite sides of the Nile near modern Elkab. Wars raged anew between the two lands. They resulted in the victory of the south and the permanent union of Upper and Lower Egypt.

It is possible that the creator of this new united kingdom was Menes, for his name stands at the beginning of the traditional roster of Egyptian rulers. Thus it is he with whom Egyptian history really begins. He is also the first ruler about whom the Egyptians themselves possessed definite information, according to which, for example, Menes was regarded as the founder of the "White Wall," later known as Memphis. Little was remembered about the earlier rulers of the two countries. They were believed to have been supernatural beings or spirits who occupied a station midway between gods and men. Their souls were accorded worship as demigods in the old capitals; in Buto they took the forms of falcons, while they were represented in Nekheb as jackals.

The material culture of this earliest period has the distinctive characteristics of the Late Stone (Neolithic) Age. On the edge of the Delta where the desert begins, a small number of Lower Egyptian sites, such as Marimda, Beni Salami, and Omari, have been located in which a Late Stone Age culture flourished, peopled by farmers with abundant pottery but lacking copper. In Upper Egypt this period left numerous cemeteries; the modern names of several of these are now the familiar designations of the different stages of later prehistoric Egyptian culture. The first, discovered sixty years ago by Petrie, has two phases known as Neqada I and II. Thirty years later Brunton uncovered a culture at Badari which proved to be roughly contemporary with Neqada I. A third, discovered at el Amrah, of approximately the same age as the other two, has given its name—Amratian—to all the Neqada I group.

The Amratians were probably seminomadic shepherds and hunters of eastern Hamitic race, among whom weapons, elephants, hippopotami, and hunting dogs played an important role. The most characteristic features represented in their pottery include polished monochrome red ware, red vessels with lustrous black tops, and others painted with white geometric and imitated basket-work designs. They buried their dead in cemeteries isolated from their settlements, in contrast to the Lower Egyptian farmers of Marimda and Omari (who were northwestern Hamites), whose graves were placed within the inhabited area.

The Neqada II culture was much more widely distributed than any of the earlier ones, numerous cemeteries having been discovered from Lower Nubia, in the south, to Gerza (whence the term "Gerzean" for this culture), Abusir el Meleq, and Maʿadi, just south of Cairo. By natural evolution the Gerzean culture directly followed the Amratian and reveals the Egyptians on a higher level. The graves are more artistically arranged and the bodies interred with greater care. Many of the earlier pottery vessels give way to new forms, and for the first time foreign influences are manifest in Egypt. Various pottery types occur which are similar in form and decoration to Palestinian and Syrian ware. Buff-colored jugs with wavy handles and vessels with red patterns and pictures of birds, animals, and crude human figures were favored. Designs on cylinder seals and other objects, as well as tombs with elaborately niched brick walls, reveal close affinities with Mesopotamia of the Jemdet-Naser period. Small figurines become common. Hunting and fishing declined to some extent in favor of agriculture and animal husbandry, which henceforth was to become the basis of Egyptian economy. The Gerzean period carried Egyptian culture down to the beginning of the dynastic era.

Several of the last predynastic kings have left monuments. One of them, a native of Hierakonpolis (Nekhen), "The Scorpion," seems to have conducted successful wars as far north as Tura, north of Memphis. His successor was probably Narmer, whose famous slate palette is one of man's first great historical records. Its reliefs reveal that Narmer carried his conquests into the Delta and claimed the Lower Egyptian crown; but it is doubtful whether he was able to muster sufficient military might to effect a union of the two lands. That achievement was assigned by tradition to his successor, Menes, the first king of the First Dynasty.

Menes' name, however, is not well attested on the monuments, and he may have been identical with Aha ("The Fighter"), unless the latter followed him on the throne. Aha had his capital at This and his tomb at nearby Abydos. In order to retain the northern conquests made by their predecessors and themselves, the presence of Menes and Aha in the vicinity of the Delta was imperative. Thus the foundation of Memphis, as is clearly suggested by its alternative name, the "White Wall," was a military necessity. The new city became a northern capital of growing importance, which soon superseded the Thinite metropolis of the south and possessed its own extensive necropolis at Saqqara, with stately tombs of immense size for the nobles and high officials of the court. While the remaining kings of the First Dynasty, Djer, Wadjty, Udimu, Adjib, Semerkhet, and Ka, were buried at Abydos, the first three of the Second Dynasty, about which little is known, prepared their tombs near the new capital of Memphis.

In this new Saqqara necropolis, King Djoser, who opened the Third Dynasty, caused his gifted architect, Imhotep, to erect for him the first royal funeral monument built exclusively of stone. Its central feature is a vast terraced pyramid which conceals the actual burial vault of the king. The sacred precinct contained in addition to the "step pyramid" a gigantic mortuary temple with a chamber for the royal statue, tombs for several princesses, an immense festival temple and festal hall adorned with columns of unique design, and many other structures. Though carried out in small-stone masonry, numerous delicate details of design betray that the entire structure was imitated from wooden prototypes. Now extensively restored, this magnificent achievement of Imhotep may still be seen in Saqqara.

It was in the reign of the Fourth Dynasty king Snefru that the true pyramid form was adopted for the royal tomb, and to this dynasty also must be accredited the three largest and best known—the pyramids of Giza. They secured undying fame to their builders, Kings Khufu, Khafre, and Menkaure, to whose unlimited wealth and power they still bear silent witness after the elapse of nearly forty-five hundred years. It is quite natural that the question should be asked how a Khufu dared to attempt the construction for his tomb of so gigantic a monument as the Great Pyramid (Fig. 4), with its height of over 480 feet and its mass of not less than 2,500,000 cubic yards of stone, since at his accession to the

FIG. 4.—THE PYRAMID OF KHUFU (GIZA)

15

throne he could have had no assurance of a sufficiently long reign to bring the stupendous task to completion. The answer is simple enough. Actually, each new king was sufficiently realistic to plan his pyramid on a scale capable of completion in a few years. As his reign continued, he simply amplified the monument with additional layers of masonry until he was content to consider it worthy of his rank.

At the foot of each pyramid there was constructed a sanctuary which was dedicated to the cult of the deceased king. It was connected by a long covered passage to a second, smaller, temple built on the desert at the very edge of the cultivated land.

Arranged in orderly rows about the pyramid of the ruler were the smaller tomb structures of princes, nobles, and other higher or lower officials who in their tomb reliefs and inscriptions have placed before our eyes a distinct picture of the state of the pyramid age and its civilization. At the head of this state stood the pharaoh as absolute monarch on whom depended the entire minutely articulated officialdom down to the last man. The most important and influential government posts—above all, the combined offices of vizier and chief justice—were placed in the hands of members of the royal family. The king himself, it is to be presumed, owned a considerable portion of the land, which was cultivated by serfs under compulsion to deliver all their produce to the court as well as to render additional forced labor for the construction of dikes, canals, temples, or pyramids (Fig. 5). The princes and barons of the provinces obviously possessed their own lands and bondslaves, but they were nevertheless subject to a certain dependence upon the court and the king.

Upon the transfer of the throne to a new house and dynasty after the death of Shepseskaf, the son and successor of Menkaure, the kingdom still maintained for a time its old power, even if scarcely perceptible tokens of the coming decay of the central authority were beginning to manifest themselves. The tomb reliefs depicting the affairs of daily life, the field operations on the great estates, or the diversions of the wealthy nobles, as well as the statues of stone and wood which have immortalized the great officials along with their male and female servants, all reflect an originality and vigor not paralleled in any other period.

The rulers of the Fifth Dynasty provided burial places for themselves at Abusir, south of Giza, in pyramids not to be compared in size or excellence of construction with those of Khufu and his successors. Each of the

Fig. 5.—The Sphinx and Pyramid of Khafre (Giza)

17

Fifth Dynasty kings erected at Abusir a special sanctuary for his "father," the sun-god. It consisted of an open court surrounding a great obelisk which soared upward from an immense substructure of hewn stone resting on a base of masonry slabs mantled with blocks of red granite. In front of the sanctuary, to judge from the single example as yet excavated, lay an enormous altar of alabaster on which the offerings were presented to the divinity. The court was surrounded by corridors richly adorned with beautiful bas-reliefs, some of which depict the celebration of a great royal festival and others some of the typical incidents which occur in the different seasons of the year. Apart from the meager information derived from the ruins at Abusir, we have but little knowledge of these rulers. The last of them was Unis, who erected for himself at Saqqara a pyramid the walls of whose inner chambers were the earliest to be inscribed with religious inscriptions in hieroglyphic writing.

The Fifth Dynasty appears not to have been overthrown without grievous inner strife. It is true that the rulers of the new Sixth Dynasty quickly restored order, but their power in the kingdom was on the wane and was doomed to give way gradually before the growing independence of the nomarchs of the various provinces or nomes. The highly centralized state of the pyramid age resolved itself by degrees into feudalism. To be sure, the reputation of the kingdom continued to spread abroad. Numerous victorious campaigns were conducted by land and sea against the dwellers of southern Palestine; their fortified cities were captured and destroyed, and their fertile estates were devastated by fire and sword. Great trading expeditions were dispatched up the Nile as far as the northern Sudan in order to bring back to Egypt rare products from central Africa.

It was, however, not long until even worse convulsions followed to shake to pieces the framework of the state. A complete lack of historical records from the period leaves us in total darkness concerning the events which occurred during the reigns of the last kings of the Sixth Dynasty. Social revolution brought the collapse of all existing institutions; the ruling classes lost their power and wealth, and confusion reigned with no visible hope for the future. An ancient sage has drawn a dreary picture of the period:

The poor of the land have become rich and the owner of property has become a nonentity. . . . . The possessors of robes are now in rags, but he who wove not for himself (because he was obliged to work for others) is now a possessor of fine linens. . . . . He who could never build a boat for himself is now a possessor of ships, while he who once owned them looks upon them, but they are no longer his. . . . . Laughter has perished and is no longer made; it is now mourning which pervades the land, mingled with wailing.

During this period of hardship and discord a prince of Herakleopolis named Kheti (*ca*. 2240 B.C.) succeeded in gaining sufficient power to establish a kingdom embracing the northern part of the Nile Valley and perhaps even a portion of the Delta. The later Greek tradition which relates that this "Akhthoes [Kheti] was more terrible than any of his predecessors and perpetrated evil on every one in Egypt" reflects the vigor of the founder of the Ninth Dynasty. Under the two Herakleopolitan dynasties (*ca*. 2240–2050 B.C.) Egyptian culture blossomed anew. Kheti IV (*ca*. 2100 B.C.) composed a famous book of "instructions" for his son Merikare, and the obscure Herakleopolitan era produced so much of the surviving classical literature that it richly deserves characterization as a golden age.

In the Upper Egyptian city of Thebes a powerful princely family ruled in complete independence of the kings of Herakleopolis. These Intefs and Mentuhoteps had played an unimportant role in the Old Kingdom and had never exercised a significant political influence. Little by little they were able to extend the authority of their house throughout the local province and to annex Abydos to their possessions. In a fierce civil war, in which the powerful princes of Assiut participated as the most faithful supporters of the Herakleopolitan kings, the Thebans carried off the victory. All of Upper Egypt and the Delta likewise recognized the sovereignty of the Theban rulers, who proudly appropriated to themselves the old title of "King of Upper and Lower Egypt." The rulers of the Eleventh Dynasty, to be sure, were unable to accomplish the full pacification of the country, the complete restoration of orderly conditions, and the suppression of every sporadic rebellion.

It was only in the next dynasty that Egypt achieved once more a state of domestic peace and prosperity comparable with the conditions which had prevailed in the Old Kingdom. The Twelfth Dynasty was opened by Amenemhet I, a Theban whose ancestors had probably held office under the preceding kings. All in all, this king had no easy task to put the unruly grandees back in their places.

He eliminated wrong . . . . and restored what he found in ruin and what one city had taken from its neighbor. He caused one town to know its boundary with another;

he established their boundary stones as firmly as the sky, for he knew their irrigated domains according to what was in the writings; they had been checked according to what was in the ancient records, inasmuch as he loved justice.

But there was one thing which the new ruler dared not attempt: he did not undertake to deprive the provincial rulers (nomarchs) of the independence which they had won under the kings of the Sixth Dynasty and during the later periods of chaos or to relegate them to the rank of mere court functionaries, as they had been under the pharaohs of the Old Kingdom. The king invested them with their dominions, which they governed and controlled. The feudal state was thus maintained for a time, until it was forever abolished under the powerful kings Senwosret II and III.

Although the kings of the Twelfth Dynasty were natives of Thebes, political expedience caused them to remove the capital northward to It-tawy, where Upper and Lower Egypt meet, beyond the Fayyum. Indeed, the kings devoted their most solicitous attention to this province. Many of the Fayyumic estates were watered by a branch of the Nile now called the Bahr Yusuf. These were protected against possible floods by the construction of extensive dikes, while the waters were controlled by the introduction of sluices which ultimately conducted them to the "Great Lake," the much-admired Lake Moeris of the Greeks, on the northwest border of the oasis. New sanctuaries were erected to the gods, or old ones renovated, in most of the cities of Egypt, but in such building activities preference was given to the Fayyum. In the capital city of Shedet, or Crocodilopolis, there was constructed for the local god Suchos (Sobek) a splendid new temple with adjacent lake in which the sacred crocodiles were kept. On the edge of the desert, west of the capital and near the present Hawara, Amenemhet III built beside his pyramid an enormous mortuary temple with countless courts and colonnades. It is the so-called "labyrinth," which was described at great length by Herodotus and Strabo. However, scarcely a stone remains today of one of the largest and most famous buildings of ancient Egypt.

The precinct of Amun at Karnak in the old Theban capital was not wholly neglected by the kings of the Twelfth Dynasty, even if they chiefly favored their new capital in the Fayyum. Senwosret I constructed at an unknown site in Karnak a lovely peripteral chapel of limestone, its walls covered with bas-reliefs engraved with exquisite detail. Toward the end of the Eighteenth Dynasty, whether because it had fallen to ruin or because it was considered old fashioned, Amenhotep III removed its limestone blocks and utilized them along with materials from other demolished temples for the core blocks of his pylon (p. 165). They have been discovered and removed in recent years; so many of the blocks were intact that it has been possible to rebuild the entire chapel on an arbitrarily selected site at Karnak—a complete little temple of delicate proportions, and the only one of its kind to survive from the Middle Kingdom.

From the earliest times Egypt had carried on trade with the Phoenician capital of Gebal (Byblos). This was the land from which the Egyptians obtained wine, certain oils for funerary use, and cedarwood from the Lebanon ranges for the construction of ships, masts, and flagstaves, for coffins, and for choice furniture of every type. In exchange for such products the Egyptians made deliveries of gold, fine metal-work, and writing materials—especially the precious Egyptian papyrus. Intercourse was carried on by traders in caravans but even more by sea in Egyptian sailing vessels so characteristic of the service in which they were engaged that they were designated "Byblos travelers." Byblos itself was greatly influenced by Egyptian commerce and culture, if it was not actually an Egyptian colony. Its prince and chief trader accepted valuable gifts from the pharaoh and was proud to refer to himself in the Egyptian language as "the Son of Re, beloved of the gods of his land," and to appropriate for himself the royal protocol of Egypt. Egyptian ornamentation and script were employed by Phoenician craftsmen in the decoration of metal-work and in other applied arts, while the Egyptians in their turn borrowed certain of the Phoenician technical processes for working metals.

The power of the Twelfth Dynasty manifested itself particularly by the extension of Egyptian authority abroad. The copper mines of Sinai, where operations had been suspended since the Sixth Dynasty, flourished once more. Expeditions were dispatched to the stone quarries of the Wadi Hammamat, between the Nile and the Red Sea, to obtain materials for the building of temples and the carving of colossal statues. Egyptian ships plied the waters of the Red Sea on the route to the remote and almost legendary land of Punt on the Somali coast in order to barter the products of the Nile Valley for the coveted perfumes of Africa. Raids against Libya were undertaken. Efforts were made to extend the authority of Egypt into Palestine and Syria. The proverbial riches and prestige of Egypt recommended her traders to the merchant-princes of Palestine, and some of them, notably the rulers of the flourishing land of Ugarit, with their capital at the modern Ras Shamra, were glad to form an alliance with the pharaohs on the Nile. Senwosret I sent gifts to the prince of Ras Shamra. A statue of the princess Khnumet-nefer-hedjet, the wife of Senwosret II, which was discovered there, a sphinx of Amenemhet III found near the entrance to the temple of Baal at Ras Shamra, and a sculptured group of the Egyptian "Vizier, Judge, and Mayor of the City," Senwosret-onekh, with two women of his family, may indicate that Egyptian influence was solidly established in this important harbor city and trading-center from the early years of the Twelfth Dynasty.

If the Egyptians of the Middle Kingdom succeeded in gaining a foothold in Palestine and Syria, their influence was not confined to the coast towns alone. For Senwosret III penetrated, according to a brief report of one of his officers, as far as Sekmem—perhaps the Shechem of the Old Testament.

During the Middle Kingdom, Egyptian sea trade with Crete assumed considerable importance, but there is no evidence that direct connections had been established with the Aegean Islands or the mainland of Greece. Conversely, a few importations of Minoan objects have been found in Middle Kingdom Egypt, including a Middle Minoan II vase in a Twelfth Dynasty grave at Abydos and some potsherds of the same period at Haraga and Lahun.

We are somewhat better informed about the Egyptian campaigns against Nubia in the upper valley of the Nile, where conditions have been more favorable for the preservation and excavation of the monuments. The possession of Nubia was vital to Egypt as much for the trade connections with the Sudan which it afforded as for the access which it provided to the desert gold mines east of the Nile. The wars with Nubia were initiated by Amenemhet I and continued with some success by his son Senwosret I, but it was Senwosret III who ultimately consummated the conquest. Nubia was then annexed to Egypt as far as the region of the second cataract of the Nile at Wadi Halfa (Fig. 23), and the frontier was marked by inscriptions nearly forty miles above that place. "Any son of mine," the king admonishes his successors, "who will maintain this boundary which I have made, he is truly my son and he was born to me. For good is the son who champions his father and maintains the boundary of him who begot him. But as for him who will lose it and will not fight for it, he is not my son and he was never born to me." The conquered districts were safeguarded by fortifications, portions of which have survived to the present time, "in order that no Nubian might pass the frontier by water or by land . . . . nor any flocks of the Nubians."

Egyptian trade naturally penetrated even farther up the Nile than political control. At Kerma, south of the third cataract, a fortified trading station, the "Walls of Amenemhet," was constructed and a mercantile colony established.

The blossoming of art and literature went hand in hand with the external development of Egyptian power. The literary creations which originated in this and in a somewhat earlier time at Herakleopolis were regarded by later generations as models, and as late as the time of the Roman emperors efforts continued to be made to imitate the "classical" language of the period.

For two hundred years the followers of Amenemhet maintained their prosperous rule over Egypt and preserved tranquillity and peace in the land. The next century and a half, however, brought division once again, with the rulers of the Thirteenth Dynasty, despite their Theban origin, based at It-tawy, while the obscure Fourteenth Dynasty held concurrent sway at Xois in the western Delta. Both dynasties consisted of innumerable rulers enjoying usually the briefest of reigns. There is reason to believe that the throne lost its hereditary character in the Thirteenth Dynasty and that elected kings of common origin served for short terms, with the affairs of state controlled, for the most part with vigor and stability, by a series of hereditary viziers. Some of the kings left numerous monuments, large and small, though often of relatively crude workmanship, throughout the land. A few of them bore Semitic names, a plain token of the increasing Asiatic population which was infiltrating the Delta and preparing the stage for that dire catastrophe which, shortly before 1700 B.C., was to burst upon Egypt—conquest by the Hyksos.

III

THE HYKSOS

MANETHO'S account of the invasion of the Hyksos, like the remainder of his history of Egypt, has perished, but a portion of it was fortunately quoted by the Jewish historian Flavius Josephus. At some time during what we now designate as the Second Intermediate Period "a blast of God smote us," Manetho relates. "And unexpectedly, from the regions of the East, invaders of obscure race marched in confidence of victory against our land. By main force they easily seized it without striking a blow; and, having overpowered the rulers of the land, they then burned our cities ruthlessly, razed to the ground the temples of the gods, and treated all the natives with a cruel hostility. . . . . Finally, they appointed as king one of their number whose name was Salitis." These invaders are designated by Manetho as "Hyksos," which he interprets to mean "king-shepherds" in the Egyptian language. "For," he adds, "*hyk* in the sacred language means 'king,' and *sos* in common speech is 'shepherd' or 'shepherds': hence the compound word 'Hyksos.'" Manetho's interpretation of the term was in fact not entirely correct. The Egyptian language does indeed possess a word *hyk* with the meaning "prince" or "ruler," while another word, *shos*, means "shepherd" in the later stages of the language. Manetho's explanation is merely a late popular etymology, and the word "Hyksos" really goes back to the Egyptian *heku shoswet*, later pronounced something like *hyku shose*, and means "rulers of foreign lands." It is thus an Egyptian title boastfully assumed by the Hyksos chiefs themselves and later perhaps transferred by the Egyptians to the entire race of the invaders.

To what race did the Hyksos then belong? While it is possible that they were not a homogeneous people, the preponderant element among them was doubtless Semitic. The presence of other racial strains (Hurrian or Aryan) cannot at present be regarded as proved. The eighteenth century B.C. was for all of western Asia a period of extensive instability, and various tribal migrations are known to have occurred. It has been supposed that the Hyksos movement into Egypt was the westernmost surge of such a migration. Nevertheless, archeological study of the material remains dating to the Hyksos period has yielded but a nebulous picture of the nature or authority of the invaders. The movement may have originated with shepherds who moved into the eastern Delta to pasture their flocks, strengthened later by bands of well-armed tribesmen led by ambitious rebels against the waning Egyptian authority in Palestine and Syria. Possible new evidence for the origin of the Hyksos invasion may be seen in the recently discovered "execration texts" which actually name foreign rebels considered dangerous to Egyptian security. The fragmentation of power in the Thirteenth Dynasty presented a perfect opportunity for either infiltration or armed invasion from the east. Manetho's much later account, that the Hyksos "treated all the natives with a cruel hostility, massacring some and leading into slavery the wives and children of others," suggests warlike inroads by armed raiders who seized political authority and established families by marriage with native women.

It has been supposed that the Hyksos were sufficiently well and long established in Syria and Palestine to have built huge strongholds there, such as Carchemish, Qatna, Gaza (Tell el-Ajjul), and Sharuhen (Tell el-Fara). But it has not been proved that the builders of such fortified cities were the conquerors of Egypt whom we call the Hyksos. If they are identical, it is a curious fact that they built no such walled cities in the only land which they are definitely known to have ruled. For it has been demonstrated that the so-called Hyksos fortifications at Heliopolis and Tell el-Yahudiah are merely the remains of Egyptian temple foundations.

Furthermore, the excavation of tombs of the Hyksos period has revealed no significant changes in burial customs and no cultural break with the past. If the invaders established a cult of Seth at Avaris, they worshiped the native gods of Egypt as well. The rulers represented themselves to be the official successors of the pharaohs. They adopted the traditional royal protocol, assumed royal names compounded with the name of Re, and designated themselves, like the native rulers whom they had displaced, as "Son of Re," or as "Horus."

The Hyksos left no literary evidence of their occupation of Egypt. Indeed, they left practically no large monuments at all. What we know about them has been painfully gleaned from a host of scarabs—those beetle-shaped amulets so characteristic of Egypt—cylinder seals, and a few other isolated objects: a tiny sphinx with royal head and Semitic face in the act of clawing to death an Egyptian; a dagger with remarkable representations of animals on the handle; a fragmentary writing palette presented by a king Apophis (one of the commonest names of Hyksos kings) to his secretary Itju. Perhaps the largest and only truly "monumental" relics of the invaders are several blocks from a stone building found at Gebelein, a few miles south of Thebes, which contain the names of the kings Khyan and Apophis Owoserre.

These meager sources, the interpretation of which requires extreme caution, may point to some sort of indefinite Hyksos political power in southern Palestine or even farther north, from which they pushed westward into the Nile Delta, with Avaris, at or near Tanis, as their capital and the subsequent fulcrum of their power. The so-called Stela of Four Hundred Years, a monument set up in Tanis by Ramesses II to commemorate the introduction there of the cult of Seth, chief god of the Hyksos, four hundred years before the foundation of the Ramessid dynasty, may record the beginning of Hyksos rule in Egypt *ca.* 1725 B.C.

At approximately that time an Egyptian king named Dedmose ruled from his ancient capital at It-tawy, near Memphis. He was probably the last independent king of the Thirteenth Dynasty and identical with the Toutimaios in whose reign, according to Manetho, the Hyksos invaded the country and appointed Salitis as king. While it is improbable that the latter or his immediate successors were able to extend their sway over all of Egypt, reliable evidence suggests that they were followed by stronger rulers who were in possession of both Egypt and Nubia. Attempts to divide them into two Hyksos dynasties, a strong Fifteenth and a weaker Sixteenth, largely on the basis of the stylistic development and the (exceedingly uneven) distribution of their scarabs and other small monuments, can scarcely be accepted with confidence. It appears certain, however, that, for a considerable time, they were strongly intrenched in Lower and Middle Egypt and in Nubia as far south as the fortified trading post at Kerma, possibly also in Upper Egypt south of Thebes.

However that may be, it is evident that a resurgence of native power occurred in the latter years of the seventeenth century (*ca.* 1625 B.C.). A fresh line of Upper Egyptian kinglets had arisen in Thebes—the Seventeenth Dynasty—and these rulers grew increasingly restive under their ignominious status as tributaries to the hated Asiatic usurpers.

The secret of their new boldness can only be imagined. Various factors may have combined to inspire them to hopes of liberation. It is just at this time that the Egyptians first utilized the services of Medjay troops, and these sturdy Nubian mercenaries became indispensable

FIG. 6.—THUTMOSE IV IN BATTLE WITH THE SYRIANS (FROM HIS CHARIOT IN THE CAIRO MUSEUM)

warriors in the campaigns of the following centuries. Furthermore, it is conceivable that the Egyptians were now beginning to arm themselves with superior types of weapons such as had been introduced from Asia by the Hyksos—new kinds of bronze swords and daggers and the powerful compound bow. Above all, the Egyptians now for the first time employed the horse and chariot. These were an innovation—possibly spurned by the conservative Egyptians until forced in desperation to adopt them—which were often assumed to have come into the Nile Valley with the Hyksos. However, we are not informed just when the northern invaders first used chariotry against the Egyptians. In any event, the latter were not slow in recognizing the advantages of this new means of warfare and in turning it against the invaders who were in occupation of their land. In fact, the subsequent employment of chariotry and Nubian mercenaries may have been chiefly instrumental in transforming the Egyptian state into a military power. They certainly revolutionized Egypt's military effectiveness and assured her success during the rapid expansion of the empire a little later (Fig. 6).

FIG. 7.—HEAD OF THE MUMMY OF SEKENENRE (CAIRO)

We are not informed which of the Seventeenth Dynasty rulers of Thebes first took up arms against the Hyksos. The struggle may have been long and cruel, with victories and defeats on both sides. A tale recorded in the time of Merenptah relates that the Theban king Sekenenre once received from the Hyksos ruler Apophis an extraordinary message of complaint to the effect that the noise made by the hippopotami in Thebes prevented him from sleeping in his palace at Avaris (a distance of four hundred miles). That Sekenenre's reply was one of conciliation implies that he was still paying tribute to the northern invaders and that he was as yet unprepared to begin a war of liberation.

However, it appears that Sekenenre was ultimately unable to avoid the struggle. Chance has decreed that the very body of this Theban king should survive to our own time. His mummy, originally buried in a small pyramid tomb on the west of Thebes, was later removed to protect it from tomb robbers and concealed along with those of numerous other pharaohs in an isolated crevice not far from the temples of Deir el-Bahri. There it rested in peace until A.D. 1875, when it was rediscovered by modern successors of the ancient plunderers. They carried on their ghoulish operations until 1881, when they betrayed themselves, with the result that the royal mummies, some still resting in their original coffins, were transferred to the Cairo Museum.

Examination of the body of Sekenenre reveals that the king died a violent death, either on the battlefield or at the hands of an assassin, at approximately the age of forty (Fig. 7). He had sustained a number of savage blows on the head. If, as may be conjectured, his tragic end came in a battle with the Hyksos, little imagination is required to reconstruct the scene. Sekenenre appears to have been struck insensible by a blow from a war club or battle-ax which shattered his left jaw. His adversary then delivered a series of deadly strokes, one of which crushed the forehead over the right eye, while another fractured the skull so severely that the brain was exposed. The body shows evidence of having lain where it fell long enough for decomposition to set in. After its recovery it was hastily bound with mummy wrappings of linen and interred in a gilt wooden coffin in his modest tomb. Such a reconstruction of events would indicate a military disaster for the Egyptians; the violent and untimely death of the Theban king would have been a serious setback in the Egyptian effort to destroy the power of the Hyksos. These invaders continued thus for a time their complacent occupation of most of Middle and Lower Egypt.

IV

THE WAR OF LIBERATION

THE Hyksos had probably ruled Egypt for about a century and a half when Kamose, the son and successor of Sekenenre, inherited the struggle for freedom. At this time the foreigners apparently ruled from Avaris while maintaining strongholds at other points along the Nile, including at least a portion of the regions from Memphis southward through Herakleopolis and Cynopolis to Hermopolis, in addition to the Bahria Oasis in the western desert, and possibly even isolated towns south of Thebes, such as Gebelein. On the other hand, Kamose's Theban capital controlled the southern frontier at Elephantine, considerable sections of Middle Egypt as far as Cusae, and important fertile areas of the Delta. But, in the south, the lost Nubian province was in the hands of a prince allied with the Hyksos ruler at Avaris. Nevertheless, in this confused situation, some freedom of movement up and down the Nile was apparently enjoyed by friend and foe alike.

The ambitious young Kamose could find no satisfaction in sharing the Nile Valley with foreigners, and he resolved to rescue Egypt from their dominion. We are informed of his plans and their execution in a remarkable record, dating from the third year of his reign and told in his own words, which has been discovered at different times over a period of nearly fifty years, the latest and longest installment having been extracted from the foundations of Karnak in 1954. Unfortunately, the beginning of the account is in fragments, most of them unrecovered, and the whole of it is difficult of interpretation.

Kamose's determination to join battle with the Asiatics met with a cool reception when transmitted to a council of the nobles whom he expected to follow him. Tolerably satisfied with the status quo, and fearful of a war on two fronts, with powerful enemies in control of Nubia and Lower Egypt, they advised action only if first attacked by the invaders. Kamose was angered but undeterred by the counsel of his court. And thus, supported largely by Medjay mercenaries, he sailed down the river to liberate Egypt. The first battle, at Nefrusi, north of Hermopolis, was a great victory for Kamose, yielding much booty and many prisoners. At this stage of the campaign horses are mentioned for the first time in any Egyptian source, and they appear to have been the exclusive property of the enemy.

Subsequent events in the war would have been unknown to us but for the newly discovered Kamose stela, which, after a long gap, resumes and completes the record. It is evident that the king had succeeded in marshaling a powerful fleet, which, "arrayed prow to rudder," advanced so far to the north and east that he was able to dispatch river raiders within sight of Avaris itself. These occupied strategic territory about the enemy capital, from which further operations resulted in the cutting-down of orchards and vineyards, the capture of horses and prisoners, male and female, the seizure of hundreds of Hyksos ships with rich cargo, and complete devastation of numerous enemy towns and cities.

Kamose's military operations seem to have been extended over a wide area in the Delta and on both sides of the Nile. While he was in one of the oases, a lucky chance delivered into his hands a messenger carrying a letter from the Hyksos king to his Nubian ally:

Owoserre, the Son of Re, Apophis: Greetings to my son, the ruler of Kush. Why do you act there as ruler without letting me know whether you see what Egypt has done to me, how its ruler, Kamose, has set upon me on my own soil (though I have not attacked him!)? He has chosen to ruin these two lands, my land and yours, and he has already devastated them. Come north, therefore; be not timid. He is here in my vicinity. There is none who can stand against you in this part of Egypt. Behold, I will give him no repose until you have arrived. And then we two shall divide up the towns of Egypt.

The pharaoh, joyful at the interception of this piece of intelligence, took advantage of the opportunity to order the courier back to Apophis with a lurid account of his successes in Middle Egypt. Having consolidated his strength at el-Kês, near Cynopolis, he dispatched a powerful troop of infantry to ravage the Bahria Oasis; then he personally led the main division of his forces in a crushing climax to the campaign, with enormous destruction to the enemy but without the loss of a single Egyptian. Finally, with the advent of the Nile inundation, an unfavorable time for fighting, Kamose sailed in triumph up the river to Assiut and Thebes to celebrate his victories in the temple of Karnak.

It is probable that Kamose died prematurely, and it remained for his younger brother Ahmose, who succeeded him, to complete the task of liberation from the Hyksos. We are relatively well informed of the later events of the war in the biography of a marine, also named Ahmose, who recorded his services to the royal house on the walls of his tomb at Elkab. While still a young man he participated in the siege of Avaris, which Kamose had apparently not been able to capture. Succeeding deeds of valor brought promotion after promotion to the young marine, and his fortune was made by the honors and decorations and other gifts of plunder and prisoners which came to him from the king.

With the fall of Avaris the Hyksos lost their last stronghold in Egypt. They withdrew into Syria, where they were welcomed by a confederation of Semitic princes. Ahmose, however, was determined to frustrate any attempt of the Asiatics to renew the threat to Egypt. Learning that the greater part of the Hyksos fugitives had established themselves in the southern Palestinian town of Sharuhen, he marched across the desert and besieged this fortress for a period of three years. The ensuing surrender of the Asiatics brought further booty and honor to our Elkab reporter.

Thus King Ahmose had completed the task begun by his elder brother. The Hyksos were driven out, Egypt was rid of "the plague," and the land was once more united under a single ruler. Nevertheless, the Nubian allies of Apophis still retained their hold of the southern province. "After his majesty had slain the Mentiu of Asia [the Hyksos]," relates our source, "he traveled southward to Nubia in order to crush the Nubian desert tribes, and his majesty accomplished a great slaughter among them." The foreign menace at an end, Ahmose was even yet unable to rest his arms. Matters at home had developed into a state of ferment. The grandees who had regained extensive privileges during the decline of the centralized state were naturally reluctant to relinquish any of them in favor of the potent Theban dynasts now in the ascendancy. It was a question, therefore, whether the old feudal state should live again in the Nile Valley or whether the Theban house of Ahmose should reign supreme in place of the expelled Asiatics. Thus, Ahmose had scarcely returned from his Nubian victories when he was faced with a series of armed revolts at home. The civil strife was promptly terminated; the leader of one of the revolts, a man named Tetian, was slain as an example, and his army was annihilated.

Ahmose died after a reign of about twenty-five years, at fifty to sixty years of age. He was buried near his predecessors, but the tomb was later violated by thieves, and the royal mummy was transferred in its unpretentious coffin to the secret crevice in which the body of his father, Sekenenre, had been hidden. The pharaoh had been married to his full sister, the princess Ahmose-Nofretari. This queen occupied in the capital the high spiritual position of "God's Wife," that is, the heavenly spouse of Amun, the principal god of Thebes. So great were her prestige and political influence that, several generations later, she and her son, King Amenhotep I, were accorded the rank of saints or demigods, and to them were addressed prayers as the protective divinities of the necropolis.

Amenhotep I, who succeeded his father Ahmose about 1546 B.C., had no sooner mounted the throne when disturbances in Nubia demanded his presence in person at the southern frontier. He journeyed on the ship of the veteran Ahmose of Elkab "southward to Kush in order to extend the boundaries of Egypt and . . . . struck down that Nubian in the midst of his army." Having shattered the forces of the enemy, he traversed the hostile country, rounding up and carrying off both people and cattle as booty. The expedition advanced as far as the Upper Well, a watering-place in the desert, after which Ahmose transported his royal master back to Egypt in two days' time, a journey so remarkably swift that he was rewarded not only with the "gold of valor" but also by promotion to the rank of "Warrior of the Ruler." It soon became necessary for Amenhotep to engage in battle with the western provinces also, for Libyan tribes had overrun the fruitful meadows of the western Delta and taken possession of numerous towns of the region. They were successfully repelled by the new king, and the frontier was protected against further attacks.

V

THE RISE OF THE GOLDEN AGE

AMENHOTEP I occupied the throne for twenty-one years and died without issue. There being no son to succeed him as the "Son of Re" on the throne, the right to the crown fell to Amenhotep's sister, the princess Ahmose, who was married to a certain Thutmose, possibly a relative of the royal family. According to Egyptian practice, it was not possible for the princess Ahmose to exercise the kingship in person. It would have outraged all tradition and convention for a woman to crown herself with the double crown of Egypt and to assume the inheritance of the gods on earth. Such a violation of precedent would have given rise to the strangest results, both in the administration of the state and in the exercise of the cult in the temples. To avoid such embarrassments, therefore, the sovereignty was passed on by the heiress to her husband, while she contented herself with the rank of "Great Royal Wife," a title reserved for the official queen. It must be understood, however, that Thutmose did not gain by this delegation of power a permanent right to the throne; in the event of the queen's death his right would come likewise to an abrupt end in favor of whatever children survived the deceased heiress of the royal line.

In his first regnal year the young king was obliged to proceed to Nubia in order to put down an uprising of the natives, who probably considered the confusion attending a change of rulers an excellent opportunity to throw off the Egyptian yoke and to escape the payment of tribute. Our old friend, Captain Ahmose of Elkab, once again had the responsibility of transporting a king and his troops to the south. The king, who participated in the battle in person, "raged like a leopard. His majesty shot his first arrow, and it lodged in the neck of that enemy" (the Nubian chief). As might be expected, the doughty Ahmose covered himself with glory in the campaign and was consequently promoted to the rank of "Chief of the Sailors," or "Admiral," as we should rate him. The war was brought to a speedy conclusion, and the Nubians were pacified again. On the granite cliffs of the east bank opposite the island of Tombos in the third cataract of the Nile, near modern Hannak, an inscription was cut during the second regnal year of the king which describes in elaborate poetic measures his victorious advance in every direction. "He marched to the ends of the earth with his conquering might, seeking one who would fight, but he found no one who would turn his face against him. He pressed on into valleys which the ancestors had not known and which the wearers of the vulture and the serpent diadems had never seen. . . . . Subject to him are the islands of the sea, and the whole earth is under his two feet." Unfortunately, these high-sounding phrases did not precisely correspond to reality. While the frontier of the vanquished country to the south was secured by a fortress erected on the island of Tombos, it was but two years later that another uprising took place. Once again, the Egyptian records inform us, the rebels were defeated and "wretched Kush" was overthrown; the king sailed down the Nile in triumph, passing on his ship through the Assuan cataract by means of a canal specially cleared for his voyage. While later times brought new revolts in Nubia and repeated attempts by Sudanese tribes to raid the Egyptian colonies, nevertheless Thutmose I had in this campaign materially expanded Egypt's Nubian possessions, and this province henceforth enjoyed with few interruptions the blessings of an orderly regime.

Between these two Nubian expeditions occurred another military venture of Thutmose I which was of the greatest importance, since it determined the direction of Egyptian foreign policy for centuries to come. This was a campaign into Syria. It will be remembered that Senwosret III had already in the Twelfth Dynasty pressed at least as far as southern Palestine, while two hundred years later Ahmose, the founder of the New Kingdom, had taken the fortesss of Sharuhen after a long protracted siege. But now, just as he had conquered the lands to the south of Egypt, so also Thutmose attempted to bring under the control of his empire the southern lands of western Asia. He traversed Syria without opposition and penetrated as far as the upper reaches of the Euphrates into the Land of the Two Rivers, Nahrin. When finally the prince of the land led out his troops to meet the Egyptian invader, Thutmose won a great victory, accompanied by a tremendous slaughter of the enemy, and "countless were the captives whom the king carried off from his victory." Before leaving the scene of his victory, Thutmose caused a triumphal inscription to be set up on the bank of the Euphrates to proclaim his mighty deeds to

all future generations. Of all the wonders which the Egyptians had encountered in the new world which had been opened to them, the river
Euphrates was itself the most astonishing by far. The Nile at home, the
only river which hitherto had come within the horizon of their experience, flowed from south to north, so that sailing vessels had the advantage of the wind on a voyage upstream to the south and that of the
current when traveling in the opposite direction. But now they found
themselves on the bank of a mighty stream which flowed from north to
south and on which, therefore—incredible as it must appear!—one could
not float northward with the current. And thus the homecoming Egyptian warriors never grew weary of telling about "that inverted water
which flows southward when (it ought to be) flowing northward"; in
fact, the "inverted water" straightway became an Egyptian designation
of the Euphrates.

The success which the young Thutmose had achieved on this first
thrust of Egyptian power into western Asia was truly brilliant, and he
was quite justified in boasting that the southern limits of his empire extended to the third cataract of the Nile, while the northern frontier was
at the Euphrates; "never had the like happened to other kings." In reality the victory over the Syrian lands was but an ephemeral one; at the
approach of the Egyptian host the Syrian princes and towns had hastened
to humble themselves by sending tribute to the pharaoh, but scarcely had
the invaders departed when they not only discontinued their gifts but
likewise made determined preparations to resist any repeated incursion
of Egyptian might.

Of the union of Thutmose I with the "Great Royal Wife" Ahmose four
children were born—two sons, Wadjmose and Amenmose, and two
daughters, Hatshepsut and Nefrubity. But the king had been married to
another princess also—a certain Mutnofret, who was a close relation,
possibly even a younger sister, of Ahmose—and she had borne to the
pharaoh a son who was named Thutmose for his father and who later
became King Thutmose II. According to Egyptian tradition, it was only
the children of Thutmose I by the crown princess Ahmose who possessed
a legitimate right to the throne. Accordingly, since Princes Wadjmose
and Amenmose and in all probability their sister Nefrubity also had died
in early childhood or youth, while their father was still living, Princess
Hatshepsut alone remained as the sole surviving lawful heir to the throne.

Nevertheless, like her mother before her, she was prevented by her sex from succeeding as "king"; she possessed no more than the right to convey the crown by marriage to her husband and to secure the succession to her children. In order, therefore, to circumvent a dynastic dilemma and to prevent the loss of the crown to another family by the union of Hatshepsut with a stranger, Thutmose I was obliged to marry his daughter to her younger half-brother Thutmose. Such brother-sister marriages were by no means abhorrent to the ancient Egyptians. Had not the god Osiris once taken his sister Isis to wife (see p. 147)? Having thus secured the succession, Thutmose I ruled on to the end of his days. Dying about the year 1508 B.C., he "went forth to heaven, having completed his years in gladness of heart. Then the hawk who was in the nest appeared . . . . as King of Upper and Lower Egypt." Thutmose II "assumed the kingship over the Black Land [Egypt] and began to rule the Red Land [the foreign countries], for he had taken possession of the Two Regions [Egypt] in triumph."

While the preceding kings who had resided in Thebes had all located their modest burial places on the desert plain west of the Nile, Thutmose I caused his tomb to be hewn in an isolated valley of the Libyan Desert known to the modern Egyptians as Biban el-Muluk ("Doors of the Kings") (Fig. 8). A contemporary noble boasts that he had charge of the excavation of the king's tomb, which was carried out in secret, "no one seeing and no one hearing." The tomb was not especially large. It consisted of a rectangular vestibule reached by a steeply descending stairway, while a second stair led to a pillared chamber which was intended to receive the pharaoh's coffin. Why Thutmose I broke with the ancient tradition which required that the royal tomb be constructed in pyramid form is difficult to determine. Perhaps he was already conscious of the fact that the earlier royal tombs of Thebes, located as they were in close proximity to the cultivated land and its settlements, were all too convenient for the predatory activities of the inhabitants. In any event, Thutmose selected a site for his tomb in this desolate valley, far from human habitation. To be sure, there was no space in the narrow desert valley for the mortuary temple which invariably comprised the essential adjunct to the royal tomb; in consequence this had to be constructed apart from the rock-hewn tomb and located as an independent building in the valley itself, on the narrow strip of desert which separates the cul-

FIG. 8.—VALLEY OF THE TOMBS OF THE KINGS (THEBES)

tivation from the declivity of rubble leading to the desert highlands. The precedent established by Thutmose I was followed by his successors for centuries, so that tomb after tomb was added to the gradually lengthening row of burial places in the solitary Valley of the Tombs of the Kings. When in the reign of the Roman emperor Augustus the Greek geographer Strabo visited Egypt, he was able to mention approximately forty splendidly executed king's tombs, the majority of which are known to us at the present time.

At the time of his accession and coronation, Thutmose II was a youth not over twenty years of age, physically delicate and so weak of will that he was wholly dominated by the queen-mother Ahmose and his exceedingly energetic and not less ambitious wife Hatshepsut.   .

About this time disquieting news reached Egypt of disturbances in the provinces of the empire, as was so frequently the situation at a change of rulers. A revolt broke out in Nubia, and the Egyptian inhabitants of the country fled with their herds to take refuge behind "the walls of the fortifications which . . . . Thutmose I had built to hold off the unruly foreigners"; these must have included the castle at Tombos and other strongholds of similar character. Being informed of the uprising,

his majesty grew furious as a leopard when he heard it. Then his majesty said: "As I live, as I love Re, as I praise my father the lord of the gods, Amun, lord of Karnak, I shall not permit one of their males to live!" Then his majesty sent a large army to Nubia . . . . to cast down all those who had rebelled against his majesty and revolted against the Lord of the Two Lands. This army reached the wretched land of Kush; the might of his majesty guided it and the terror of him cleared its course. Then the army of his majesty cast down these barbarians, and not one of their males was permitted to live, even as his majesty had commanded, with the exception of one of the sons of the prince of Kush who was brought as a prisoner along with [some of] their subjects to the place where his majesty was and placed under the feet of the Good God [the king].

Thutmose appeared on the balcony of the palace and caused the captives to be led into his presence. Thus Nubia became once more "the possession of his majesty as it had been originally, the people were in jubilation, the nobles rejoiced; they gave praises to the Lord of the Two Lands and extolled this eminent god [the king] in accordance with his divinity."

Little else is known of Thutmose II's military exploits, except of a campaign in the land of the Shosu, which can scarcely have been more than a raid against the Beduin of the Sinaitic peninsula or the Syrian Desert.

By a curious trick of fate the legitimate marriage of Thutmose II, like that of his father, had failed to supply a male heir to the throne. Since he had but two daughters, anxiety rose once more as to who should succeed to the throne in the event of his early death—a not unlikely contingency in view of the precarious state of his health. Thus in order to safeguard the survival of the dynasty, Thutmose named to succeed him a young son by a minor wife, a boy who likewise bore the name of Thutmose. He appointed this lad as coregent and in order to lend greater force to the choice he married him to his half-sister Merytre, who was Thutmose II's daughter by Hatshepsut and therefore the true heir to the throne.

Thus on the death of Thutmose II (*ca.* 1504 B.C.), this young prince ascended the throne and was crowned as Thutmose III. He did not, however, succeed in taking over the reins of office. During the years of his minority, his stepmother and mother-in-law (through his marriage to Merytre), the royal widow Hatshepsut, assumed the kingship. A contemporary official has recorded this significant situation in characteristic Egyptian language:

> Thutmose II went forth to heaven and mingled with the gods. His son [Thutmose III] advanced to his place as King of the Two Lands and ruled on the throne of him who had begotten him. His sister [really Thutmose II's half-sister], the "God's Wife" Hatshepsut governed the land; the Two Lands were at her will and served her. Egypt was in submission . . . . for she was a dictator excellent of plans who reassured the Two Regions by her speaking.

Even though she was in full control of the government, while the youthful king was kept in the background, Hatshepsut was nevertheless officially no more than the royal widow, the "Divine Consort [God's Wife] and Great Royal Wife" of the deceased king. Reliefs from the period of the regency depict her standing *behind* Thutmose III.

Not more than a few years at most had elapsed, however, until she abandoned her restraint, whether through ambition or for other reasons unknown to us. Instead of surrendering her regency as soon as Thutmose III reached his majority, Hatshepsut usurped the titles of a sovereign ruler of Egypt. She now called herself "the [female] Horus, the Queen [the Egyptian word for 'queen' is written exactly the same as that for 'king'] of Upper and Lower Egypt, the Daughter of Re," and assumed, in accordance with the old tradition, a special king's name, Kamare. Of the long series of royal titles and epithets which Egyptian kings were accustomed to employ, there was one alone which she refrained from adopting; this was the designation "Mighty Bull," which was obviously hardly applicable to a woman, even if she were a queen.

In order to justify her usurpation, the ancient dogma of the divine origin of the king was produced and applied to her own birth. When she was begotten it was the god Amun who had visited her mother, thus Hatshepsut came into the world by direct intervention of the gods. When this divine princess had grown up, she informs us, her father Thutmose I intrusted to her the royal office, and she was acclaimed king by the joyful people. She describes herself as "exceedingly good to look upon, with the form and spirit of a god, ... a beautiful maiden, fresh, serene of nature, ... altogether divine." She accompanied her father on his voyages of inspection in the Delta; and on such occasions all the gods "came to her, ... Hathor of Thebes, Wadjet of Buto, Amun Lord of Karnak, Atum of Heliopolis, Montu [the god of war] Lord of Thebes, Khnum Lord of the Cataract, all the gods of Thebes, in fact, all the gods of Upper and Lower Egypt," promising her protection and good fortune for her reign if she would in future years devote herself to the gods and the temples.

Reliefs, statues, and sphinxes represent Hatshepsut in the conventional garb of a king. She frequently appears in the customary royal skirt, wearing on her chin the ceremonial beard which had been a badge of kingship since time immemorial, while her head is usually adorned with one of the numerous royal crowns or the folded headcloth characteristic of kingly rank. There is no reason to doubt that she was a beautiful woman gifted not only with every feminine charm (Fig. 9) but also with an extraordinary intellect and a powerful personality and will. Moreover, in addition to these qualities, she had the unusual good fortune to possess in the person of the official Senenmut an adviser and chancellor who was able both to encourage her thirst for power and to carry out her plans.

Of humble origin, Senenmut had in early youth entered service in the temple of Amun at Karnak and before very long had successively occupied a series of important posts. In what manner he forged the bonds which brought him into close relations with his royal mistress and by which he won not only her trust and favor but possibly even her love is a closed page of history. We know only that she heaped upon him endless honors, such as had never been found "in the writings of the ancestors,

Fig. 9.—Statue of Queen Hatshepsut (Metropolitan Museum of Art)

and that she appointed him to be the tutor or, as the Egyptians expressed it, the "Great Nurse" of her daughter, the princess Nefrure. He is depicted in this capacity in several granite statues which were set up in the temple of Karnak (Fig. 10). He squats on the ground, holding his pupil wrapped in his ample robe, which is entirely covered with a long hieroglyphic inscription. The princess, after the manner of Egyptian children, wears a long lock of hair on her right temple, while the uraeus serpent on her brow and the ceremonial beard on her chin identify her as the future legitimate "king."

For the first time since the collapse of the Middle Kingdom, Egypt enjoyed a period of economic prosperity during the reign of Hatshepsut. Extensive building operations were carried on in the capital at Thebes as well as in other cities of the land. Magnificent temples were erected, while the sanctuaries which had been destroyed or neglected by the Hyksos were restored and the cults re-established. But the queen's special consideration was devoted to the great temple of Amun. Eloquent witness to her building activities in Karnak is borne to this day by her halls and courts and, above all, by the two giant obelisks, each about ninety-seven feet in height, which she erected. These colossal monoliths of red granite were hewn from the Assuan quarries under the direction of Senenmut within the short space of seven months. Then they were transported on the Nile to Thebes and erected in a forecourt of the great temple of Amun, where one of them still stands and proudly lifts its lofty spire above the surrounding chaos as a distinctive landmark of the ancient sanctuary (Fig. 11). It is difficult to convey an adequate idea of the amount of labor which must have been expended in the creation of these two remarkable monuments. The shaft which survives intact is ninety-seven and one-half feet in height, contains approximately one hundred and eighty cubic yards of granite, and weighs something like 700,000 pounds. What inestimable tenacity of purpose, what levies of laborers, must have been mustered to fashion these colossi in the quarries, to remove them to the Nile, to embark and disembark them, and finally to erect them upon their pedestals! The points of the obelisks were covered with gold in order that they "might be seen on both sides of the river, and their rays inundated the Two Lands whenever the sun rose between them, just as it appears in the horizon of heaven." Long inscriptions carved at the base of the shafts proclaim to future generations that the

Fig. 10.—Statue of Senenmut and Nefrure (Berlin Museum)

Fig. 11.—Obelisks of Thutmose I and Queen Hatshepsut (Karnak)

queen made the obelisks "as her monument for her father Amun, Lord of Karnak," each one of them consisting of a single block of granite, and that she had ordered their erection in order that her "name might remain enduring in this temple forever and ever."

It must have been very much against his will that the energetic young Thutmose III watched from the side lines the high-handed rule of the "pharaoh" Hatshepsut and the chancellorship of the upstart Senenmut. But at length his hour also struck. He succeeded in overthrowing Senenmut and in banishing along with him Hatshepsut's not inconsiderable galaxy of satellites. Thus about 1482 B.C., she came to what we may well believe was an unnatural end. Her daughter Nefrure had apparently preceded her in death. The passing of these two women saw the last branch of the old royal house in the grave, and Thutmose III had achieved undisputed possession of the crown. His ambition had at last been realized, and sole rule over Egypt was assured to him and his descendants. And now the king wreaked with full fury his vengeance on the departed ones who in life had thwarted his ambitions. He was resolved that their memory should perish from the earth. Wherever the names or representations of Hatshepsut occurred on temple walls, they were chiseled away and replaced by those of Thutmose I, II, and III. Excepting in places either inaccessible to or overlooked by the persecutors, her name was utterly obliterated. The statues and sphinxes which she had erected in her beautiful temple at Deir el-Bahri were broken to pieces and cast into a near-by stone quarry.

Thutmose III (Fig. 1) was about thirty years old when he attained the sole reign, and twenty years had elapsed since he had acceded to the throne on the death of his father. While he appears to have met with no opposition to his assumption of the royal power in Egypt itself, on the eastern frontier of the empire in Palestine, where Egypt's strength had never been very great, storm clouds were gathering which threatened to break at any moment with devastating violence. The king therefore determined to forsake the Nile Valley at once in search of the laurels of foreign conquest. He would win for Egypt the Asiatic provinces the subjection of which his grandfather Thutmose I had already begun, and he would make them a permanent part of the Egyptian empire.

VI

WESTERN ASIA IN THE MIDDLE OF THE
SECOND MILLENNIUM B.C.

THE main goal of the Egyptian conquest was the land of Syria with its prosperous cities and fruitful plains, its strategic harbors and vital caravan routes leading to Asia Minor and the mighty empires on the Tigris and the Euphrates. Syria itself is a mountainous country cut off from Egypt on the south by the desert and the mountain range extending into the Sinai Peninsula. The Taurus Mountains constitute a similar barrier between Syria and Asia Minor on the north. The terrain falls abruptly to the Mediterranean on the west, with a narrow strip of coast land which broadens out somewhat in the south. Toward the east the dry and uninviting steppes of the Syrian Desert extend as far as the banks of the Euphrates and, in fact, across this river on to the Tigris. The entire Syrian highland is cut from north to south by a deep cleft. The northern part of this is watered by the Orontes River; the central part takes in the valley bounded by the Lebanon and the Anti-Lebanon—the Coelesyria of the ancients—and drained by the Upper Orontes and the Litany; and the southern extension of the gigantic gorge embraces the valley of the Jordan and the Dead Sea. The usual Egyptian designation of Syria and Palestine was first Retenu and later Khor, from the Hurrians (the biblical Horites) who long dominated the land. The territory along the Mediterranean from Askalon north to the Lebanon and as far inland as the Sea of Galilee was called Djahi, while the region north of the Lebanon was known as Amurru (Amor). All "national" boundaries were naturally shifting and uncertain.

At the period when the Egyptian pharaohs and especially Thutmose III were campaigning in Syria, the Hebrews had not yet come into possession of the country. Palestine, Coelesyria, and the coastal plain as well were inhabited by Semitic tribes commonly designated as the Canaanites, who spoke a language almost identical with the Hebrew. Here also the Hyksos still possessed fortified towns after the withdrawal from Egypt. Farther to the north, in the Orontes Valley and extending eastward to

Damascus, the land was occupied by the Aramaeans, a Semitic people some of whom as nomads roamed the broad plains of the Syrian Desert. They too spoke a dialect not widely different from that of the Canaanites. We encounter these Semitic "barbarians" everywhere on the Egyptian monuments, and we are never left in doubt as to how completely foreign and outlandish in dress and appearance they were regarded by the Egyptians. Even their very stature was in strong contrast to that of the Egyptians; the latter were a slender race, slight of build, while the Syrians were more heavily constructed and often inclined to corpulence. The inhabitants of the Nile Valley were accustomed to shave their hair and beards and to wear wigs, but the foreigners permitted their hair and beards to grow long. In fact, their hair fell in thick masses about the back of their heads as low as the neck and was usually confined by a sort of fillet above the forehead; and their yellowish-brown faces were framed by heavy dark beards which ended in a point beneath the chin (Fig. 12). While the Egyptians as a rule wore white, unpatterned garments, the Asiatics preferred clothing woven or embroidered with gaily colored designs.

During the period with which we are concerned, in consequence of the natural configuration of the land, Syria never possessed a powerful united state. We find instead small communities, each headed by a king who had probably risen to power from the landed nobility. The center of such a community consisted of a city fortified by crenelated walls and towers, to which the entire rustic population fled whenever it was threatened by an invading enemy. Only too frequently these cities were dominated by a spirit of strife and discord among the nobles, each of whom was constantly hopeful of winning for himself the sovereignty. In addition, there was endless warfare among the numerous cities, with interludes of peace as a rule only when danger to all was threatened by a common enemy. Thus the division of the land into small city-states, together with its situation midway between Egypt and Babylonia, was mainly responsible for the fact that since the earliest times it had fallen under the political domination of one or another of the great powers of the ancient Orient.

Already at the beginning of the third millennium B.C. Babylonian trading-parties in search of the coveted wood from the forested heights of the Lebanons traveled industriously the busy caravan route which led from Babylonia up the Euphrates and thence via Aleppo and Hamath into the valley of the Orontes. It was not long until armed hosts followed the traders. In approximately 2350 (or 2600, according to the "long" chronology of other authorities) northern Syria as far as the Lebanon and the Taurus Mountains was conquered by the Babylonian king Sargon I. As a result Syria received additional stimulus in the development of its already ancient culture. Babylonian legends of the gods were transmitted to Syria and were told and retold there. Thus it may be assumed with little doubt that the account of the great flood through which the entire human race, with the exception of a single god-fearing man and his family, came to destruction originated in Babylonia, migrated thence to Syria, and ultimately found its way into the biblical story of the deluge and the survival of Noah.

The most far-reaching evidence of the cultural influence of Babylonia on the Syrian lands is, however, the fact that the Babylonian language

Fig. 12.—Syrian Tribute-Bearers (British Museum)

(Akkadian) and its cuneiform system of writing were introduced and became for centuries the international means of diplomatic and commercial intercourse in all of western Asia, as did Aramaic under the Persian kings and French in the Europe of the eighteenth and nineteenth centuries. This diffusion of the cuneiform is all the more significant since it was by no means easy to acquire a mastery of the script; with its numerous word- and syllable-signs it made heavy demands of skill on writer and reader alike. We shall nevertheless see that the Syrian princes still composed their letters to one another in this unique script in the fifteenth century and that even the scribes of the Egyptian court were obliged to devote their study to it in order to translate for their royal master the documents which flowed into Egypt from all parts of western Asia. In Ugarit (Ras Shamra) a special, simplified script was developed which was impressed in cuneiform characters on clay tablets after the fashion of the more complex Akkadian system of writing. It consisted of twenty-nine alphabetic characters, mostly consonants, which were employed for writing a Semitic language unknown before the discovery of the Ras Shamra tablets.

While then Babylonia stood in close relation with northern Syria and exercised a substantial influence on its culture, Egypt likewise from the time of the earliest kings had developed lively trade connections with southern Syria and the Phoenician coastal cities, especially with Byblos. We know that King Snefru, the predecessor of Khufu, had caused forty ships laden with cedar of Lebanon to be brought to Egypt for use in his building operations. There is no doubt that these ships took on their cargoes in Phoenician harbors. The tutelary goddess of Byblos was known to the Egyptians and identified with their own Hathor, who in this manner became for the Egyptians the mistress of the Syrian lands. We have already seen what vigorous commercial relations Egypt carried on during the Middle Kingdom with Ras Shamra and possibly with other cities of Palestine and Syria as well (p. 22).

In addition to the various small Syrian states, the period down to the fourteenth century B.C. witnessed the development in the Near East of four great empires which came into contact with Egypt, in war or in peace, during the following centuries.

The first of these was the Babylonian empire on the Euphrates, which reached a conspicuous peak of power about the end of the eighteenth century under the strong Semitic dynasty of King Hammurabi. Its profound cultural influence on the other lands of western Asia has already been mentioned. It gradually gave way before the obscure Kassites, a people who may have infiltrated southward from a previous home in the Caucasus region. Their nearly four centuries of rule in Babylonia have left astonishingly little information about them. They apparently possessed little originality or individuality and soon absorbed the native culture which they found in their new environment. Their religion was of a singularly abstract character, with considerable emphasis on ethics. The gods expected righteousness of men, protected the upright, and abandoned sinners. Anthropomorphization of the gods was avoided—a tendency which greatly affected the Kassite art: their sculpture is not significant, and even the cylinder seals display cuneiform texts rather than figures of the gods. The Kassite rulers carried on a busy correspondence with their "brothers" the Egyptian kings, chiefly in repeated pleas for gold and vain hopes for interdynastic marriage.

By the second half of the second millennium, Assyria had fallen into a state of decline, overshadowed first by the Babylonian successors of Hammurabi and later by the growing domination of the Hurrians. The resurgence of this second of the Asiatic empires was destined to come several centuries later, when it expanded in every direction from its capital at Asshur on the Tigris.

West of Assyria lay the third great empire, that of the Hurrians, known to the Egyptians as Mitanni and Nahrin. The populace appears to have been subject to an Aryan ruling class (the Marianni) of horse and chariot owners with Indian names, worshipers of such Indian divinities as Indra, Varuna, Mitra, and the Nasatyas. Beginning with numerous tiny city-states, Mitanni in the fifteenth and fourteenth centuries was forged into a powerful empire extending from the Zagros to the Mediterranean and from Lake Van to Asshur and Arrapha (Kirkuk). The precise location of its capital Wassukanni has as yet defied discovery by archeologists, and the language and literature are still in the early stages of interpretation. Among the chief Hurrian divinities—who have to be considered apart from the Indian gods of the Marianni—were Kusuh, Simigi, Teshub, Hepat, and the important father-god Kumarbi, who bears a striking resemblance to the Greek Kronos. Both the religion and the literature of the Hurrians wrought a profound influence on the

Hittites to the north. Mitanni's rivalry with Egypt for control of western Asia was vigorous from the beginning of the Eighteenth Dynasty; it was eventually tempered by royal intermarriages. At length inner strife, owing possibly to the racial disparity of the population, undermined the short-lived Hurrian empire, and it eventually succumbed to the Hittites, to become a pathetic buffer state against the resurgent Assyria.

The fourth and most powerful empire of western Asia was that of the Hittites (Hatti), which centered in Anatolia in the heart of Asia Minor, the region watered by the great bend of the Halys River. Its capital was Hattushash (Boğazköy), about ninety miles east of modern Ankara. Excavation of its ruins has turned up state archives and libraries consisting of many thousands of clay tablets inscribed in the various languages spoken throughout the empire. The Hittites themselves spoke an Indo-European tongue which they wrote in cuneiform on tablets or carved with an unrelated system of hieroglyphs on stone monuments. However, Akkadian continued in use as the international language of diplomacy. The Hittites consisted of several different strata, who dwelt in a far-flung series of city-states. These were gradually welded into a monarchy with a king who considered himself as purely human and subject to the gods, in contradistinction to the usual oriental theories of divine kingship. In the beginning he was chosen by the nobles, and only later, after bitter and murderous contention for the throne, was he empowered under strict limitations to name his successor. During several centuries of fluctuating fortunes, the Hittite kings developed a stable government and promulgated an enlightened legal "code," with its chief emphasis on restitution and individual welfare rather than penal law and blood revenge. A dynasty of able rulers succeeded in conducting their conquests over a large area in spite of the Mitannian pressure from the south. A little later, with Mitanni deprived of Egyptian support during the Amarna period, Shuppiluliuma, greatest of Hittite emperors, marched out with his armies in every direction and rapidly added to his dominion northern Syria as far as the Lebanon, the countries of Asia Minor, and the once mighty Mitanni itself. It was at this climax of Hittite power that Tutankhamun's widow dispatched her desperate plea for a Hittite prince to become her consort on the throne of Egypt (cf. p. 241). Henceforth for several centuries the Hittite empire was to rank as Egypt's keenest rival for the control of the East.

VII

THE CONQUESTS OF THUTMOSE III

IT WAS on the twenty-fifth day of the eighth month, in the twenty-second year of his reign, that King Thutmose III passed the fortress of Tjaru (Sile) on the eastern frontier of Egypt "in order to repel those who had attacked the boundaries of Egypt" and to overthrow those who "were inclined to rebel against his majesty." In central and northern Palestine there had been organized a confederation of three hundred and thirty native princes the very soul of which was constituted by the Hyksos who had been driven from Avaris and Sharuhen. At its command was the king of Kadesh, who was determined to resist by force of arms every attempt to bring Syria under Egyptian dominion. Southern Palestine alone appears to have remained loyal to the pharaoh. After his preparations were complete, Thutmose marched forth along the great military road which then as now, beginning at Qantara (on the present Suez Canal), followed the coast of the Mediterranean. On the fourth day of the ninth month, in his twenty-third year, the anniversary of his accession to the throne, he arrived at Gaza. The march continued by way of Askalon, Ashdod, and Jamnia, where the Egyptian army apparently left the desert road which connected Jamnia with Joppa to follow the caravan route inland along the foothills and past the Carmel Ridge. Eleven days after leaving Gaza, Thutmose reached the town of Yehem at the foot of the mountain. There he was informed that the enemy were stationed on the other side in the Plain of Esdraelon and that they had chosen the fortified town of Megiddo as the fulcrum of their defense.

It was imperative to penetrate the mountain range and engage the enemy forces at Megiddo; the only doubt in the matter was the route by which the march must be undertaken. There were three possibilities in all. The first and nearest led from Yehem via Aruna directly to Megiddo; it was a narrow pass in which the army could make but slow progress, marching "horse after horse and man after man." Besides, there was a very real danger that the enemy might join battle with the van of the Egyptian forces as soon as it debouched from the valley on the plain and destroy it very easily before the remaining body of troops could come up with reinforcements. Both of the other two routes were longer but less dangerous.

The king called a council of war in order to reach a decision on the proper line of march. It was the general opinion that the nearest but most dangerous route should be rejected in favor of one of the others. Thutmose, however, interpreted this advice as a mark of cowardice and expressed his opinion that the enemy would likewise attribute to fear a choice of any but the most direct road to the field of battle. "As Re loves me and my father Amun praises me," cried the king in the presence of his troops, "I will march on this road to Aruna; let him of you who will go on these other roads which you have mentioned and let him of you who will follow my majesty." Thus the most difficult and hazardous road was selected. The army set forth and arrived in Aruna after a march of three days. After a night's halt at the summit the descent was made in the early hours of the next morning to the Plain of Esdraelon. The king proceeded in person with the van of his troops and, pressing slowly forward through the narrow pass, had already descended into the valley while the main body of the army was still in the mountains and the rear had not even left Aruna. Nevertheless, the dreaded attack of the enemy did not occur; they had stationed themselves in battle array before the gates of Megiddo and for some incomprehensible reason made no attempt to hinder the advance of the Egyptian host. Thutmose was accordingly able to lead his troops without disturbance into the plain and to settle them in a fortified camp. There they refreshed themselves by a night's rest and gathered strength to meet the enemy on the morrow. The battle began at dawn. The king mounted his "golden chariot, arrayed in his panoply of war like Horus mighty of arm and Theban Montu," and stationed himself at the head of his army. The enemy retreated before the furious onslaught of the Egyptians and fled headlong toward the city walls. They found the gates already barricaded by the inhabitants, so that the fugitives, including the prince of Kadesh, who was leader of the revolt, and the prince of Megiddo himself, had to be drawn up over the walls by employing their clothing as ropes. The enemy losses were small, thanks to their speedy flight; there were but eighty-three dead, the hands of whom were severed and laid before the pharaoh, and three hundred and forty prisoners. However, the entire camp of the confederates fell to the Egyptians, including an enormous quantity of war chariots and horses which had been abandoned by their owners. The Egyptian troops fell so greedily upon the rich plunder that they completely overlooked their opportunity to pursue the foe and to capture the city. The chiding of the king was useless—it came too late. Thus he was obliged to settle down to a siege of Megiddo, "the capture of which was the capture of a thousand cities," and by a blockade which lasted for seven months to starve it into submission. Trenches were constructed about the town, and strong ramparts were erected to forestall any attempt at a sally. Ultimate capitulation was of course inevitable; the princes came out in person and fell at the feet of the pharaoh to "beg breath for their nostrils."

Then that fallen one [the chief of Kadesh], together with the chiefs who were with him, caused all their children to come forth to my majesty with many products of gold and silver, all their horses with their trappings, their great chariots of gold and silver with their painted equipment, all their battle armor, their bows, their arrows, and all their implements of war—those things, indeed, with which they had come to fight against my majesty. And now they brought them as tribute to my majesty while they stood on their walls giving praise to my majesty in order that the breath of life might be given to them.

Then my majesty caused them to swear an oath, saying: "Never again will we do evil against Menkheperre [praenomen of Thutmose III]—may he live forever—our lord, in our lifetime, for we have witnessed his power. Let him only give breath to us according to his desire. . . . ."

Then my majesty allowed to them the road to their cities, and they went, all of them, on donkeys. For I had taken their horses, and I carried off their citizens to Egypt and their property likewise.

Thus the booty taken in the initial assault before the city walls was greatly augmented at the raising of the siege. There were 2,041 horses, 191 colts, 924 chariots in all, 892 of which were of ordinary quality, while the remainder were richly wrought with gold and silver mountings as described above, as well as a multitude of valuable weapons. The royal palace of Megiddo was plundered, the booty consisting of not only the 87 children of the prince himself and his royal confederates but 1,796 male and female slaves of lesser rank, together with other persons, besides a vast amount of costly household equipment, including gold pitchers and other vessels, articles of furniture, statues, and other objects too numerous to mention. Of the animals which fell into Egyptian hands there were, in addition to the horses already mentioned, 1,929 bulls, 2,000 small cattle, and 20,500 other animals. Furthermore, the entire crop of standing grain in the fields surrounding the town was harvested by the besiegers, and, in so far as it had escaped being cut in secret by individual soldiers, this was carefully measured and shipped by sea to Egypt.

In the conquest of Megiddo the pharaoh had re-won at a single stroke all of northern Palestine; the remaining princes of Syria made haste to announce their allegiance by dispatching gifts to the conqueror. Even the king of Assyria sent from far away on the Tigris his quota of "tribute," consisting of huge pieces of lapis lazuli and a number of costly Assyrian vessels. The vanquished princes were compelled to provide hostages, who were sent to Egypt, and it is not to be doubted that many a Syrian king's daughter was received into the harem of the pharaoh. As a permanent memorial of this great victory, Thutmose caused to be carved in the great temple of Karnak three different lists of the conquered cities. Each one of them is represented by an ellipse containing its name in hieroglyphic characters and surmounted by the bust of a human figure with arms bound behind the back and clearly designated as a Syrian by the large crooked nose, the prominent cheek bones, and the pointed beard. In one of the accompanying scenes the king is depicted as conqueror of Asia, wearing on his head the crown of Lower Egypt and holding by the hair a group of kneeling Asiatics whom he is in the act of smiting with his mace, while the goddess of Thebes approaches from the right, leading on a rope the various Syrian towns in fetters in order to present them to the king.

However great the victory which Thutmose III had won in the battle on the Plain of Esdraelon before the gates of Megiddo, his ultimate goal—the overthrow of all Syria as far north as the banks of the middle Euphrates and the Taurus and Amanus Mountains, whose rich and powerful commercial cities offered stiff resistance in order to preserve their liberty—had not been achieved. Wartet, which was defended by troops from nearby Tunip, was captured, and Ardata was plundered and destroyed. Here the Egyptian soldiers made merry in the sumptuous houses and bursting wine cellars of the inhabitants. They became drunk every day, and they were "anointed with oil as at the feasts in Egypt." In order to leave the city in a state of utter submission and impotence, the king ordered the grain fields, vineyards, and fruit trees of the adjacent territory to be destroyed, thus putting an end to the principal source of income of the people. While the army returned to Egypt by land, two captured ships were utilized to transport the spoils of the campaign. Ardata, however, was not crushed in spite of all this punishment. Thus the pharaoh found it necessary in the following year—the thirtieth of his reign—to march once more against the defiant city, which he captured and sacked a second time. More impressed than on the previous occasion, the population decided to recognize the authority of the Egyptian king and to pay the regular demands of tribute. The fate of Ardata was extended to Simyra and Kadesh as well.

On the coast of Palestine, somewhat farther to the south, the harbor city of Joppa—the modern Jaffa—appears likewise not to have surrendered to the Egyptians without opposition. It was laid under siege and, if a later Egyptian legend may be trusted, was ultimately taken only by stratagem. While the Egyptian general Djehuti was encamped before the walls of Joppa, he contrived by some device to persuade the prince of the town to visit his field headquarters. Accepting the invitation, the prince appeared at the camp of the foreigners in the company of a body of his retainers. These were richly entertained, their horses were properly fed, and after a short time the company of guests lay drunk on the ground. The prince of Joppa himself, in the meantime, was sitting in conversation with Djehuti. At length he expressed a desire to examine "the great war club of King Thutmose," which Djehuti had with him. The latter ordered it to be produced, whereupon he grasped its handle and brought it down with a sudden blow on the temple of the "enemy of Joppa," who fell unconscious to the floor and was promptly secured with rope. After the enemy leader had been thus eliminated, two hundred baskets were brought in, and into them were stowed two hundred Egyptian soldiers, together with lengths of rope and wooden handcuffs. Djehuti then sent a message to the charioteer of the prince of Joppa, who was presumably waiting outside in complete ignorance of what had happened to his compatriots and his master, ordering him to return to the city to announce to the princess of Joppa that her husband had captured the Egyptian commander and that he was already on his way home with his booty. Sure enough, a long procession was actually approaching the city: the baskets heavy with "booty" and attended by five hundred "prisoners" filed through the city gates. As soon as all of them were within the walls, the "prisoners" released their baggage, and in a trice the garrison was overpowered and the stronghold taken. That night Djehuti sent a dispatch to Egypt to the king reporting his success: "Rejoice! Your good father

Amun has delivered to you the enemy of Joppa, all his people, and his city. Send people to lead them off as captives, in order that you may fill the house of your father Amen-Re, king of the gods, with male and female slaves who will fall under your feet forever and ever." However legendary the details of the story—the Egyptian version of the Trojan horse—there can remain little question of the authenticity of the nucleus of the tale, that Joppa was captured by a trick. The hero Djehuti is himself a well-authenticated historical personality. He bore titles which indicate him to have been a sort of governor of Syria who accompanied the king abroad and remained to administer the conquered territories. A number of objects from his tomb have survived, including two magnificent basins, a fine dagger, and several beautiful oil vases of alabaster.

Much more critical were the contests which Thutmose III had to face in northern Syria, especially those against the town of Kadesh on the Orontes, whose prince had been the leader of the great revolt against Egypt in year 22, and the distant land of Mitanni. The first attack on Kadesh occurred in year 30, when the town was captured and plundered, "its groves laid waste and its grain pulled up." But Kadesh made a speedy recovery from its defeat; the fortifications destroyed by the Egyptians were rebuilt, and measures were taken to ward off a new attack. Thutmose now realized that extensive preparations were essential before undertaking the future expeditions which he contemplated. These were made during the seventh campaign, in year 31, when he captured Ullaza on the Phoenician coast and stocked enormous supply bases in "every port town" which he reached. Two years later he was ready to march forth on his greatest campaign. Having crossed the Orontes near Homs, he captured Katna. In the next battle, at Aleppo, he was joined by the general, Amenemhab, who had been diverted to southern Palestine to quell a riot in the Negeb. From Aleppo the course lay northeasterly to Carchemish, which promptly capitulated. Then, with boats of firwood ("cedar") built in the mountains behind Byblos and transported on oxcarts all the way to the Euphrates, he ferried his army across the great river to his ultimate goal of conquest in Nahrin. Another great victory was won, but the king of Mitanni led the bulk of his forces into one of his remoter provinces, leaving only 636 captives to the Egyptians. Thutmose thoroughly devastated unhappy Mitanni; then, after erecting a victory stela on the east bank beside that of his father, he recrossed the Euphrates and turned to the southeast for a series of victories on his homeward trail. Sindjar was taken, and at last, three years after its first surrender, Thutmose once more arrayed his horses and chariots beneath the walls of Kadesh. Still stinging under the memory of his previous defeat, the prince of Kadesh contrived an ingenious *ruse de guerre*. He released a mare before the line of Egyptian war chariots, each of which was drawn by a pair of stallions. The horses instantly grew restive; the entire rank wavered and appeared ready to break up in confusion. At this exciting moment the heroic Amenemhab sprang from his chariot and darted forth to intercept the galloping mare. With a neat stroke of his sword he "slashed open her belly, cut off her tail, and tossed it before the king," while the troops shouted their loud admiration. The trick had failed, but the prince of Kadesh stood safe within his reconstructed fortress with no thought of surrender. Thutmose ordered the indomitable Amenemhab to reduce the city. The general with a few picked troops advanced to attempt a breach, and he records in his surviving tomb at Thebes that he was the first Egyptian to pierce the wall. Thus the attackers poured into the city and occupied the citadel, and great was the spoil that fell into their hands. After other successes in the Takhsy country near Kadesh, Thutmose turned again to the north and led his forces to Niy, where he set up another commemorative stela.

While he was still bivouacking with his troops in this region, the pharaoh was informed of the presence of a herd of elephants which was feeding and basking in the rocky pools of Niy. A mighty hunt was arranged as a diversion from the routine of war, and the king met a herd of a hundred and twenty animals. However, Thutmose came near to disaster while on this hunt. One of the infuriated beasts charged him and would certainly have killed him had not the valiant Amenemhab rushed to his aid and struck off the elephant's trunk with his sword, "while standing in the water between two rocks."

This victorious campaign left a deep impression on the peoples of northern Syria. Gifts were heaped upon the king from all sides, including costly offerings from Babylonia and the Hittite country, great quantities of which were transported to Egypt as "tribute" in ships specially built for the purpose at one of the conquered Lebanon ports.

While Thutmose III during several decades of campaigning in western Asia pushed the northern frontier of Egypt as far as the Euphrates, his records indicate that two expeditions up the Nile sufficed to fix the southern boundary of his empire at Napata. He constructed a small temple at Gebel Barkal and set up in it in year 47 a gigantic gray granite stela in order to impress his Nubian subjects with all the prowess and power of their Egyptian overlord. Three years later the king cleared an obstructed channel through the first cataract and ordered it to be maintained permanently by the local fishermen. On the seventh pylon of the temple of Karnak, as a counterpart to the lists of Palestinian towns which he had conquered on the Megiddo campaign, Thutmose compiled a similar "catalogue of the southern lands and Nubian peoples which his majesty subjugated," most of which, however, had come under Egyptian sovereignty at an earlier period, while others had never belonged to the empire. But even if this list, like the others, is not to be taken literally in every respect, it cannot be doubted that Thutmose III did actually extend his sway over a mighty empire, just "as his father Amun had commanded him." In the name of the Theban king of the gods the pharaoh had marched forth to war; under his protection he had smitten the ignominious foe; finally to his temple fell the lion's share of the booty which was brought home to Egypt from the conquered lands.

In order to portray the deeply felt debt of gratitude which the king owed to Amun (Fig. 13), the priests at Karnak composed a marvelous ode of victory in which the returning king is greeted and eulogized by his divine protector.

> Come thou to me, rejoicing to see my beauty, O my son, my champion, Thutmose. . . . .
> I give unto thee valor and victory over every land;
> I place thy might and the fear of thee in all lands,
> And the terror of thee as far as the four supports of the sky. . . . .
> The chiefs of all lands are united in thy grasp—
> I stretch forth mine own hands to bind them for thee;
> I bind the Nubian Beduin in ten thousands and thousands, and the northern peoples in hundred thousands.
> I cast thine enemies beneath thy sandals, and thou destroyest the recalcitrant,
> Even as I have committed unto thee the earth in its length and in its breadth,
> While the western peoples and the easterners are under thy control.

FIG. 13.—GOLD STATUETTE OF THE GOD AMUN (METROPOLITAN MUSEUM OF ART)

61

Thou treadest every foreign land with joyful heart, and none ventureth himself in thy vicinity;

But as I am thy guide, so thou reachest out unto them.

Thou hast crossed the waters of the great bend of Nahrin, in the victory and the might which I have decreed unto thee.

They hear thy battle cry and they creep into their holes;

I rob their nostrils of the breath of life; I cause the terror of thy majesty to pervade their hearts.

The uraeus serpent on thy head, it consumeth them; it burneth with its flame the inhabitants of the distant moors;

It severeth the heads of the Asiatics, and not one of them escapeth.

I cause thy victories to penetrate to all the lands; that which my uraeus serpent illuminateth is subject unto thee.

None is rebellious against thee as far as the span of heaven;

They come with gifts on their backs in obeisance to thy majesty, even as I have commanded.

I cause to collapse every attacker that cometh near unto thee: their hearts burn up and their bodies quake.

I have come to cause thee to trample the chiefs of Djahi; I disperse them beneath thy feet throughout their lands.

I cause them to see thy majesty as the lord of rays: thou shinest before them in mine image.

I have come to cause thee to trample the dwellers of Asia; so smitest thou the heads of the Asiatics of Retenu.

I cause them to see thy majesty adorned in thy regalia when thou takest thy weapons into the war chariot.

I have come to cause thee to trample the Orient; so treadest thou the inhabitants of God's Land.

I cause them to see thy majesty like a comet that streweth its flames and unfoldeth its train.

I have come to cause thee to trample the Occident; Keftiu and Isy are subject to thy dignity.

I cause them to see thy majesty as a young bull firm of heart and sharp of horns, wholly unassailable.

I have come to cause thee to trample those who dwell in their distant moors: the lands of Mitanni quake from fear of thee.

I cause them to see thy majesty as a crocodile, master of terror in the water, and one approacheth him not.

I have come to cause thee to trample the people of the islands; those who dwell in the midst of the sea bow to thy battle cry.

I cause them to see thy majesty as the Avenger crowned in glory on the back of his victim.

I have come to cause thee to trample the Libyans; the Utentiu have succumbed
  to thy might.
I cause them to see thy majesty as a fierce lion: thou makest them into corpses
  throughout their valleys.
I have come to cause thee to trample the tail of the world; that which the sea
  encircleth is enclosed in thy grasp.
I cause them to see thy majesty as a soaring falcon that taketh what it per-
  ceiveth according to its desire.
I have come to cause thee to trample those who dwell at the head of the world;
  thou bindest the sand-dwellers in captivity.
I cause them to see thy majesty as an Upper Egyptian jackal swift of feet, the
  runner that prowleth throughout the Two Lands.
I have come to cause thee to trample the Nubians; everything is in thy grasp
  as far as Shatiu-djeba.
I cause them to see thy majesty like thy two brothers [Horus and Seth], whose
  arms I have joined with thee in victory.

This song of praise, which was a model of form and style, with a structure easily discernible even in translation, became exceedingly popular
and in later times was widely imitated and adapted to the glorification of
other kings.

In the thirtieth year of his reign Thutmose was able to celebrate for the
first time the thirty-year jubilee commemoration of the day on which he
had been designated heir to the throne. Since from of old it had been
customary to repeat this jubilee every three or four years after its first
celebration, he enjoyed in the remaining twenty-three years which were
destined for him a total of such celebrations quite unusual for an oriental
potentate. According to an old tradition the celebration of these *heb-sed*
festivals was signalized by the erection of obelisks. Four of these wonderful monuments of Thutmose III have survived to us—two which once
stood in Thebes and a pair originally erected before the temple of Re in
Heliopolis. By a curious trick of fate not one of them still stands in its
ancient site. Some of them already in antiquity, the others in modern
times, have been removed to widely separated localities. One of the Theban obelisks was taken by order of the emperor Constantine the Great to
Byzantium, the eastern capital of the Roman Empire, which had been
renamed Constantinople in his honor; it was not, however, until the year
390 that the emperor Theodosius caused it to be erected in the Hippo-
drome, where it stands to this day. The mate to this obelisk—a shaft a
hundred and five feet in height—to which Thutmose IV had added an

inscription during his reign, was removed to Rome and set up in the Circus Maximus about 363. It was overturned in some manner, however, and lay buried in rubbish for centuries, until Pope Paul V excavated it in 1588 and had it erected on a new foundation before the palace of St. John Lateran. Still more remarkable were the wanderings of the two Heliopolitan obelisks. By order of the prefect Barbarus they were brought in the eighth year of Augustus (23 B.C.) to the Egyptian capital Alexandria in order that they might be erected before the Caesareum in the new suburb of Nikopolis. These shafts are the famous "Cleopatra's Needles," as they were named for the great queen by the Arabs. But they were both destined for still further travels. After one of them, a shaft of about sixty-eight feet in height, had lain on the ground for over a thousand years, it was presented by Muhammad Ali to the British government and removed at the expense of a private citizen to London in 1877, to be erected on the Thames Embankment, where, nearly ruined by smoke and soot, it stands today. Its mate was brought in 1880 to New York as a gift of the Egyptians to the United States government, and it has now become one of the most famous landmarks of Central Park. And thus, in four modern cities of the Old and the New World, these four colossal shafts of red granite proclaim the renown of the ancient "world-conqueror," Thutmose III, and fulfil far beyond his expectations the wish of the greatest of the pharaohs that "his name might endure throughout the future forever and ever."

If according to the Egyptian point of view the virtue of a ruler proclaimed itself primarily through his service to the gods and in the temples which he erected for them, then was Thutmose III without doubt one of the best of pharaohs. From the booty of his wars he made rich gifts to the various priesthoods, and there is scarcely a single one of the larger cities of Egypt which lacks remains of his building activities. Unfortunately, few of the sanctuaries which owe to him their existence, with the exception of those which he built at Thebes (to which we shall return later), have survived to modern times.

Near the end of his reign, Thutmose III appointed as coregent his only son Amenhotep, whom his second wife, the "Great Royal Wife" Hat-shepsut-Merytre, had borne to him. The father and his son had but a short time to share the throne. For on the last day of the seventh month, in the fifty-fourth year of his reign, Thutmose III "fulfilled his time; he flew up to the sky, united himself with the sun, and mingled with him who had created him." He had attained approximately the age of sixty-five. As late as his fiftieth regnal year he had conducted his last campaign into Nubia, and shortly before his death he had participated with his son and coregent Amenhotep in a review of his troops.

Thutmose III had provided for his last resting-place a great cliff tomb in the lonely Valley of the Kings, where his father was buried and where Hatshepsut also had excavated for herself a tomb. It begins with a corridor more than sixty-five feet in length which leads from the entrance by a steep descent to a great shaft twelve to fifteen feet square and fifteen to twenty feet in depth. On the far side of the shaft is a large hall with two square pillars, the walls of which are adorned with no fewer than seven hundred and forty-one pictures of Egyptian divinities. In the floor at one of the rear corners of this hall is the opening of a second corridor which descends by a series of shallow steps to the main hall of the tomb. The roof of this chamber is also supported by two rectangular pillars. Its walls are covered with pictures and hieroglyphic inscriptions all of which are drawn rather than painted in a cursive style in black or red color on a yellowish-gray background. The resulting impression is much as if the walls of the entire chamber had been tapestried with an enormous inscribed papyrus. The beholder finds here spread out before his eyes a complete and undamaged copy of one of the best-known and most-appreciated books of the time—the "Book of What Is in the Netherworld," a sort of guide to the hereafter, the knowledge of which was necessary to the king if he would successfully undertake the nightly journey through the lower world in the company of the sun-god Re. On an alabaster pedestal in this hall stood the sarcophagus of yellow quartzite which at one time contained the wooden coffin with the mummy of the king. But Thutmose III, like various of his ancestors, was not destined to rest forever in the place which he had chosen. About five centuries after his death the subterranean burial chambers were penetrated by the indefatigable robbers, who not only broke into the stone sarcophagus and looted the mummy but even hacked the body into three pieces. It was discovered in this state by the necropolis guards, who carefully re-wrapped it in the original bindings and mummy cloths and transferred it to the "royal cache," in which it was discovered with the other royal mummies in 1881. The coffin and mummy of the king are now preserved in Cairo.

There is no doubt that Thutmose III was one of the most significant personalities who ever appeared on the throne of the pharaohs. If any Egyptian ruler deserves to be honored by being designated "the Great," he is a far more fitting candidate than any other, certainly more than the later Ramesses II, to whom this title has been unjustly applied by more than one modern historian of ancient Egypt. The Egyptians were fully conscious of his stature and "how greatly the gods had loved him." For centuries his praenomen Menkheperre was regarded as a potent good-luck charm, and it was inscribed on countless amulets to protect the wearers from adversity. The exploits of the king who had founded an Egyptian world-empire survived in the memory of the people and were embroidered with numerous legendary adornments. His name alone was forgotten. When Germanicus, the nephew of the Roman emperor Tiberius, visited Thebes in A.D. 19 and wandered about the vast precinct of Karnak, he prevailed upon one of the priests to explain the long inscriptions on the walls which to this day preserve almost the sole record of the military exploits of Thutmose III. The accommodating priest according-ly explained to him how the king with an army of 700,000 men had overthrown Libya and Ethiopia, the Medes and Persians, the Bactrians and Scythians, Cappadocia, Bithynia, and Lycia—in fact, almost all of Asia Minor. He also read the tribute which had been imposed on all these peoples, the weight of the gold and silver, the quantities of chariots and horses, the ivory and grain, and all the other objects which each tribe was required to deliver—everything, indeed, which the annals of Thutmose III actually describe. But when asked who it was who had achieved all this glory, the priest named not Thutmose III but Ramesses—the Ramesses whom the modern dragoman is still accustomed to designate whenever he elucidates to an open-mouthed tourist the astonishing wonders of an ancient monument.

VIII

THE GOLDEN AGE: THE SUCCESSORS OF THUTMOSE III

ON THE death of Thutmose III (*ca.* 1450 B.C.) his son Amenhotep II (Fig. 14) assumed the sole rule over the Egyptian empire. It was only natural that Thutmose should have given special attention to the education of the heir to his throne. While we have but meager knowledge of the training considered appropriate for an Egyptian prince, it is evident that no little emphasis was placed on archery, hunting, aquatics, and horsemanship. Records survive of several of Amenhotep's teachers, among them an expert bowman named Miny, who gave him lessons in shooting. The enthusiasm for sports and contests of skill which was imparted to the royal pupil by his tutors, as well as the prince's great love for horses, has recently been revealed in one of the best characterizations which has survived from the ancient world. It consists of a series of episodes in the life of Prince Amenhotep before his accession to the throne recorded on a stela discovered several years ago not far from the great sphinx at Giza.

Now, moreover, when his majesty appeared as coregent while still a fine young stripling, when he had developed his body [to maturity] and had completed eighteen years on his legs in valor, he was one who knew every work of Montu—there was no equal to him on the field of battle. He was one who knew horses, without his like in this numerous army, nor was there one in it who could draw his bow. He could not be approached in fleetness. Strong was he of arms, one who never wearied when he took the oar; but he rowed at the stern of his falcon-boat as the best of two hundred men. After casting off when they had finished half an *iteru* [three-quarters of a mile] they were worn out and their bodies exhausted, nor could they draw breath any more. His majesty, however, was mighty under his oar of twenty cubits [about thirty-three feet] in length. He cast off and finally moored his falcon-boat after completing three *iteru* [four and a half miles] in rowing without a rest from pulling [the oar]. The faces [of the spectators] were joyful at watching him.

He did this also: he drew three hundred stiff bows, comparing the workmanship of the artisans who had made them, in order to distinguish the ignorant from the clever. And he came also and did the following, which I wish to call to your attention. He entered his northern garden and found set up for him four targets of Asiatic copper of a span [three inches] in their thickness and with twenty cubits [nearly thirty-five feet]

FIG. 14.—STATUE OF AMENHOTEP II (CAIRO MUSEUM)

between one pole and its fellow. Then his majesty appeared in a chariot like Montu in his power. He seized his bow and grasped four arrows at once. He rode northward, shooting at them [the targets] like Montu in his regalia. His arrows came forth from the back of [one of] them while he attacked another. And that is a thing, indeed, which had never been done nor even heard of in story: that an arrow shot at a target of copper came forth from it and dropped to the earth, excepting [at the hand of] the king, rich of glory, whom Amun has strengthened, ... Okheprure [Amenhotep II], heroic like Montu.

Now, indeed, when he was still a youth he loved his horses and rejoiced in them. It made his heart strong to work them, to learn their nature, to become skilled in taking care of them, and in being initiated in the [proper] methods. When it was heard in the palace by his father, the Horus: Mighty Bull, Appearing in Thebes [Thutmose III], the heart of his majesty was pleased when he heard it, and he rejoiced at what was being said about his eldest son, saying in his heart: "He shall exercise the lordship of the entire land without his being attacked; his mind already entertains valor and he rejoices in strength, even though he is still but an innocent lad, my beloved, and one yet without understanding and not yet at the time of doing the work of Montu; he is still unconcerned with thought of self, but he loves strength; it is God who puts it into his heart to act so that Egypt will be preserved for him and the land will defer to him." Then said his majesty to those who were with him: "Let there be given to him the very best horses from the stable of my majesty which is in Memphis, and tell him: 'Care for them but let them fear you. Trot them but break them if they resist you.' " Thereafter it was intrusted to the prince to take care of the horses of the stall of the king, and he did that which had been intrusted to him: Resheph and Astarte rejoiced at him because of his doing everything which his heart desired. He trained horses without their equal. They never grew tired when he took the reins nor did they ever sweat even on a long gallop. He used to yoke them in the harness in Memphis and stop at the sanctuary of Harmachis [the sphinx]. He would tarry a while there encircling it and gazing at the perfection of this sanctuary of Khufu and Khafre. His heart desired to perpetuate their names, and he kept reminding himself of it, indeed, until that came to pass which his father Re had commanded him. After this, when his majesty was crowned as king, ... then he remembered the place where he had enjoyed himself in the vicinity of the pyramids and sphinx, and it was ordered that a sanctuary should be built there in which there was set up a stela of white stone, the face of which was engraved in the great name of Okheprure, beloved of Harmachis, given life forever.

It is not surprising that a prince with this background would possess an uncommonly democratic spirit toward his people. Amenhotep II appears always to have retained intimate contact with the friends of his youth and to have surrounded himself with loyal officials selected from their ranks. If he appointed one of them to a distant post in his empire, he was not above reminding him on occasion by a personal letter of his continuing interest. Consistent with his character and training, Amenhotep's surviving records of his principal wars emphasize his personal exploits and adventures.

His first campaign was probably incited by the revolt of certain of the North Syrian districts conquered by Thutmose III, including Takhsy, near Kadesh. It took him as far north as Alalakh on the great bend of the Orontes and to Shemesh-Edom, but he apparently did not lead his army eastward in the footsteps of his father to cross the Euphrates. Somewhere, however, he "smote Nahrin." On the homeward march he captured Niy and Ugarit and forced the surrender of Kadesh and many other still unidentified cities of northern Syria. While near Kadesh the sport-loving king relaxed for a time for some target shooting and a hunt in a specially constructed game inclosure in the forests of Rebiu. Subsequently, while driving his chariot through the Plain of Sharon, he captured a courier of the prince of Nahrin, whose dispatch on a clay tablet fastened to a cord hung from his neck, and conveyed him to Egypt "on the side of his chariot." Returning with much spoil and many prisoners to Memphis, the king celebrated a great triumph, which, he takes pride in relating, was witnessed by the queen. While in revolting Takhsy, Amenhotep had slain with his own hand seven of its princes and had brought their bodies home to Egypt. Now, as the crowning act of his vengeance, he suspended them heads down on the prow of his Nile boat and transported them to Thebes. Six of the bodies were displayed on the face of the wall of the capital; the seventh was taken to Napata and exposed on its wall as an example to any would-be rebels.

The second campaign was confined to Palestine, where the king captured numerous towns (mostly unidentified), enormous quantities of booty, and no fewer than 89,600 prisoners. After the surrender of Iteren and Migdol-yun, their spoil and captives were assembled in an inclosure surrounded by a double ditch filled with fire; and the king relates that he stood guard throughout the night, "his battle-axe in his right hand, alone, there being no one along with him, for the army was too far distant from him to hear the call of pharaoh." This campaign created a deep impression on the powers of western Asia, for, after hearing of Amenhotep's victories, "the prince of Nahrin, the prince of Hatti, and the prince of Babylonia imitated one another in making presents and . . . . begging peace from his majesty."

Amenhotep II caused his burial place to be excavated in the Valley of the Kings not far from that of his father and on much the same plan. The sarcophagus of yellow quartzite was placed in a crypt adjoining the great pillared hall of the tomb. When it was opened in 1898, the body of the king still lay in the sarcophagus, along with the floral decorations placed on it by pious hands at the burial. Festoons of leaves and flowers were laid about the neck, and on the breast rested a small bouquet of acacia blossoms. The other offering-objects which had once reposed with the pharaoh had been stolen or destroyed by tomb-robbers in antiquity. When the violation of the burial occurred in the tenth century B.C., the authorities for some reason decided to leave Amenhotep in his own tomb, but before sealing it again they removed to it the bodies of nine other kings, including the two immediate followers of Amenhotep II—Thutmose IV and Amenhotep III—which were no longer safe in their own burial places. These continued in undisturbed slumber century after century, until the tomb was discovered and the chamber reopened in 1898.

The pharaoh Amenhotep II was succeeded by his young son Thutmose IV, who had been borne to him by Queen Tyo; we have but the meagerest information about his reign. Minor campaigns in Syria and Nubia resulted in the maintenance of the outposts of the empire as far as Nahrin on the north and Karoy (Napata) in the south. One of the principal events in the king's reign was the excavation of the great sphinx (Fig. 5) from the drifting desert sand which had partially covered it. The sphinx is a huge couchant lion with the head of the king wearing the customary cloth headdress and with the uraeus serpent on the brow. It was probably a natural rock which from a distance bore some resemblance to a lion; when the pyramid of Khafre was built, it was in part chiseled from the spur of rock and in part built up with blocks of stone into the form of a sphinx, and the head was supplied with the features of Khafre. How the impulse to liberate the sphinx from the drifting sand came to Thutmose IV is vividly described by the king himself on a monument which he caused to be installed between the forepaws of the colossal figure. According to this inscription, Thutmose frequently entertained himself as a prince before his accession to the throne by desert hunts in the vicinity of Memphis and "drove in his chariot whose horses were swifter than the wind," while killing lions and gazelles with his javelin. On one of these hunting excursions the youth seated himself during the heat of the day "in the shadow of this great god." At the time when the sun reached its highest point he fell asleep and beheld the majesty of the august god, who spoke to him with his own mouth, as a father speaks to his son.

Look upon me and behold me! O my son Thutmose, I am your father, Harmachis-Khepri-Re-Atum. I shall give to you my reign upon earth over the living and you shall wear its red crown and its white crown on the throne of Geb the Prince. To you shall belong the earth in its length and its breadth, together with that which the eye of the All-Lord illuminates, and to you shall be apportioned provisions from within the Two Lands and the great products of every foreign country. For prolonged years already my face has been turned to you and my heart likewise. You belong to me. Behold, my state is like [that of] one who is in pain, and my entire body is out of joint. For the sand of the desert, this [place] on which I am, presses upon me. I have been waiting to have you do what is in my heart; for I know that you are my son and my champion. Approach; I am with you; I am your guide.

When Thutmose awoke, he was still conscious of the words of the god, and they remained in his memory until his accession to the throne. Immediately upon the beginning of his reign he fulfilled the request of the god who had given him the sovereignty and caused the removal of the sand which had almost buried the sphinx. Only a few years ago, in 1926–27, the Egyptian Service des antiquités followed the example of their ancient king and freed the sphinx once more from the encroaching sands. Thus it may be viewed today, reclining majestically with outstretched paws as it gazes toward the rising sun, much as it must have appeared after Thutmose IV had excavated it in response to the appeal of his father Harmachis (Fig. 5).

After the death of Thutmose IV and his burial in the Valley of the Tombs of the Kings, his son by the "Great Royal Wife" Mutemwiya ascended the throne as Amenhotep III (Fig. 15). His reign of thirty-eight years was in the main a peaceful one, attended with blessings for Egypt beyond those of the past. Toward its end, however, ominous signs of decay began to reveal their presence. Amenhotep himself is the most brilliant representative of this happy era—the perfect picture of a magnificent oriental potentate reveling in the utmost fulness of life. In seeking a single term to epitomize his character, no more fitting epithet for him could be found than "Amenhotep the Magnificent."

As far as we know, Amenhotep III was obliged but once during his reign—in year 5—to take the field in a military campaign. On that occasion certain Nubian tribes had staged an uprising, but the pharaoh defeated them and brought back to Egypt seven hundred and forty Negroes as captives. It is improbable that Amenhotep ever set foot on Syrian soil. He sought, nonetheless, to convey the impression on his monuments that he himself had "with his valiant sword" subjugated the foreign lands, including wretched Kush, Nahrin, and Syria, and placed all of them "under his feet." He also would perform the exploits of his great ancestor, Thutmose III; the loyal clergy complied with his wishes and immortalized him in all his temples as the "victorious ruler." He is depicted, for example, on a magnificent stela, as he stands in his chariot, whip and bow in hand, and drives his horses in triumph over the prostrate forms of his foes. In reality, however, Amenhotep contented himself with driving out on the hunt where in place of human foes he could slay wild bulls or lions. His account of the hundred and two lions which he

FIG. 15.—COLOSSAL GROUP OF AMENHOTEP III AND QUEEN TIY (CAIRO MUSEUM)

had killed with his own hand during the first ten years of his reign is probably much more credible than his attempt to depict himself as a great conqueror.

Amenhotep carried on unusually energetic building activities during his reign. Like his predecessors, he obviously utilized the greater part of the slaves and material wealth which were pouring into Egypt as tribute from the provinces of the empire in order to make rich gifts to the gods

Fig. 16.—Head of Queen Tiy (Berlin Museum)

and to adorn their temples or build new ones. The majority of this wealth naturally fell to the chief divinity of Thebes, Amun the king of the gods, to whom Amenhotep built no fewer than three great temples, not to mention a fourth in faraway Nubia, near the modern Soleb.

At the beginning of his reign Amenhotep III was already married to a woman named Tiy (Fig. 16), the daughter of a commoner by the name of Yuya and his wife Tuya. In spite of her humble origin, Tiy was elevated to the rank of "Great Royal Wife," which established her as queen consort. This fact was commemorated by Amenhotep by the issue of a series of large scarabs (Fig. 17) which mention the lowly background of the queen, her parentage, and the fact that she is nevertheless the official queen of a pharaoh whose realm extends southward to Karoy and northward as far as Nahrin. The young queen apparently exercised considerable influence over her husband and played an important role in political life. She is frequently depicted on monuments beside her husband in a manner totally unprecedented in Egyptian art; and scarabs bearing the names of the king and queen side by side were commonly used as seals or

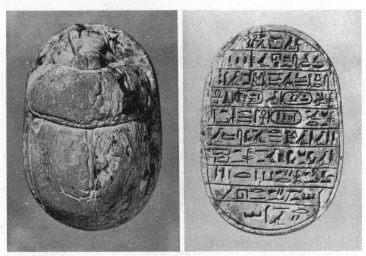

FIG. 17.—SCARAB ANNOUNCING MARRIAGE OF AMENHOTEP III WITH TIY (ORIENTAL INSTITUTE MUSEUM, UNIVERSITY OF CHICAGO)

amulets. Thus there is ample evidence to conclude that the queen had issued forth from the customary seclusion of the past in order to take a prominent position in public life. Not far from the great royal palace on the west bank of Thebes, the pharaoh excavated for her an enormous lake, approximately 6,400 feet in length and 1,200 feet in width, which, in spite of its vast size, was completed in the space of only fourteen days. The event was deemed worthy of the issue of a new series of large "historical" scarabs. Furthermore, the parents of Queen Tiy were accorded a princely burial (which was discovered intact) in the Valley of the Kings.

No discussion of the reign of Amenhotep III can ignore the most famous of his contemporaries. This was a man named Amenhotep, like

FIG. 18.—STATUE OF AMENHOTEP THE SON OF HAPU (CAIRO MUSEUM)

the king his master, though he was familiarly known as Huy. The son of a certain Hapu, he was a native of the Lower Egyptian city of Athribis. His far from handsome but animated old face has been preserved to us in one of the best portrait sculptures of the time (Fig. 18). In the early years of his reign the king's attention had been directed to this man because of his exceptional knowledge of the "divine words" (the hieroglyphs), and he had appointed him to an undersuperintendency of royal scribes. After a period of loyal service, as we learn from his autobiography, Amenhotep was promoted by the king to the position of "Chief Royal Scribe of Recruits."

I mustered the young men of my lord; my pen reckoned the number of millions. I inducted the sturdiest men from the seat of their families. . . . . I levied the estates according to their numbers and drafted the troops of their respective estates. I filled out the ranks with the best of the captives which his majesty had smitten on the battlefield. I inspected all their troops and rejected the weakling[s]. I stationed troops on the road[s] to repel foreigners to their [own] place, and this "girdle of the Two Regions" stood guard against encroachment by the Beduin. I acted similarly on the shores of the Nile mouths, which were blocked under my troops except to the crews of the royal fleet.

But all of Amenhotep's achievements as an administrative official and military leader were greatly surpassed by his accomplishments in his third sphere of activity as chief architect. "My lord honored me a third time . . . . he appointed me overseer of all works, and I perpetuated the name of the king forever. I did not imitate what had been done before." He then proceeds in stilted phrases to relate how he had completed a royal statue in one of the quarries near Heliopolis and how he had transported it to Karnak and erected it in one of the courts of the temple.

I directed the operations on a great and broad statue, taller than his colonnade, the beauty of which enhanced the pylon. Its length was forty cubits [sixty-nine feet] in the august mountain of quartzite beside Re-Atum. I constructed barges and transported it upstream, and it was erected in this great temple, enduring like the sky. My witnesses are you who will come after us. All the soldiers were united under my charge, and they worked with joy, their hearts happy, rejoicing and praising the good god [the king]. They landed in Thebes in exultation.

What other monuments were created by Amenhotep, or whether the wonderful temple of Luxor and the king's enormous mortuary temple behind the still-surviving colossi in western Thebes (Fig. 19) were his work, we do not know. Long and verbose as his autobiography is, he has left us with but few precise details of his important career.

In order to provide for the requirements of his own mortuary cult, he constructed on the edge of the western desert at Thebes, not far from the great temple of his lord, an imposing temple with pool and gardens. By royal decree this was provided for all time with rich and inviolable endowments, including male and female slaves, and it was placed under the protection of Amen-Re, "the king of eternity and guardian of the dead." The memory of this Amenhotep, like that of Imhotep, the architect of the great mortuary monuments of Djoser (p. 14), survived for many centuries. He was reckoned as one of the sages of Egypt, and sayings attributed to him were still current in the Ptolemaic period. Because of his wisdom and his alleged ability to foresee coming events, he was held to be of divine nature. Finally, under one of the successors of Alexander the Great—probably Ptolemy Euergetes II about 140 B.C.—he was deified and henceforth worshiped as a god.

FIG. 19.—THE COLOSSI OF AMENHOTEP III (WESTERN THEBES)

Amenhotep III was afflicted with a severe illness in his latter days. We find him depicted as a weary old man, seated on his chair in the palace with drooping head and with his corpulent body collapsed to a certain flabby lethargy, while his hand hangs listlessly over his knee (Fig. 20). All possible medical assistance proving to be of no avail, he wrote as a last resort to the king of Mitanni, requesting him to send to the Egyptian capital a certain wonder-working statue of the Ninevite goddess Ishtar in the hope that her famous healing powers might bring him some relief.

FIG. 20.—AMENHOTEP III AS AN OLD MAN, WITH QUEEN TIY AT HIS SIDE (BRITISH MUSEUM)

During the last decade or more of his life the ailing pharaoh associated with himself on the throne his son Amenhotep, who had been borne to him by Queen Tiy shortly after his accession. It was not a promising decade for the future of the empire. The king's failing health, in addition to his natural indolence, left him in no condition to attend to the affairs of state. Thus, while he had enjoyed in a magnificent way the heritage of his ancestors, he had made no serious effort during his long reign to maintain it as a permanent possession for himself or his family line. And the young coregent, who might have become the staff of his father's old age, took no interest whatever in administrative duties. Possessed

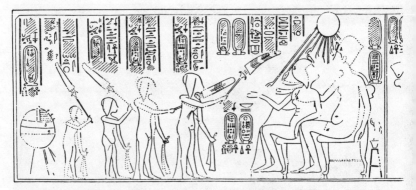

FIG. 21a.—AKHNATON, NOFRETETE, AND FOUR OF THEIR DAUGHTERS AT AMARNA (TOMB OF HUYA)

of a mystical temperament and perhaps of an unsound body as well, he had already begun to devote all his energies to the promulgation of a new religious doctrine as remarkable as it was unfortunate for that critical time and situation. For while Amenhotep III was sitting incapacitated as a semi-invalid at Thebes, his extraordinary son was either absent at Amarna, where he had already begun to build a new capital for the decaying empire, or devoting his time and energy to a bitter religious controversy with the priesthood of Amun at Thebes. In the meantime Syria was in a state of unrest, and hostile forces in the north and east were crossing the frontiers and everywhere attacking the cities which remained loyal to the pharaoh. There were apparently no garrisons in the provinces which were equal to the occasion. Calls for help which were sent to Egypt in close succession echoed unheeded, while the requests for spe-

cific military reinforcements disappeared into the state archives with
scarcely the courtesy of even a hasty perusal.

During the latter half of the coregency, after Amenhotep IV had
changed his name to Akhnaton and taken up his permanent residence at
his new capital of Akhetaton (Amarna), Amenhotep III spent a portion
of his time there in the palace of his son (Fig. 21b). At last, about the year
1375 B.C., the languishing pharaoh passed on to his ancestors and was
buried in a lonely rock-hewn tomb at Thebes which he had prepared for
himself somewhat apart from those of his fathers. With his death passed
also the zenith of the empire on the Nile. For after the accession of Amen-

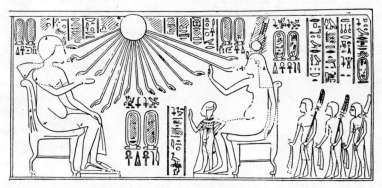

FIG. 21b.—AMENHOTEP III AND QUEEN TIY AS GUESTS AT AMARNA (TOMB OF HUYA)

hotep IV (Akhnaton) to the throne as sole ruler, matters were permitted
to grow from bad to worse. The new king not only made no attempt to
reassure or lend material aid to the faltering representatives of Egyptian
power in western Asia but rather, through his fanatical devotion to his
religious innovations, brought Egypt to the brink of ruin.

IX

THE KING AND THE ADMINISTRATION
IN THE GOLDEN AGE

THE flowering of the pharaonic empire may be considered to have taken place in approximately the period of the fifteenth century B.C., between the accession of Thutmose III and the death of Amenhotep III. Neither before nor after this time did Egypt ever extend its boundaries so far to the north or south, nor was there such a remarkable condition of prosperity in the land. Within seventy years after the expulsion of the Hyksos, Egypt had developed into a world-power such as the Orient had never before witnessed. This situation, of course, had arisen only after the Egyptian state had passed through a complete transformation and had acquired an authority which was undreamed of in the bureaucracy of the Old or Middle Kingdom.

From time immemorial the Egyptian king had been considered the lord of the world. He was held to be the embodiment of the falcon-god Horus, the youthful sun-god who destroyed his enemies; or he was the son of the sun-god Re, who had placed himself on the throne of Geb, the father of the gods; in this latter form he was likewise the son of the principal god of the imperial age, Amun of Thebes, who had become identified with Re. This father-and-son relationship was not conceived by the priesthood as a mere figure of speech but was interpreted as a definite reality. Long rows of relief sculptures in various temples illustrate how the king was begotten by Amun and how he came into the world under the protection of the gods. In a room of the Luxor temple, for example, the god Khnum is shown seated at the potter's wheel, where he fashions in the presence of the goddess Isis two baby boys, the future king Amenhotep III and his ka—a sort of tutelary genius identical in appearance and nature with the king himself. In the next episode Amun approaches the "Great Royal Wife," Mutemwiya, and begets the royal child already created by Khnum. In another scene the god Thoth appears before the queen and announces her prospective confinement, while in an adjoining representation she is led off by Khnum and Isis to the scene of her delivery. This is depicted near by in the presence and with the assistance of numerous divinities and demigods; after it is successfully consummated, the newborn prince is presented by Isis to his father Amun, who takes the child into his arms and promises him "millions of years like Re." The royal infant is suckled by goddesses and sacred cows. He grows up under the protection of the gods, until he is at length installed by his father on the throne of Egypt.

It is obvious that this son of the gods surpassed all mundane creatures in wisdom and power and that the court eulogists never tired of chanting their laudations of the superhuman wisdom of the "good god."

Every speech of thy mouth is like the words of Harakhti; thy tongue is a balance: more accurate are thy lips than the tongue of the balance of Thoth. What is there that thou dost not know? Who is there that is as wise as thou? What place is there which thou hast not seen? There is no land which thou hast not trodden. Every circumstance hath come to thine ears since thou hast administered this land. Thou madest the plans while thou wert still in the egg, in thine offices of child and crown prince. To thee were delivered the affairs of the Two Regions when thou wert still a child with the side-lock. . . . . Thou becamest commander of the army while yet a lad of ten. . . . . If thou sayest to the waters, "Come upon the mountain," a flood floweth directly at thy word, for thou art Re . . . . and Khepri. . . . . Authority is in thy mouth and perception is in thy heart; the activity of thy tongue is the temple of Maat [the goddess of Truth], and God sitteth upon thy lips. Thy words are consummated each day, and thy heart hath made thee like unto Ptah who created the arts. Thou art destined for eternity. All is done according to thy will, and whatever thou sayest is obeyed.

Even if the king was considered as a god, it was but rarely, at least in the time of Thutmose III and his immediate successors, that the concept was carried to its logical conclusion, so that worship was accorded to the pharaoh as a god in temples built for the express purpose of carrying on his divine cult. There were, however, noteworthy exceptions, as in the temple of Soleb in Nubia, where Amenhotep III was worshiped as the "living image of Re on earth," and in the Nubian town of Sedeinga, where Queen Tiy was similarly honored in a chapel built for her worship.

The ruler was outwardly distinguished from commoners by a multitude of insignia which had originated in the remote past but which had been retained, with inevitable alterations, through the ages as a sacred legacy of the ancestors. A characteristic symbol of the kingship was the deadly cobra—the uraeus—which coiled itself upon the forehead of the king in order to destroy all his enemies, just as it had once annihilated the adversaries of the sun-god Re. The official dress of the king consisted of a short or a long skirt thrown about the hips and falling down in front in a curious broad triangular construction. On top of this was frequently hung a narrow band of stiffened material decorated with fine embroidery and ending in a pair or sometimes a row of uraeus serpents. The skirt was supported by a broad belt from the back of which hung a long animal tail, probably an ancient North African badge of chieftaincy. The royal headdress consisted of a whole collection of crowns: the white crown ⩗ of Upper Egypt; the red crown ⩗ of Lower Egypt; the double crown ⩗, a combination of the white and red crowns (Fig. 85), which symbolized in the person of the king the "uniter of the Two Lands" and therefore the ruler of all Egypt; the blue crown ⩗, a cap of cloth or leather which the king often wore on the battlefield (Fig. 98); the linen kerchief which covered the head and extended in front over the shoulders and chest in two broad lappets, while it ended behind the head in a sort of queue hanging below the back of the neck (Fig. 15). Other insignia of the king included a considerable number of different scepters: the crook ⩗, the so-called flail ⩗ (Fig. 39), the mace ⩗, and the scimitar ⩗. It is quite evident that court etiquette prescribed precisely with what dress and insignia the king must adorn himself on each of his appearances and that the keepers of the king's wardrobe maintained a careful watch to insure that the regulations devoted to that end were meticulously observed.

At public audiences the pharaoh was accustomed to appear seated on his throne under a canopy supported by light columns and adorned at the top with a row of uraeus serpents. The splendor of such a royal throne has recently been revealed by the discovery of an actual example of one which was once provided for Tutankhamun, first in his palace and later as mortuary equipment in his rock-hewn tomb in the Valley of the Tombs of the Kings (Fig. 90).

A pharaoh possessed no fewer than five different names, according as he was manifested as the embodiment of the god "Horus," the "Two Ladies" (the tutelary goddesses of Upper and Lower Egypt), the "Horus of Gold" (or the "Falcon of Gold"), the "King of Upper and Lower Egypt," or the "Son of Re." Thus Thutmose III was the "Horus: Mighty Bull, Appearing in Thebes; the Two Ladies: Enduring of Kingship; the Horus of Gold: Splendid of Diadems; the King of Upper and Lower Egypt: Enduring of Form Is Re [Menkheperre]; the Son of Re:

Thoth Is Born [Thutmose]." Of all these names, the last one alone was the original one which was given to the king at birth and by which he was known before the beginning of his reign; the other four were all adopted upon his accession to the throne and were often amplified by the addition of supplementary epithets in the course of his reign. In official intercourse and in letters addressed to him by foreign rulers, the king was addressed by the "great name" which he bore as "King of Upper and Lower Egypt" and which was inclosed when written in hieroglyphic, like the personal name given at birth as the "Son of Re," in an elliptical cartouche. In daily life there was a tendency to avoid the mention of the king by name; instead, he was referred to by various titles or circumlocutions, such as "His Majesty" or the "Good God," while it was customary to say "one commanded" for "the king commanded." Finally, in the New Kingdom he was addressed or spoken of as the "Greatest House," originally a designation of the palace (compare the Turkish title "Sublime Porte"); this title, which was pronounced in Egyptian something like *per-o*, eventually suppressed most of the others and came into current use even in foreign countries, so that it survived into modern times through the medium of the Hebrew form "pharaoh."

What constituted the activities and duties of an Egyptian pharaoh? Whoever would seek to answer such questions on the basis of the representations on the temple walls with their countless pictures of the ruler in association with the gods would necessarily conclude that he spent most of his time in prayer or in the presentation of offerings. That would, however, be far short of the truth. He did, of course, as high priest of the land, participate in the great religious festivals; he personally conducted foundation and dedication ceremonies in the temples which he built for the gods, as well as other priestly functions. These were, nonetheless, not his chief business. There is no doubt that most of his time was devoted, as in the case of rulers in other lands and in other ages, to the transaction of the actual business of ruling and in the administration of the empire. He had to read and dispose of the countless documents and reports which were brought to his court by the high officials, and even if most of the routine duties were performed by clerks and other assistants, there must have been a large amount of work which demanded his personal attention. He was accustomed to give audience and to receive oral reports from the chief dignitaries, who kept him informed, for example, of the condition of the harvest, the amount of tax collections, the height of the Nile inundation, and the like. Moreover, the king was traditionally the chief justice of the nation, with the responsibility of settling all controversies. In reality, of course, he delegated this important power to various administrative agencies, above all to the vizier. The king not infrequently forsook the capital, sometimes for the relaxation of the hunt but probably more often to journey up and down the land on tours of inspection of new buildings which were under construction or of the canals, dikes, and wells of the highly developed irrigation system. His military duties were of primary importance. He not only took part in the recruiting and arming of troops but, as we have observed in the careers of Thutmose and his followers, also often went to war in person and as commander-in-chief led his troops into battle.

From the very earliest period the highest minister in the administration of the state was the vizier, who was likewise the commandant of the capital and the chief justice. During the pyramid age the office of vizier was at first held by a royal prince; a little later, in the Fifth Dynasty, it became for a considerable time a hereditary office in one of the noble houses; at length the king followed the practice of offering the vizierate to a deserving or otherwise favored noble of his own choosing. Up to the reign of Thutmose III the whole of Egypt fell within the sphere of the vizier's authority, but under this pharaoh a division of labor was instituted in the appointment of two viziers. One of these served Upper Egypt as far north as Assiut, while the authority of the Lower Egyptian vizier extended throughout the northern part of the empire. The powers of the vizier had from time immemorial been rigidly determined by a code of regulations. He sat at judgment in a special hall in which no other official was permitted to give a hearing or cause punishment to be administered. All administrative business had to pass through his hands. He gave judgment in boundary controversies, wrote reports to the king, and controlled the lists of recruits who were to "accompany his majesty to the north and the south." To him as "Superintendent of Works" was intrusted the supervision of the artisans who were engaged by the state and the temples in the capital. Thus, for example, the vizier Rekhmire, who held office under Thutmose III, was charged with the construction of a great entrance portal at the temple of Amun in Thebes. Even the required brick were manufactured under his supervision: the Nile mud was broken up with mattocks, moistened with water from a near-by pool, mixed with sand and chopped straw, and formed in molds, just as the children of Israel are described to have done in the Old Testament account (Exod. 5:6–19). The bricks were then taken from the molds and baked in the sun, after which they were ready for use in construction. The colossal statues and sphinxes, the great gateways, the manifold furniture and implements, the vessels and precious objects which were required for use in the temples, were likewise prepared under the control of the vizier. Above all, it was his duty to receive and to transfer to the proper authorities all the tribute which came to Egypt from the surrounding rulers. The office of the vizier was the administrative center of the entire land.

In consideration of the vast importance of the vizierate, it is not surprising that the installation of the vizier was undertaken by the king in person. The ceremony took place with great pomp in the audience hall before an assembly of the underofficials of the department. According to old custom, the king gave a formal charge to the new appointee in which he offered his personal injunctions for the conduct of the office, with particular emphasis on the great moral responsibilities which devolved upon him.

Look after the office of vizier and watch over everything that is done in it, for it is the constitution of the entire land. As to the office of vizier, indeed, it is not pleasant; no, it is as bitter as gall. . . . . He is one who must give no special consideration to princes or councilors nor win to himself anyone as a follower. . . . . Now if a petitioner comes from Upper or Lower Egypt, ... then you must on your part see to it that everything is done according to law and that everything is conducted in the proper manner, while every man is accorded his rights.

Now as for an official who hears in public, the water and the wind announce everything that he does, so that no one is ignorant of his actions. . . . . Now the [best] safeguard for a prince is to act according to regulation. . . . . For one whose case has been decided must not say: "I have not been accorded my rights." . . . . Look upon him whom you know as on him whom you do not know, the one who is close to you as the one who is distant from you. For an official who so conducts himself will succeed here in this position. Pass over no petitioner without hearing his case. . . . . Show anger to no man wrongfully and be angry only at that which deserves anger. Instil fear of yourself that you may be held in fear, for a true official is an official who is feared. The distinction of an official is that he does justice. But if a man instils fear in an excessive manner, there being in him a modicum of insincerity in the estimation of men, then they do not say of him: "That is a just man." . . . . What one expects of the conduct of the vizier is the performance of justice; for it is the vizier who has been its proper keeper since [the rule of] the god. . . . . The vizier is the one who before all other men shall practice justice.

Now a man shall continue in his office, while he officiates in accordance with the instructions which have been given to him. Unassailable is the man who acts according to what has been said to him. Perform not your own desire in affairs about which the law is known. And touching on arrogance—the king prefers the timid to the arrogant. Conduct yourself, therefore, according to the instructions which have been given to you.

The most important of the various ministries in the Egyptian government was the ministry of finance. The treasury was under the control of numerous "overseers," who stood next after the vizier in rank. All sorts of taxes and other payments were delivered to the treasury, and the salaries of the officials and numerous other disbursements were paid out of its coffers. All payments were made in kind: the peasant brought a portion of the produce of his fields; the artisan, specimens of his handiwork. Taxes were collected by the state for each cow, each donkey, each ship, for palm trees and vineyards. It goes without saying that the ancient Egyptian peasant paid this burden of taxes with no less resistance than the modern fellah; not infrequently he paid his current dues only under the weight of the cudgel. The number of officials engaged in the finance ministry must have been exceedingly large, and equally great must have been the multitude of storehouses, granaries, and stables in which the deliveries of produce and animals were kept until they were paid out again to meet the expenses of the government. In this connection it is of interest to recall that since the expulsion of the Hyksos the greater part of the Egyptian land and fields were the property of the pharaoh, that is, of the state. In other words, the situation was very similar to that described in the Book of Genesis as having been instituted by Joseph during a famine (Gen. 47:13 ff.). The temples in the land alone, with the possible exception of some of the old landholders, possessed free landed property. Most of the artistocracy had probably been permitted to remain on their estates at the reorganization of the state after the expulsion of the Hyksos, but they will have been compelled to deliver to the treasury a specific portion of their harvest—according to the biblical record it amounted to a fifth—in addition to the other taxes. It is probable that the amount of this ground rental was reckoned according to the height of the Nile inundation and that it consequently fluctuated from year to year. Certain officials, chief of whom was the "overseer of the granaries," were intrusted with the collection of the payments in field produce. They were responsible for bringing in the maximum deliveries and for reporting directly to the pharaoh the state of the harvest in Upper and Lower Egypt.

Unfortunately, we are very ill informed about the details of the finance administration. Though we know a multitude of officials with the most varying titles, there is but little available information concerning their respective duties. The situation is no better in connection with the interior administration of the land. We know that from the earliest times the country was divided into various provinces or nomes which were ruled by independent princes. Already under the powerful kings of the Twelfth Dynasty the places of these princes had come to be supplied by governors who were appointed to office by the ruler. They continued to bear the old princely title and were responsible as "overseers of gardens, cattle, and granaries" for the collection of the imposts from the orchards and herds and fields. As "overseers of works" they were liable for the building and maintenance of roads, dikes, canals, and other public works in their provinces, while as "overseers of the treasury" they were held accountable for the administration of finance.

In the early period there had never been a standing army ready to answer the call of the king as commander-in-chief. On the other hand, each nome possessed its own militia, which was drawn from the able-bodied men and equipped by the local prince. In addition, the temple provided small contingents of troops, while even the treasury department maintained a quota of soldiers for the purpose of protecting the corps of workmen which were sent to the quarries and mines. There was a police force also, but it was chiefly if not entirely recruited from certain Nubian tribes. In case Egypt was faced with the threat of war, all these diverse contingents were equipped with weapons from the royal armory and organized under a commander chosen to meet the emergency. The troops were classified according to their arms into spearmen and archers. The former carried long spears equipped with copper or bronze points and large shields covered with leather. The archers were provided with bows and arrows (Fig. 22). Among the other weapons carried were axes, slings, and short daggers. The uniforms of this Egyptian militia were simple in the extreme. They consisted merely of a short linen skirt to the front of which was attached a narrow heart-shaped leather guard for the better protection of the lower part of the body. Helmets and armor appear to have been quite unknown in the early period, and swords are never found in the hands of the soldiers.

The expulsion of the Hyksos was accompanied by a sudden alteration in the military organization of the empire. The irregular and loosely organized militia gave way to a large standing army which received extensive discipline and training in the wars against the armies of the western Asiatic states. The war of liberation awakened in the traditionally peace-loving Egyptians a thirst for military prowess, while Syria of-

FIG. 22.—A COMPANY OF EGYPTIAN SOLDIERS (CAIRO MUSEUM)

fered a broad new field of exploitation. The nucleus of the army consisted of native Egyptians, who were augmented increasingly as time passed by the employment of mercenary troops from all the surrounding countries.

The infantry of this period are armed much the same as before, and their dress likewise shows but little change. Both spearmen and archers, however, carry in addition to their regular equipment small clubs or battle-axes and, a little later, short swords or daggers. On parade they appear customarily to have laid aside all their weapons except the ax. Officers of lower rank are distinguished from common soldiers by somewhat lighter and more conveniently portable arms; the higher officers bear, in addition to the ax, a ceremonial fan as a mark of rank.

A much more drastic and significant innovation in the arms of the New Kingdom was the addition to the infantry of an entirely new type of fighting equipment—the war chariot, which henceforth played a role in the conduct of war not less in importance than the tank of modern warfare. It is certain that the Egyptians first encountered this type of equipment in their wars with the Hyksos. They realized instantaneously that effective operations against such weapons demanded the employment of the same means of fighting. As a result, they imported multitudes of horses and chariots from Asia and integrated them into their growing military machine. It can be safely assumed that the conspicuous success enjoyed by Thutmose I and III in their Asiatic campaigns was the outcome of their employment of well-equipped and highly trained ranks of war chariots and their drivers. The Egyptian chariot, which was widely used for various purposes in time of peace as well, was a two-wheeled vehicle drawn by a span of horses (Fig. 6). It was usually manned by two persons—the driver, who controlled the reins and on whose skill much depended on the field of battle, and the fighter, who was armed with spear and bow and arrows. Riding horseback was evidently something repulsive to the Egyptians, and it is but seldom that we encounter an armed rider on the battlefield. Several centuries were to elapse before cavalry came into use. When on the march the army was accompanied by an extensive baggage train consisting of donkeys and four-wheeled oxcarts loaded with supplies, gear, and the shelter tents of the troops.

It appears that the Egyptian army as a whole was divided into two main sections—one from Upper Egypt, the other from Lower Egypt—each of which was regularly stationed in its respective part of the country. Each one of these armies was, in turn, composed of divisions bearing their own names. There were, for example, a "Division of Amun," a "Division of the Beauty of Re," and a "Division of Pharaoh." The strength of the different divisions or regiments or how they were individually equipped is beyond our knowledge. We do know, however, that smaller units which we might designate as squads possessed their own insignia, such as a fan or a standard consisting of an emblem mounted on the end of a staff.

It is unlikely that the soldiers received a fixed wage; they were provided with food on a campaign and they were rewarded with a share of the booty. If a front-line officer was able to distinguish himself before the eyes of the king, like Ahmose of Elkab (p. 33), Djehuti the conqueror of Joppa (p. 57), or Thutmose III's commander Amenemhab (p. 58), he not only received his due portion of the booty but was rewarded in addition with the "gold of valor"—decorations in the form of flies or lions, with chains for suspending them round the neck—and sometimes with grants of land in Egypt after the return from the campaign.

The bureaucracy, which proudly and not altogether unjustly considered itself as the firm foundation of the state during the Eighteenth Dynasty, regarded the military with contempt. In the schools the lot of the soldier was painted in the blackest colors, and scholars were warned against following the profession of arms. When a young recruit entered military service, his training consisted of endless blows and brutality. When on the march to Syria

his bread and water are on his shoulders like the burden of a donkey. His neck is made as sore as a donkey's and his spinal column has [developed] a crook. He drinks stinking water. He halts only to mount guard. When he encounters the enemy he is like a snared bird, with no strength in any of his limbs. When he succeeds in returning to Egypt he is like a stick which the worms have eaten; he is ill and bedridden. He is brought back on a donkey, neatly stripped of his clothing, and his comrade has deserted.

Vastly different, however, were the position and life of the military officialdom who sat in the office of the army administration, the "scribe of the soldiers," the "overseer of the soldiers" (general), as several designations of rank may be translated. These were officials versed in the art of writing and therefore entitled to greater respect and a higher station in the government. They were frequently appointed to high public office; a general of Thutmose IV named Harmhab became, in addition to his military rank, an "overseer of fields," an "overseer of the buildings of Amun," an "overseer of the priests in Upper and Lower Egypt," with duties quite apart from the responsibilities of his military career. Much the same situation may be pointed out in the case of another general named Harmhab who served under Tutankhamun and later occupied the Egyptian throne (p. 244).

What became of the large army in time of peace, after the end of a campaign? A portion of it remained in foreign parts to make up the various garrisons left in the conquered cities and states; these were maintained at the expense of the vanquished people. Of that part which returned to Egypt, the drafted peasants were probably mustered out of the service to resume their former labors at home in the fields. The professional troops, especially the mercenaries, were probably settled in special quarters, either in the large cities or, often enough, in the country. They were sometimes granted fields by the king, with peasants to carry on the agricultural work in their behalf, or they were provided with a living from the royal magazines. If such payments were delayed for any reason, it is not at all improbable that this hungry military rabble wandered about from village to village, robbing and plundering as they went, in order that they might obtain a living by force at the expense of the peaceable inhabitants of the farms. As time passed, these hordes of mercenaries developed into a military class which became the chief mainstay of the kingdom. It was an easy matter, however, to turn its power against the ruler; this military class, in fact, was destined to develop such power and influence that it eventually altered the course of Egyptian history (p. 254). Thus, like the Mamelukes of the Middle Ages, the foreign mercenaries in antiquity, especially the Libyan tribes, were transformed from a safeguard of the state into its most serious source of danger.

X

THE OUTSIDE WORLD

OF THE various foreign lands by the possession of which the Thutmosids elevated Egypt to the position of a great world-power, the "southern lands" were the most valuable, even if Syria surpasses them in our estimation because of our historical and religious interest in the Holy Land. Efforts toward the conquest of the Upper Nile from Elephantine southward through the cataract had been attempted already in the Old Kingdom, and, though some success in this direction was attained in the Middle Kingdom, the south was first brought under permanent control of Egypt by Thutmose I.

This land, known to us today as Nubia (Fig. 23), was as a rule divided into two regions by the ancient Egyptians. The northern part as far as modern Wadi Halfa was designated as Wawat, while the more southerly section of the Nile Valley, reaching into the Sudan, was termed the land of Kush. The Egyptians called the inhabitants of the region the "Nehsi"; this term embraced not only the southern Nubians but also the Beduin, who eked out a bare living in the desert valleys and plains between the Upper Nile and the Red Sea. They dwelt in the caves and crevices so common in their mountainous land, and from the manner of their houses they became known to the Greeks as the troglodytes (cave-dwellers). They did not practice agriculture but supported themselves on the produce of their flocks and herds or from the plunder which they carried off from raids on the Nubian meadows. To the south they bordered on the Negroes, whose northern advance in antiquity had reached as far as the region of the White Nile above Khartum.

While Egypt and Lower Nubia possessed in the earliest time—before 3200 B.C.—not only a homogeneous population but also a fundamentally unified culture, by the second half of the fourth millennium they had become gradually more and more differentiated from each other. The establishment of a united nation rewarded Egypt with enormous cultural dividends; already in the first dynasties a national Egyptian art had come into being, and the first pinnacle of her culture had been achieved as

Fig. 23.—The Nile in Nubia

early as the pyramid age. Nubia, on the other hand, persistently held to her primitive cultural level and preserved without change the forms and techniques of the remote past with inevitable loss of youthful vigor. By the Old Kingdom, Nubia had sunk to the lowest cultural ebb of her history. The burials of this epoch bear witness to the utmost poverty of the population and to an almost complete absence of connection with Egypt.

But Nubian culture made a great upward surge about the third millennium B.C., when a Hamitic race strongly mixed with Negro blood pressed northward from the Sudan and established itself in Lower Nubia between the first and second cataracts of the Nile. The new arrivals carried with them to their new homes their native customs and practices. On the withered soil of decadent Nubia a new art developed which was in sharp contrast to that which had previously existed in the land, though there was much in the old which could be utilized by the new. Especially characteristic of the new culture was its pottery of manifold varieties among which beautiful baked clay bowls with attractive incised patterns are conspicuous. A new period of highly developed Nubian culture had arrived.

During the same period, somewhat farther to the south, above the third cataract in what is now the province of Dongola, a much more barbarous Nubian culture grew up at Kerma. An Egyptian trading-post had been established here as early as the beginning of the Twelfth Dynasty. The native chieftains of this region prepared burial places for themselves in the form of great circular tumuli of stone, and their funerals were marked by the ruthless slaughter of numerous members of their retinue in order that they might follow their lords into the beyond. They manufactured peculiar ivory inlays of animals for their furniture, ornaments of mica to be sewn on their clothing, and beautiful red polished pottery of a type entirely different from that of the more northerly culture. Indeed, the Kerma culture in many of its details reflects a strongly African character.

About this time significant changes were taking place in the population of northern Africa outside of Egypt. Along the coast of the Mediterranean appeared a European race, the Temeh—a race of light-skinned, blond, blue-eyed people—who apparently reached their new home by way of the Straits of Gibraltar. They now encountered the older brunet Libyan Tehenu, but, pressing beyond the latter, they advanced eastward through the oases and onward to the Upper Nile and Nubia, where they settled and mingled with the older population.

What, then, was the attraction in the south which made the possession of Kush so desirable to the Egyptians? Why did the pharaohs persist so energetically in their efforts to vanquish the regions of the Upper Nile and to incorporate them into their growing empire? Of course, taxes in the form of field products and cattle could be extorted from the native peasants. Of much greater importance, however, were the extensive and highly productive mines of Kush, which yielded enormous quantities of gold. Besides, Nubia was, like Egypt, a land on the great river, and the Nile was the connecting-link between Egypt and the regions of the Sudan with which rich trade was carried on for all the coveted commodities of Africa, for ivory and ebony, for ostrich feathers and eggs, for leopard skins and cattle and slaves. From remotest antiquity almost to the present time, Egyptian trade was chiefly directed toward the lands of the Upper Nile and the Sudan, and this could be successfully maintained only if these regions themselves and all the connecting desert routes were under Egyptian control.

It was unquestionably a mark of great administrative genius that Thutmose I incorporated the newly conquered land of Nubia into the Egyptian empire and united it along with his southernmost province into a great administrative district, as in fact it is at the present time. A viceroy was appointed to govern the province with the title, "Prince of Kush and Overseer of the Southern Lands." His position, as the title suggests, was much more independent than those of the other Egyptian officials. His domain extended from Elkab in Upper Egypt to the southern frontier of the empire, which from the time of Thutmose III was located in the district of Karoy, in the region of Napata. The authority of such a governor, who had his residence at Mem, the modern Ibrim and Aniba, was very extensive indeed. He was the chief commanding officer in his province, which he had to protect against uprisings as well as against Beduin raids. His was the responsibility for the construction of temples and fortifications, magazines and canals, while in his hands rested the administration of justice and, above all, the obligation to deliver to his lord in the Egyptian capital all the dues and imposts of his province in the proper amount and at the proper time. These consisted of gold, either in the form of dust packed in sacks or in the rings which were the nearest approach to coin known to the ancient Egyptians; various kinds of cattle; male and female slaves; and "the ships laden with ivory, ebony, and every other beautiful product of the land in addition to the yield of the harvest." All these things were transported to Thebes, where the viceroy himself often appeared in person to render an account of his stewardship and to deliver the tribute with his own hands. A private tomb in Thebes has preserved to us a beautiful painting of such an event (Fig. 24), when the prince of Kush, Amenhotep-Huy, who held office under Tutankha-mun, conducts the Nubian grandees with their tribute into the presence of the king. We meet in these pictures the Negroes, whose districts the Egyptians of the Eighteenth Dynasty had reached for the first time and with whom they may only then have come into really close relation. They are for the most part clad in the prevailing Egyptian fashion; some of them even affect Egyptian modes of dressing the hair, though the majority have retained their native coiffure, which is attractively set off by an ostrich feather. Among the grandees appears no less a person than the Negro princess, who, sheltered by a gorgeous sunshade, drives along in an elegant Egyptian chariot drawn, curiously enough, rather awkwardly by oxen instead of the usual spirited steeds. It is not difficult to imagine with what astonishment the inhabitants of the Egyptian capital must have viewed this exotic procession, especially the Negro women leading their naked children by the hand or, in one case, carrying the tiniest baby in a basket on the back, the tall giraffe accompanied by two keepers, and the stately cattle with their sumptuously decorated horns.

Nubia developed rapidly under the well-ordered Egyptian administration. The irrigation system was much improved, so that there was a noteworthy increase in the yield of the cultivated lands. New cities were established, and on every hand rose beautiful temples which in size and equipment were scarcely inferior to those of the mother-country. We know of no fewer than twelve Nubian temple edifices which owe their existence to the kings of the Eighteenth Dynasty. The most beautiful of all was without a doubt the great temple of Soleb, which belongs to the most brilliant period of Egyptian architecture—the reign of Amenhotep III. As indicated in a dedicatory inscription, it "was made very broad and great, its beauty was transcendent, its entrance towers reached the sky, and its flagstaves mingled with the stars of heaven. It was visible on both sides of the river. . . . . It was surrounded by a great wall the battle-

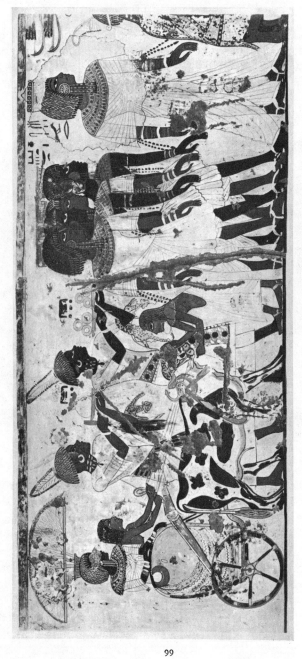

Fig. 24.—Nubians Bringing Tribute to Tutankhamun (Thebes, Tomb of Huy)

99

ments of which gleamed more than the sky and resembled the obelisks which King Amenhotep had erected for a million millions of years." After passing through an avenue flanked by statues of sacred falcons, rams, and lions (Fig. 25), the images of Sopdu, Amun, and the king, one arrived at an imposing colonnade which led to the gigantic double-towered portal of the sanctuary, inside which was a great court sur-

FIG. 25.—STONE LION WITH INSCRIPTION OF TUTANKHAMUN (BRITISH MUSEUM)

rounded by colonnades on every side. Behind the first court was another of the same type, to which was attached a hall whose ceiling was supported by twenty-four palm-leaf capitals; this hall opened into a second, still larger, one containing forty columns of a different style, while at the rear of the great building was situated the holy of holies and a series of smaller chapels of which but the meagerest of traces have survived.

The cults celebrated in these Nubian temples were for the most part devoted to the great Egyptian divinities, Amun of Thebes and Re-Harakhti of Heliopolis, though some attention was given to other gods as well, especially the native god of Nubia, Dedun, the deceased king Senwosret III, who, as the first conqueror of Nubia, had been elevated to the position of a sort of patron saint, and in Soleb to the reigning king, Amenhotep III himself. The inscriptions on the walls of the temples were composed in the Egyptian language and writing, just as Egyptian was the official tongue of administration and commerce, though the great mass of the population continued to employ their native Nubian dialect or dialects.

Thus Nubia gradually became completely Egyptianized, so completely, in fact, that it tenaciously held fast to Egyptian culture in later times when Egypt itself succumbed to foreign influences. When the Greeks came into the valley of the Nile in the seventh century B.C., it was Nubia—the Nubia at one time scornfully referred to as "wretched Kush" —which was considered the seat of orthodox Egyptian character, and the visiting Greek writers jumped to the conclusion that the entire civilization of Egypt had originated in Ethiopia, the land of the black race, and had been exported thence down the Nile to Egypt proper.

An important event of the early Eighteenth Dynasty was the resumption of commercial intercourse with the people of the wonderland of Punt on the Somali coast. In the ninth year of Queen Hatshepsut an expedition consisting of five great sailing vessels was dispatched to that distant land under the command of one of the royal favorites. The fleet arrived after a long voyage at the "myrrh terraces" on the coast of Punt, where the Egyptian sailors marveled at the sight of the huts of the inhabitants, which were built on piles in groves of palm and myrrh trees and accessible from the ground only by means of ladders (Fig. 26). The Egyptian marines disembarked the manifold wares—the weapons, strings of beads, rings, and the like—which had been brought from the Nile; soon there appeared from the village of Punt its prince, accompanied by his hideous fat wife and their sons and daughters, that they might greet the strangers and inquire how and why they had come (Fig. 27). In the meantime trade went on apace; the Puntites brought the products of their land, especially great quantities of myrrh and gold, and bartered them for the curiosities from Egypt. The trading completed, the ambassadors of Hatshepsut lavishly entertained the chief of Punt with a banquet consisting of "bread, beer, wine, meat, fruits, and all the good things of Egypt." Meanwhile the Egyptian vessels were being "heavily laden with the wonders of Punt, consisting of all kinds of beautiful plants of God's Land [the region east of the valley of the Upper Nile], heaps of myrrh, live myrrh trees, ebony, genuine ivory, gold, costly woods, incense, eye cosmetics, apes, monkeys, greyhounds, leopard skins, and slaves together with their children." At last the queen's fleet cast off, and, after a successful return voyage, the soldiers of the Lord of the Two Lands disembarked in Thebes with an embassy from the "chiefs of the land of Punt," who had accompanied the expedition in order to bring gifts to her majesty and to seek peace "from her whose name had penetrated to the uttermost reaches of heaven." The successful return of the expedition with its huge array of rare treasures caused the greatest rejoicing in the capital. There was no end of astonishment at the wonderful products of the voyage, especially at the thirty-one flourishing myrrh trees which had been transported in tubs. The queen, "her limbs fragrant as the dew of the gods with ointment and myrrh," and her consort Thutmose III presented with thanksgiving the greater portion of the treasures to Amun of Thebes, at whose command and under whose protection the mission had been conducted, and who had "placed all lands under the sandals of the king and the queen."

FIG. 26.—THE LAND OF PUNT (THEBES, TEMPLE OF DEIR EL-BAHRI)

After this great voyage to Punt intercourse with that distant country was permanently maintained, and from that time forth the Egyptian records inform us repeatedly of the wonders which were brought thence to the Nile Valley as the result of trading rather than military expeditions.

The most momentous event of the entire age was the conquest of Syria and Palestine, which had been gradually achieved by dint of hard fighting ever since the expulsion of the Hyksos. The Egyptians had, nevertheless, not succeeded in reducing this region to the status of an Egyptian province or in establishing a unified administration, as they had done in Nubia. In a land split by nature into so many unrelated divisions and so politically disunited, such an organization could have been achieved only by a far greater employment of military and administrative force than was actually available to the pharaohs. In consequence, they were obliged to content themselves with requiring the Syrian com-

FIG. 27.—THE QUEEN OF PUNT (CAIRO MUSEUM)

munities to recognize the sovereignty of Egypt. The princes who, either of their own free will or by armed compulsion, had submitted to the Egyptians were forced to recognize the king as their lord and to pledge themselves to regular payments of tribute in precisely determined quantities. They were likewise bound to serve in the army of the king in time of war and to supply the Egyptian troops "with food and drink, with cattle, sheep, honey, and oil" whenever they were obliged to march through their domains. Not infrequently an Egyptian resident commissioner supported by a division of soldiers was stationed in their cities to represent the pharaoh and guarantee a proper respect for the Egyptian name and authority. According to the official point of view, the territory of the individual states was the property of the king. Any prince who had been permitted to retain his power or any newly appointed one was accordingly taken under the king's protection, in order that his local sovereignty might be supported with Egyptian assistance against all internal or external enemies. "If you show yourself submissive," the king assures his vassal, "what is there that the king cannot do for you?" Thus if the domain of a prince was attacked or plundered by a neighbor, he was able to turn to the court at Thebes for aid, and in most cases it was provided. There were exceptions, however; the precept "divide and rule" was honored by the pharaohs also, and they endeavored, if not to foster, at least not always to suppress the perennial dissensions and petty rivalries which beset the little states from time immemorial. Obviously, as long as the local princes battled one another and thus dissipated their wealth and strength, there was no danger that they would conspire against Egypt and venture in a united effort to throw off the foreign yoke. Any attempt at defection was severely punished. If the report of one came to the ears of the pharaoh, he threatened the suspect with the harshest penalties. "If for any reason you entertain a desire to exercise hostility or harbor any thought of enmity or hatred in your heart, then you and all your family are condemned to death; therefore, submit yourself to the king your lord and you shall live."

It would naturally have been a great political blunder to have left a vanquished land to its own devices and the delivery of tribute to the good will of the princes, after the departure of a large Egyptian army. On the very day on which the last Egyptian soldier would have been withdrawn from Syrian territory the princes would certainly have declared their independence, the resident commissioners with their entire staffs would have been "purged," and the tribute withheld. This did in fact happen often enough, and the constantly repeated invasions of Syria by Egyptian armies are unmistakable evidence that the states of "wretched Retenu" did not submit lightly to Egyptian supremacy. In order, therefore, to prevent as largely as possible the occurrence of revolts, to hold the vassals in obedience, and to provide firm strongholds for any contingency of war, military stations or "halting-places" were established everywhere in the land; these were fortified with walls and defense towers and manned by a garrison of archers and charioteers. Great magazines were provided in them for the storage of a portion of the tribute delivered by the surrounding towns, in order that the "halting-places" might be supplied with every good thing when next the Egyptian army marched in and had to be provisioned.

The Egyptians employed still another effective means of securing the obedience of the tributary princes; they carried off to Thebes their sons or other members of their families as hostages. These were quartered in the capital in a great palace where they were handsomely treated even though it was a sort of princely prison. They were given an Egyptian education and became acquainted with the Egyptian mode of life at the imperial capital. Whenever a prince died in the Syrian homeland, the pharaoh designated his Egyptianized son to succeed him, and, after "anointing his head with oil," the king sent him off to occupy the princely throne of his father. Thus in the course of time a body of loyal vassals was built up who "kept watch over their cities" and in later years gratefully recalled the time when "they had been taken to Egypt as children to serve the king their lord and to stand at the door of the king."

Intercourse between Egypt and the Syrian vassal princes was maintained through the medium of royal couriers who traveled from city to city, collected the tribute, delivered written orders from the pharaoh, and carried letters from the princes to the Egyptian court. We are quite well informed about this correspondence, which was carried on in the cuneiform writing of the Akkadian language, for in the year 1887 a portion of it, together with numerous letters of Babylonian and other western Asiatic kings, was discovered in the ruins of Amarna in Upper Egypt. These letters came from many different cities of Palestine and Phoenicia. There are communications from the princes of Jerusalem, Byblos, Tyre, and Sidon, as well as others from Accho, Megiddo, Askalon, and Beirut. Their content is of the most varying character. A prince assures the pharaoh in the humblest possible terms of his abiding loyalty, requests aid against his enemies, complains when after numerous pressing demands it does not arrive, or announces to the king the peace and safety of the region intrusted to his care. Above all, eloquent expression is found in these letters of the quarrels and intrigues among the various princes, each of whom is, of course, more faithful than any of his fellows. Thus Prince Abdihepa of Jerusalem defends himself against charges of treason which have been reported at court in the following communication:

To the king, my lord, speaks Abdihepa, your servant: Seven and seven times do I fall at the feet of the king, my lord. What have I done to the king, my lord? They are calumniating me before the king, saying, "Abdihepa has fallen away from the king, his lord." But see, neither my father nor my mother has set me in this place, but the mighty hand of the king has invested me with the house of my father. Why then should I commit a crime against the king, my lord? As long as the king, my lord, lives I shall say to the commissar of the king, my lord, "Why do you love the Habiru and hate the resident vassal prince?" And that is why they are slandering me before the king, my lord.

Full of obsequiousness is likewise the following epistle which Prince Ammunira of Beirut addressed

to the king, my lord, my sun, my gods, and the breath of my life. . . . . I have heard the words of the tablets of the king, my lord, my sun, my gods, the breath of my life, and the heart of your servant, the dust under the feet of the king, my lord, my sun, my gods, and the breath of my life, rejoices very, very much because the breath of the king, my lord, my sun, my gods, has gone forth to his servant and the dust under his feet. When, furthermore, the king, my lord, my sun, wrote to his servant and the dust under his feet, "Make everything ready for the troops of the king, your lord," I have understood it completely. And behold, I have prepared everything, my horses, my chariots, everything of mine which the servant of the king, my lord, possesses, for the troops of the king, my lord. May the troops of the king, my lord, my sun, my gods, crush the head of his enemies. And may the two eyes of your servant look upon the life of the king, my lord.

Not all the letters are in the same tone, however. Some of them are expressions of bitter complaint that the pharaoh has failed to send the promised protection against the adversaries of his vassal. Such a prince was Ribaddi of Byblos, one of the most loyal of all the friends of Egypt. Sorely pressed by King Aziru of Amurru, son of a certain Abdashirta, who was certainly conspiring against the pharaoh, he had written to the court in a vigorous appeal for assistance. Receiving a negative reply from the king, he answered with a good deal of agitation as follows:

If the king, my lord, says, "Protect yourself and protect the city of the king which is in your charge!" with what, then, shall I defend myself and the city? In the past there was a garrison of the king's troops here with me, and the king delivered grain from Iarimuta to provide for their sustenance. But behold, Aziru has repeatedly attacked me, so that I have left neither cattle nor provisions—Aziru has taken them all away. There is no grain left for my sustenance here, and the peasants have departed to the cities where there is grain for their sustenance. Furthermore, why does the king compare me with the other vassal princes? Their cities belong to them, and their chiefs are at their feet; but my cities belong to Aziru, and he is courting my allegiance. Why should I make an alliance with him? What dogs the sons of Abdashirta are, that they should act according to their interests and leave the cities of the king to the flames!

The pharaoh concerned himself over these dissensions but little as long as the payments of tribute kept coming and there was no interruption of the trade with the Nile Valley. What was of supreme importance to him and to the Egyptian government was to extract the highest possible revenue from the vassal states. A portion of the harvest from field and garden had to be delivered in the form of taxes which were either sent by ship to Egypt and stored in the royal granaries or, as we have already seen, were utilized to provision the military stations. Important other items of tribute which came from Syria were male and female slaves, who were assigned to work in the construction of temples and public buildings or to labor in mines and quarries; horses and chariots; great herds of all kinds of cattle, sheep, and goats, as well as rarer animals such as elephants and bears; incense, oil, wine, and honey; ivory and desirable metals, including gold, copper, and lead; semiprecious stones, especially lapis lazuli and rock crystal; and countless manufactured products of Syrian craftsmanship, including gold and silver vessels and pitchers, some of which were remarkably executed in the shape of animal heads. The inhabitants of the wooded slopes of the Lebanons were forced to make deliveries of useful woods, especially the conifers, which were highly valued in almost treeless Egypt, where they were employed in building operations and in the manufacture of large and small articles of furniture, chests, small dishes, and the like. This tribute arrived in Egypt regularly each year, when it was received and registered by certain high officials in the name of the king. It must have been an impressive spectacle when "the chiefs of Retenu and all the northern lands came from the ends of the earth, bowing in humility, bearing their tribute on their backs," for it became a favorite subject chosen for the wall paintings used in the decoration of their tombs by the dignitaries in charge of the reception of tribute (Fig. 12).

Admittedly, it is a great question whether everything designated and depicted as "tribute" by the Egyptians was actually tribute. Gifts were returned by the king in acknowledgment of many of the objects sent by foreign princes, so that it would be more accurate to regard the transactions as a type of trade. In any event, a considerable trade developed between Egypt and western Asia after the conquest of Syria, and the pharaoh himself may well have been the chief trader. Great caravans plied the military roads which connected the Delta with Palestine, while both Egyptian and Syrian trading vessels cruised along the coast of the Mediterranean in order to transport the manifold wares from one country to the other.

This commerce extended far beyond the boundaries of conquered Syria, northward beyond the Taurus and Amanus Mountains to Asia Minor and the land of the warlike Hittites, in Mesopotamia as far as the empire of Mitanni, eastward to Babylonia and Assyria, westward to Cyprus, Crete, the islands of the Aegean Sea, and perhaps even as far as the mainland of Greece.

Since the time when Thutmose III had crossed the Euphrates with his army and put to flight the people of Nahrin while plundering their cities and devastating their fields, Egypt's relations with that empire had undergone a marked change. The people of the Nile had come to realize that this land was ruled by a king not inferior in birth to their own pharaoh, and they were persuaded that it was more to their advantage to live at peace with the land than to carry on a succession of wars which under no circumstances of victory could ever assure permanent Egyptian control over such a remote state. Thus, under either Thutmose III or his successor it is probable that a treaty of friendship was concluded beween the two empires, and it was confirmed by the marriage of Thutmose IV with a daughter of the Mitannian king Artatama. Emissaries traveled freely between the two courts, and there ensued an extensive correspondence on cuneiform tablets of which some of those written by King Tushratta of Mitanni to the pharaohs Amenhotep III and IV have survived in the royal archives at Amarna.

The desire of the pharaoh to take a Mitannian princess into his harem was not immediately acceptable to the friendly court on the Euphrates. In fact, it was not until Amenhotep III had sent five or six times to Shutarna, the successor of Artatama, that the Mitannian king at last consented to have his daughter Giluhepa become the wife of the Egyptian. When, accompanied by three hundred and seventeen ladies of her harem, she finally arrived in the Nile Valley, there was great rejoicing, and Amenhotep III followed his usual custom of issuing a series of large memorial scarabs in order to celebrate this significant event in the foreign relations of Egypt. Still later, when Shutarna's son Tushratta came to the throne of Mitanni, Amenhotep sent his ambassador Meni to him with the message: "My brother, send me your daughter to be my wife, the mistress of Egypt." Tushratta, on his part, "grieved not the heart of his brother and made a favorable decision. He showed her to Meni, even as his brother desired. And Meni saw her and when he had seen her he rejoiced greatly." Thereupon Meni traveled back to Egypt in order to communicate to his lord the result of his inspection of the bride; finally, armed with a letter from Amenhotep, he made a second journey to the Euphrates so that he might escort Princess Taduhepa to Egypt. "I read the tablet which he brought," Tushratta writes, "and I understood the words of my brother. Exceedingly good were the words of my brother, as if I could see my brother himself." He went on to say that he was willing to "give the wife of his brother, the mistress of Egypt, and that she should be brought to his brother," but only after he had received for her a huge bride price, "without limit, reaching from the earth to the sky." It was not until six months had passed that the messengers were able to travel off to the Nile with the princess and her dowry, which was recorded to the smallest item on two large clay tablets, and accompanied by Tushratta's blessing: "May Shamash and Ishtar go before her! May they cause her to be pleasing to the heart of my brother, and may my brother rejoice on that day. May Shamash and Ishtar bring rich blessings and great joy to my brother, and may my brother live forever."

Taduhepa reached Egypt in safety and was welcomed with great joy and laden with honors and gifts. The purpose of cementing by this marriage the friendship between the two courts "tenfold more closely" than it had been before appears actually to have been achieved. When Amenhotep III fell ill, Tushratta sent the "figure of the goddess Ishtar of Nineveh, which had traveled to Egypt on a previous occasion," in order that it might restore the pharaoh to health. As we have seen (pp. 79–81), this was destined to be ineffective, and the king died, to be succeeded on the throne by his son Amenhotep IV, whom the cuneiform tablets officially call Napkhuriria. He notified the Mitannian king of the death of his father and requested that their old friendship might be extended to him as well, especially since he had determined to take his father's wife Taduhepa into his own harem. Tushratta's reply to this letter is also preserved to us:

When I was informed that my brother Nimmuria [as Amenhotep III was known in the cuneiform tablets] had gone to his destiny, then I wept on that day. I sat here day and night; on that day I partook neither of food nor drink, for I was in sorrow. And I said, "If only another in my land or in the land of my brother had died, and my brother whom I loved and who loved me were still alive! For our love would endure as the heaven and the earth endure." But when Napkhuriria, the great son of Nimmuria by his great consort Tiy, assumed the rule I said, "Nimmuria has not died if Napkhuriria his great son rules in his place. He will turn no word from its former place." And now, my brother, we shall maintain ten times the friendship of your father.

Such conduct of mutual interests was actually the nucleus of the entire friendship, which was, of course, built upon a purely materialistic foundation. Not for nothing were the Mitannian princesses sent to Egypt, not for nothing were they outfitted with sumptuous trousseaux and provided with rich dowries, not for nothing were ambassadors sent to the pharaoh's court with horses and chariots, with precious stones and all sorts of trinkets. Gifts of not inferior value were expected in return, but what was desired above all else was gold, "which is present in the land of my brother in quantities like the sand." If these return favors were denied or delivered in quantities smaller than had been anticipated, there was no hesitation in demanding the arrears in a tone anything but kingly. Amenhotep III had, for example, promised his father-in-law Tushratta as the price for his daughter, among other things, two gold statues the material for which he had even shown to the Mitannian envoy. As a matter of fact, "when they were cast the envoys had seen them with their eyes that they were perfect and of full weight. And he had been shown much other gold, without measure, which he intended to send, saying to the envoys, 'Here are figures and here are much gold and countless objects which I am sending to my brother. See them with your eyes.' And the envoys saw them with their eyes." However, Amenhotep III died before these articles went off, and Akhnaton withheld the objects which had been designated for shipment, and instead of the two gold statues he sent to Mitanni a pair made of wood and merely covered with gilt or gold foil. Small wonder that Tushratta was greatly disappointed and vexed at them, especially as the pharaoh was well aware of his father's obligation and was consequently guilty of a transaction which was anything but honorable or in keeping with his motto "Living by the Truth." Thus the "gifts" which had been withheld became the object of bitter complaints and may even have been sent back to Egypt by their dissatisfied recipient. It is evident that, despite the mutual protestations of friendship, each of the kings remained ever the crafty merchant who never became "vexed" at his brother—who, in other words, never permitted himself to be taken in. By the term "gifts" nothing was intended but "goods," and a brisk exchange of trade was carried on between two princes but very poorly concealed under the pretense of an exchange of the visible marks of friendship.

On a very similar plane were the relations which existed between Egypt and the two great powers on the Tigris and Euphrates—Assyria and Babylonia—as they are illustrated in another series of cuneiform tablets from Amarna. A particularly active exchange was carried on with the Babylonian kings Kadashman-Enlil and Burnaburiash. The letters which we possess from these rulers are composed in a much more vigorous and self-assured tone than those from the Mitannian court and indicate that these princes of a great and mighty empire considered themselves at least the equals of the pharaoh. No Mitannian ruler had ever ventured to seek in marriage the hand of an Egyptian royal princess. It was quite otherwise with the Babylonians. When Amenhotep III requested a daughter of Kadashman-Enlil for his harem, she was given to him without hesitation, but at the same time he was confronted with the counterdemand that an Egyptian princess be sent to Babylon. This unreasonable proposal was curtly rejected as contrary to every tradition. But Kadashman-Enlil replied to "his brother" most logically and consistently in another letter:

If, my brother, you write that you will not permit your daughter to marry, saying, "Never has the daughter of an Egyptian king been given to anyone," why not then? You are the king and able to act according to your own will. If you desire to give her, who can say anything?

He proceeds naïvely to state that he would, after all, be quite content with another beautiful woman, since it would be easy for him to claim that she was a king's daughter, and no one would be the wiser.

But if as a matter of principle you will send none at all, then were you not taking consideration of brotherhood and friendship when you wrote of forging closer relations with each other by a marriage? It was to that end . . . . that I have written to you concerning a marriage. Why, then, has my brother not sent to me even one woman? Well, you have not sent a woman to me; shall I then, like yourself, withhold a woman from you?

The letter takes up another topic:

And concerning the gold about which I have written to you—send me gold, all that there is, much, even before your envoy comes, right away, during the present harvest, ... in order that I may complete the work which I have undertaken.

He goes on to say that the gold will not be acceptable later on and that, unless he receives the proper amount immediately, he will return it and will likewise be unable to give his daughter to the Egyptian king.

Thus it is evident that repeated requests for gold and other gifts constitute the most important part of these letters. In addition, political questions occasionally come up for consideration. The king of Assyria turned to Egypt for assistance against his feudal lord, the Babylonian king Burnaburiash. When the latter heard about this request, he wrote to the friendly court that the petition should be unconditionally refused, since, in a similar circumstance, when certain Canaanites under Egyptian sovereignty had requested support from Babylon, he had denied it to them.

That Egyptian trade and its mightiest and richest representative, the pharaoh himself, came into contact with the Hittites in Asia Minor and with Cyprus has already been mentioned. Letters on cuneiform tablets as well as "tribute" in the guise of gifts were exchanged with the princes of those regions also. Cyprus dealt chiefly in copper, the Hittite empire in treasures of silver, while Egypt traded with gold and the products of the applied arts.

Among the princes "who had heard of the victories of Thutmose III in all lands" and who had come to Egypt to present their gifts were numbered "the chiefs of the land of Keftiu and of the Islands in the Midst of the Sea." They were fair-skinned men wearing costumes in strong contrast to those of the Syrians. Their dress consisted of a short, gaily colored kilt with a patterned border and ending in a point in front. Their feet were incased in high shoes also decorated with bright colors. They had beardless faces, while their glossy hair fell in long locks about the shoulders and often in abundant curls over the forehead. These peoples were frequent visitors to the Nile Valley, to which they came with the products of their lands: elaborately wrought vases, jugs, and bowls of gold and silver, goblets, and gold animal heads. All these objects and many other articles were eagerly bartered for the coveted wares of Egypt.

The Keftians were the inhabitants of the island of Crete, and from their capital at Knossos, the seat of the legendary King Minos, they had probably extended their empire to include most of the Aegean Islands and perhaps even the southern mainland of Greece. Their ships plowed the waves of the Mediterranean to its remotest recesses as they carried on a brisk trade with the various peoples about its shores. Most important, however, was the commerce with Egypt, with which they had been in contact from the earliest times and to which they came laden with various fine oils and other products in demand among the inhabitants of the Nile Valley. After Crete had suffered a terrible catastrophe about 1400 B.C., and tribes from the Greek mainland had brought about the fall of the brilliant island empire of Minos, the commercial and cultural connections of Egypt with the Aegean world continued to flourish. These relations are witnessed by numerous Aegean (late Minoan) vessels and potsherds found at various Egyptian sites, as well as by Egyptian objects which have been discovered in graves and city ruins throughout the Aegean world and which belong to the time of Amenhotep III and Akhnaton.

Thus, in the fifteenth century B.C., the ancient world had for the first time achieved an important system of international trade. Its routes connected the Sudan with Asia Minor and continued from the Tigris and Euphrates to the coasts of Syria, the islands of the Aegean Sea, and the mainland of Greece. Products of the remotest races were the objects of barter, and the representatives of widely separated cultures mingled and exchanged ideas with one another. Through the lack of contemporary monuments it is exceedingly difficult to follow foreign influences into Babylonia and Assyria; it is quite probable that Egyptian importations were insufficient to divert into new channels the not less ancient art and culture of Mesopotamia. The situation is much different in the Syrian countries. Since they had become political dependencies of Egypt, a lively exchange of commercial relations developed between them and the empire of the pharaohs. Egyptian officials stationed in Syria took with them all sorts of objects for their personal use, including the most excellent creations of Egyptian craftsmanship; at the same time the natives received in trade enormous quantities of the most diverse wares—Egyptian vessels, jewelry made of precious metals and fayence, scarabs, and amulets—all of which found ready acceptance and soon became the object of imitation in Syrian workshops. Just as the Egyptian domination put an end to Babylonian political influence, so it likewise replaced the Mesopotamian cultural supremacy; somewhat later, as a result, a peculiar mixed culture and art developed in Phoenicia, concrete testimony of which has been preserved in numerous surviving objects. In the Aegean world as well there is evidence that the contacts with Egypt were not without permanent effects, chiefly in the technique of the applied arts, in the manufacture of stone vessels, and the like.

Was there, then, any reciprocal influence of these foreign cultures on that of the Nile Valley? With the overthrow of Syria and the resulting growth of an international trade, a transformed spirit and a renewed life electrified the dwellers on the Nile, and the horizon of this people, which had not previously extended beyond the cataracts on the south or the "mountains of light" which formed the eastern and western limits of the valley, suddenly became enormously expanded. There awakened a delight in luxury and the comforts of life which became increasingly nourished by the riches that came pouring in from the conquered countries of the northeast. The simple fashions of dress for men and women alike, which had remained essentially unchanged from the earliest times, now vanished, to be replaced with more elegant styles; the simple skirt was abandoned for ample pleated robes which enveloped the entire body, while the plain, old-fashioned wigs gave way to large and elaborately dressed periwigs (cf. Figs. 57 and 64). Noble ladies now began to affect the same richly adorned ear ornaments which were fashionable in Asia. The art likewise underwent marked transformations. The circle of ideas was greatly extended, and the methods of presentation began to throw off the shackles of old tradition and to move in new directions. Thus Egyptian art forms were affected by borrowings from Babylonian and Syrian sources, on the one side, and from Aegean originals, on the other; strange ornamentation was imitated and foreign forms were adopted, so that the rich Egyptian treasury of patterns was greatly enhanced by accretions from without.

The Egyptian language also benefited from its exposure to the new horizon of Egyptian experience. A multitude of Syrian and therefore chiefly Semitic words, largely names of products unknown to the Egyptians until they were imported either as tribute or in channels of trade, were fused into the language. These consisted primarily of designations for such objects as wagons and horses, weapons and implements new to Egypt, and secondarily of expressions for commoner objects such as river, sea, scribe, house, and the like, for which the Egyptian already possessed words, but which the Egyptian writer enjoyed employing in order to exhibit his adherence to the latest fashions. The larger Egyptian cities were by this time swarming with Semitic tribesmen who either had been brought to the Nile Valley as hostages, prisoners of war, or slaves or had immigrated voluntarily to engage in trade. Many of these in the course of time rose to high positions in the government. They had imported with them their own gods—Baal, Astarte, the tutelary goddess of Kadesh, and the war-goddess Anath—to all of whom sanctuaries were erected and priests appointed, until at length they were accorded official recognition and were honored by the offerings of native Egyptian worshipers.

Egyptian culture was in itself too firmly confined and circumscribed by tradition to retain permanently all these Semitic innovations of the hour. Later, when the Egyptian control of western Asia was relaxed, most of them were speedily sloughed off, though a few of them had, of course, taken hold so firmly that they became, as a relic of the golden age, the abiding possession of the very soul and substance of Egypt.

XI

THE EGYPTIAN HIEROGLYPHS

PROBABLY the greatest single achievement for the entire intellectual life of the Egyptian people was the development of their writing, which, following the Greeks, we are accustomed to designate as the "hieroglyphic" script. The language of the Egyptians was no less of a mixture than the people among whom it developed. In the earliest form in which it is available to us, it exhibits an essentially Semitic character, with an especially far-reaching resemblance to the Semitic in structure and mode of thought. There are, however, significant differences in the vocabulary, while countless expressions of commonplace ideas are wholly unrelated. It is evident that the Egyptian and the Semitic languages, as well as the originally closely related Hamitic and Semitic tribes themselves, became separated from one another in remote antiquity, so that each one of them underwent an exceedingly long period of independent development. Thus Egyptian had acquired already in primordial times countless foreign elements, mostly of African origin, at the expense of gradually expiring native idioms. Primitive Egyptian, indeed, suffered somewhat the same fate as the Semitic tongues of Abyssinia—the Tigré, the Tigriña, and the Amharic—all of which were so radically affected by the African environment that they almost entirely lost their original character.

The Egyptian hieroglyphic system of writing is a picture script consisting of a multitude of pictures of concrete objects the significance of which may in most cases still be readily recognized. During the earliest period Egypt was unacquainted with true writing. In the many hundreds of graves from this era not the slightest trace of any sort of script has ever been discovered; even among the prehistoric rock drawings of the Upper Egyptian desert valleys, in which some stimulus to the development of writing might have been expected, nothing has been found which could be classified as a written character. It is only at the very end of the prehistoric culture that signs appear on scattered monuments which, without the slightest doubt, represent an attempt at writing, though we are unable to interpret them. We are, nevertheless, justified in assuming that the prehistoric Egyptians employed certain picture-signs as a means of communicating ideas. In such a manner, likewise, facts which an individual desired to record for himself or for posterity were perpetuated by a series of pictures arranged side by side. For example, to indicate the possession of six cattle and nine donkeys a picture of an ox accompanied by six strokes and a donkey with nine strokes might be used; everyone would recognize at once what was meant by such a combination of signs. In order to express a more involved idea in pictures, it was necessary to em-

FIG. 28.—EGYPTIAN PICTOGRAPH FROM THE PALETTE OF NARMER

ploy symbols according to an accepted system which could be interpreted only by those who were acquainted with it. A pictograph was produced in which all the elements of a thought were united into a single group or scene. One existing picture of this sort contains a falcon holding in its claw, which has been converted into a human hand, a length of rope which passes through the upper lip of a man (Fig. 28). The bearded head alone of this man is shown, and this is attached to a long rectangle with rounded corners from which rise six plant stems. This remarkable composite was a symbol readily comprehended by everyone acquainted with the system. It was intended to convey the message that the falcon-god Horus has subdued the northerners—designated by the head and the elongated piece of land with the six water plants—and has led them to the victorious ruler (depicted elsewhere on the monument on which the scene occurs) at the end of a rope. The true picture script developed from such simple and symbolic pictorial compositions. Each picture of this script represents, first of all, the object which it depicts. A bearded face ϙ seen from the front is the word ḥr for "face"; the crescent moon ⌒ designates i͗ʿḥ, "moon"; for the word "eye" an eye ⟳, and for "star" a star ✶, is written. These signs are known as ideograms (from Greek *idea*, "form," and *gramma*, "writing"). Verbs designating an action perceptible to the eye were likewise written by means of ideograms, by representing either the action itself or the implement by which it was performed. Thus the word ʿḥꜣ, "to fight," was expressed by the picture of arms holding a shield and battle-ax 𝈂; the verb ḫni͗, "to row," by two arms engaged in rowing with an oar ⧖. The verb zẖ, "to write," was indicated by the picture of a scribe's outfit 𓏞, consisting of a palette, water bowl, and reed-holder; the verb ḥkꜣ, "to rule," by a crook or scepter ⌐. In other cases the writer was obliged to depend on symbols. Thus, Upper Egypt was designated by a plant ⚘ regarded as typical of Upper Egypt, and Lower Egypt correspondingly by a clump of papyrus 𓇅, since the latter occurred in countless numbers in the marshes of the Delta. For the word "day" the Egyptian made use of the picture of the sun ⊙; for "month," that of the moon ⌒. A large number of concepts could be expressed by means of ideograms. A more advanced step in the development of the script came with the complete disregard of the literal significance of the pictures and the employment of signs for the writing of words with which they had no conceptual relation but with which the connection was one of sound alone. English parallels which could be cited would take a picture of a ham ("meat") to denote, rebus fashion, the verb "to meet," or that of a deer for the noun or adjective "dear." The Egyptian, in a similar manner, wrote the verb pri͗, "to go forth," with the picture of a house ⊐ (shown in plan), because the word for house contained the same consonants as the verb. And since the word tpy contained the consonants used in the words "dagger" and "first" in Egyptian, the word for "first" was written with the picture of a dagger ⌐; the picture of a bowstring ⟩ rwd was in the same manner utilized for writing the similarly sounding word meaning "firm" or "hard," and the dung beetle 𓆣 ḫprr for the verb ḫpr, "to become." Such transfer of pictures from one word to another was greatly facilitated by the fact that the consonants alone were considered in writing, while the vowels and endings of words were entirely disregarded; it was very simple under those circumstances to write with the same hieroglyph ⊏⊐ the words *pēry*, "house," and *paryet*, "to go forth," since the principal consonants in both are identical. The same principle would be effective in English if we should in a rebus use the picture of a fan for such diverse meanings as "fan," "fun," "fin," "fane," or "fine."

This system was, nevertheless, still somewhat cumbersome and offered no opportunity to express certain necessary grammatical elements. Besides, there were many words which could not be expressed by a picture either directly or symbolically. This difficulty was ultimately met by the employment of certain pictures not only for entire words with identical consonants but also for parts of words containing the same succession of consonants. Thus the picture of a small clay vessel ʊ, which originally signified a "pot" (*nw*), simply became a general sign for the two consonants *n* and *w*, in that order, whether they both belonged to the same syllable or successive syllables of a word; ⬳, originally the word *wn*, "hare," became the customary two-consonant sign *wn;* and ⊟, perhaps originally a word *mn* for "draught-board," developed into a general sign for the consonantal group *mn*, as in *mun*, "to remain," *sminet*, "to establish," *hosmen*, "natron," and *emnudj*, "breast."

Following a similar course of development, single-consonantal signs—that is, alphabetic characters—were derived from word-signs containing in fact or in appearance but one consonant. Thus the sign ⚊, which originally constituted the essential element in the word *z* for "bolt," came to represent the letter *z;* ⌣ *ro*, "mouth," the letter *r;* ∤ *i*, "reeds," the consonant *i* or *y;* ⊂ *shei*, "pond," the consonantal sound *sh* (one consonant ꜣ in Egyptian); and the picture ⌒ *t*, "bread," the consonant *t*. In this manner the old Egyptian script obtained twenty-four letters. Their discovery was of the most far-reaching consequence, for in later times they had an important influence on the formation of the Semitic alphabetic script, the mother of all modern alphabets.

It would now have been comparatively easy to have put aside the word-, and the two- or three-consonant, signs and to have written all words with alphabetic characters alone. That, however, was a step which the Egyptians never took. Instead, they continued as before to make extensive use of the old ideograms and phonograms; the word *dwn*, "to stand up," was, for example, not spelled out merely with the three letters *d* ⊂, *w* ⬊, and *n* ⌁, but rather with the *d* plus the biconsonantal sign ⬳ for *wn*, with the further addition of what appears to us to be a quite superfluous *n* ～.

Since the Egyptians were not accustomed to separate their words by spaces and since many of their signs had more than one meaning, in order to avoid ambiguity and to promote easier comprehension of the script, they utilized still another type of sign, the so-called sense-sign or determinative, which was placed at the end of the word in order to offer a clue to its meaning. Thus, to the word ⬳, "to stand up," which has just been mentioned, a final sign ⋀, depicting two walking legs, was added to indicate that the action of standing is an activity of the legs. According to these principles, the verb *swr*, "to drink," was written ⎮⬳～⿴, with ⎮ *s*, the two-consonant sign ⬳ *wr*, to which was added the final consonant ⌒ *r* of the word, and at the end of the entire consonantal skeleton the "determinative" ～, the Egyptian picture-sign representing "water," to indicate that water is involved in drinking, and finally another "determinative," ⿴, a man holding his finger to his mouth, to show that the action designated by the root *swr* is performed by the mouth.

A closer examination of the development of hieroglyphic writing as here described makes it possible to distinguish two classes of signs. The first of these embraces the phonograms or sound-signs; above all, the twenty-four letters of the alphabet:

⿳ 3 (a sound which our ears do not distinguish)	⊖ *ḫ, kh* (like the *ch* in Scotch *loch*)
⎛ *y*	⌖ *ẖ, kh* (perhaps like the *ch* in German *ich*, but different from the preceding consonant)
⌐ *ᶜ* (a guttural common in Semitic languages but foreign to English)	⎯ *z*
⿳ *w*	⎮ *s*
⎰ *b*	⌐ *š, sh* (one consonant in Egyptian)
▫ *p*	⋀ *k* (rather like *q* in "queen")
⌐ *f*	⌒ *k*
⿳ *m*	▨ *g*
～ *n*	⌒ *t*
⌒ *r*	⌐ *ṯ, tj* (one consonant in Egyptian)
⬚ *h*	⌐ *d*
⎛ *ḥ* (an intensified *h*)	⎞ *ḏ, dj* (one consonant in Egyptian)

To this class must be assigned also the numerous signs which represent two or three consonants, such as ⳺ *mr*, ⳺ *tm*, ⳺ *wr*, ⳺ *nw*, ⳺ *ḫpr*, ⳺ *nfr*, etc. The second class consists of the determinatives or sense-signs, the use of which has already been described above. These originated from pure word-signs which were later added to words in order to clarify their meaning.

All these signs were used side by side according to definitely fixed laws which had been established in the orthography at a very early period and in which every first-rate scribe was obliged to receive instruction. Thus, for example, the word "to live" is written ⳺, *ʿnḫ*, that is, with the word-sign ⳺, to which the second and third consonants, *n* ⌁ and *ḫ* ⊜, respectively, have been added in order to facilitate the reading; ⳺, *Km.t*, "the Black Land" (Egypt), is written with the phonetic sign ⳺ *km*, which depicts a piece of crocodile hide with spines, to which have been added a second phonetic character, the alphabetic ⳺ *m*, and the feminine ending ⌁ *t*, while the meaning of the entire word as a place name is indicated at the end by the determinative ⊛, which depicts a village with crossroads dividing it into quarters.

As the preceding examples have shown, the Egyptian system of writing was a consonantal script; as in such old Semitic languages as the Hebrew, Phoenician, and Arabic, the vowels of the words were not written. Everyone versed in the language could supply them without difficulty. Hieroglyphic writing was characterized by another peculiarity which it possessed in common with the Semitic languages: it was usually written from right to left and in exceptional cases alone, perhaps for artistic reasons, the reverse direction from left to right was chosen.

If writing was not to be done on stone with a chisel but on wood or papyrus—the ancient Egyptian "paper," which was made from the pith of the papyrus stem—with a reed pen, the signs quite naturally assumed a simpler and more rounded form. Thus, in addition to the monumental hieroglyphic writing, there developed an abbreviated book script which was employed on coffins, mummy wrappings, and papyrus for mortuary use. But when letters and business accounts had to be written hastily in the course of daily life, this script was simplified still further in such a manner that the individual signs were frequently joined together in a sort of running hand. The result of this development was the cursive script which is known today as the "hieratic" writing; it bears the same relationship to the carefully drawn hieroglyphs as our handwriting does to printing.

At a still later time a new cursive type of writing was evolved from the hieratic by means of further abbreviation and joining of characters. It was widely used during the Greco-Roman period, and it is known as the

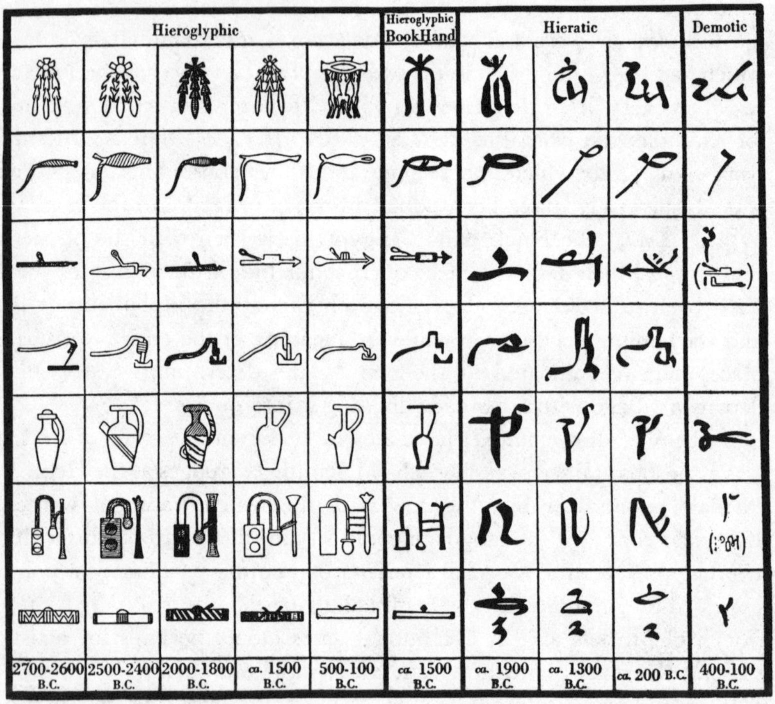

Hieroglyphic					Hieroglyphic BookHand	Hieratic			Demotic
2700-2600 B.C.	2500-2400 B.C.	2000-1800 B.C.	ca. 1500 B.C.	500-100 B.C.	ca. 1500 B.C.	ca. 1900 B.C.	ca. 1300 B.C.	ca. 200 B.C.	400-100 B.C.

FIG. 29.—EGYPTIAN HIEROGLYPHS AND THEIR CURSIVE EQUIVALENTS

"epistolographic" or "demotic" writing. The accompanying sketch (Fig. 29) illustrates seven different characters, first in five varying monumental forms in which they were carved on stone at different periods, in the hieroglyphic book hand, in three different eras of hieratic writing, and finally in the demotic script of the late period. The hieroglyphs depict (1) three foxskins tied together, *ms;* (2) a whip, *mḥ;* (3) a single-barbed harpoon, *wᶜ;* (4) an adz at work on a block of wood, *stp;* (5) a stone jug with handle, *ḫnm;* (6) a scribe's outfit, *zš;* and (7) a roll of papyrus tied with a cord.

This complicated system of writing demanded rigorous training of would-be scribes and government servants, whose careers, as we have seen (p. 92), were painted in strong contrast to that of any other profession. A recently discovered papyrus offers delightful testimony to ancient Egyptian appreciation of "education."

As for those learned scribes who lived after the [reign of the] gods, ... their names will endure forever, though they are gone . . . . and all their relatives are forgotten. They did not make for themselves pyramids of copper with tombstones attached of iron. They were unable to have children as heirs to pronounce their names, but they made heirs for themselves in the writings and teachings which they created. They gave themselves the papyrus roll as a lector-priest, the writing-board as a loving-son; [books of] teachings were their pyramids, the reed-pen was their child, and the stone surfaces a wife. From the greatest to the least, [these] served as their children, and the scribe, he is the chief of them.

Though doors and houses were made for them, they are fallen to ruin. Their mortuary service is gone, their tombstones are covered with earth, and their burial-chambers are forgotten. Their names, however, are [still] pronounced because of the books which they made, for they were good, and the memory of him who made them continues forever. Write, therefore—put that in your heart—and your name shall fare likewise. More beneficial is a book than a carved stela or a solid tomb wall. . . . . A man decays, his corpse is dust, and all his relatives are defunct; but the writings cause his name to be remembered in the mouth of the orator. More beneficial is a book than the house of the builder or a mortuary chapel in the west. It is better than a finished pylon or a stela in the temple.

Is there anyone like Hordedef? Is there another like Imhotep . . . . Nofry and Akhtoy, ... like Ptahhotep and Ka-ires? . . . . Those wise men who foretold what was to come—that which came forth from their mouths happened. It is found as spoken and written in their books. . . . . They are gone and their names are neglected, but [their] writings cause them to be remembered.

The range covered by Egyptian literature to the end of the dynasty of Thutmose I, whether written in hieroglyphic or the more cursive hieratic in rolls of papyrus or carved on stone, is exceedingly wide. Nearly every type of literature is represented—only the drama and the epic are nearly completely lacking. The latter is represented in Egypt by but a single surviving example, which dates from the Nineteenth Dynasty (thirteenth century B.C.); it commemorates a great military exploit of Ramesses II. Drama survives largely in texts devoted to the religious cults. Furthermore, just as the names of none of the great master builders and architects of the wonderful buildings erected by the ancient Egyptians have been preserved, so also the works of Egyptian literature were, with few exceptions, left unsigned by the poets and other writers who created them.

By far the largest place in the surviving literature is occupied by religious works, chief of which are three great collections known to modern science as the "Pyramid Texts," the "Coffin Texts," and the "Book of the Dead." They consist of compilations of magical spells by the use of which the journey to the hereafter and the existence there were facilitated for the king. The origin of the Pyramid Texts goes back to the beginning of the Old Kingdom and in part even to the prehistoric period, but the first copies discovered in modern times occur in the subterranean burial chambers of the pyramids of the Fifth and Sixth dynasties. The Coffin Texts, which were written chiefly on the sides of coffins for private persons, must be dated to the Middle Kingdom; while the Book of the Dead, written for the most part on papyrus book rolls, belongs to the New Kingdom.

In the New Kingdom these collections were augmented by the addition of another type of mortuary literature in which the ancient conceptions of the nightly journey of the sun-god in the netherworld were related in inscriptions and illustrated with pictures. To this group of texts belong the "Book of What Is in the Netherworld" (usually known to science as "Am Duat"), which has already been mentioned (p. 65; see also p. 150), and the "Book of Gates," first recorded in the kings' tombs at Thebes but certainly dating from an earlier time. In addition, countless hymns were composed in honor of the gods.

The creations of the so-called "fine" literature transport us to a unique sphere of existence, especially the romantic stories and folk tales which relate in simple fashion all sorts of wonderful adventures. We may read, for example, of great sorcerers who practiced their art in the reign of Khufu and in still earlier times or of two brothers who lived together in harmony until they became alienated through the faithlessness of the wife of the elder and of the adventures which subsequently befell them. Another tale, strongly reminiscent of the story of Sindbad the Sailor in the *Thousand and One Nights* relates the account of a sailor who suffered shipwreck and was cast ashore on a lonely island inhabited by a giant serpent who claimed to be the ruler of Punt. In other stories the simple folk spirit is abandoned in favor of a more pompous and artificial tone which must have had no less appeal to the educated Egyptian of old than it does to the Arab of today. In this "fine" style was written a widely circulated narrative of an Egyptian noble who was obliged for some obscure reason to flee to Syria at the accession of Senwosret I to the throne and to remain there for many years among the Beduin, until at last, at an advanced age, he was summoned back to the court of the pharaoh.

That the military exploits of the Egyptian armies in Syria worked their influence on the telling of stories has already been illustrated in the tale of the capture of Joppa by the general Djehuti (p. 57). The joy which the Egyptian found in everything strange and wonderful reigns in all these stories; like his descendants of today, the Egyptian of long ago loved nothing better after the burden of the day's work than to hear from the mouth of the talkative story-teller these tales of the marvelous world beyond the borders of his home.

Unfortunately, we possess but a limited number of secular songs, and these are of very uneven quality. The eulogistic verses in honor of the kings, like the hymns to the gods, abound in grandiloquent and turgid phrases; a few of them, however, reach a certain sublimity of poetic inspiration and are characterized by frequent highly effective metaphors. A stanza from a hymn to Senwosret III is well worthy of quotation:

> How great is the lord for his city:
> He alone is a million, and the other people are of small account.
> How great is the lord for his city:
> He resembles a dike which restrains the waters at flood time.
> How great is the lord for his city:
> He resembles a cool dwelling which invites a man to sleep far into the day.
> How great is the lord for his city:
> He resembles a rampart which protects the timid one from his adversary.
> How great is the lord for his city:
> He resembles the shade, fresher than a cool place in summer.
> How great is the lord for his city:
> He resembles a warm dry corner in the wintertime.
> How great is the lord for his city:
> He resembles a mountain that turns aside the storm when the heaven rages.
> How great is the lord for his city:
> He resembles Sekhmet when facing the enemies who trespass his boundary.

Several charming collections of love songs exist, all closely reminiscent of the Song of Solomon. Perhaps more remarkable, however, are the pessimistic poems, one of which, in praise of death, may be accounted the greatest surviving example of Egyptian lyric verse.

> Death is in my mind today
> As when a sick man regains his health,
> Like rising again after illness.

Death is in my mind today
Like the fragrance of myrrh,
Like sitting in shelter on a windy day.

Death is in my mind today
Like the perfume of lotus blossoms,
Like tarrying at the brim of the winebowl.

Death is in my mind today
Like the retreat of a rainstorm,
As when men return home from the wars.

Death is in my mind today
Like the clearing of the sky,
As when a man grasps suddenly what he has not understood.

Death is in my mind today
Like the longing of a man for his home,
When he has passed long years in captivity.

The Egyptians were exceedingly fond of aphoristic verses, and numerous collections of didactic sayings similar to those in the Bible, especially the Book of Proverbs and the apocryphal Book of Sirach, provide all sorts of rules of wisdom and good manners. One of the most interesting of these wisdom books is the "Teaching for Life and Instruction for Prosperity," which the "Overseer of Grains," Amenemope, the son of Kanakht, composed for his son to "lead him aright in the ways of life." Many of its passages are so closely parallel to certain verses in the Book of Proverbs that it seems necessary to conclude that some verbal relationship existed between the two works. A single illustration will suffice to point out the parallelism:

Prov. 22:24	Amenemope 11:13–14
Make no friendship with a man that is given to anger; And with a wrathful man thou shalt not go.	Join thyself not to the passionate man, And approach him not for conversation.

Closely related to the wisdom books is another remarkable type of Egyptian literature in which are set forth reflections and complaints over the wretchedness of the world and the evil of humanity. The author not infrequently expresses a pessimistic view of the prospects for future betterment of this unhappy situation. Sometimes, however, he points with prophetic eye to a pleasanter future either on earth or in the hereafter subse-

quent to the death which, after all, does ultimately come to release a
humanity struggling under the burden of misery.

All these classes of poetry are distinguished from ordinary prose narrative by their choice of language; most of them are likewise dominated by
a special verse form accompanied by a definite rhythm and by that same
parallelism of members which is a characteristic mark of Hebrew poetry.
A thought which has been stated in one verse is reiterated in a second,
often in a somewhat expanded and embellished form, and perhaps in a
third verse as well. An ancient eulogy of the king well illustrates this
characteristic of Egyptian poetry:

> Praises to thee who protecteth the land and extendeth its boundaries,
> Who overcometh the foreign lands by his crown and embraceth the Two
>   Lands with his arms;
> Who slayeth his foes without a blow of the ax, and shooteth the arrow without
>   drawing the bow.
> His might hath smitten the Beduin in the land; and the fear of him hath slain
>   the Nine Bows.

The science of the Egyptians is renowned; yet what has been revealed
to us by those of their scientific works which have been discovered largely
gives the lie to the panegyrists of old. It is true that the Egyptians possessed a highly developed power of observation, that their perception of
the phenomena of the external world was often faultless, and that they
gained considerable empirical knowledge as the result of experience.
However, in distinct contrast to the Greeks, they rarely succeeded in ar-
ranging their individual observations into a homogeneous system in accordance with fixed points of view. Perhaps their greatest success lay in
the field of astronomy, for already at an early date they had begun to
observe the stars and to analyze the fixed stars into constellations, each
with its own name. In order to find their way about in the great multitude of the heavenly bodies, they divided the celestial equator into thirty-
six parts called decans; then the positions of the stars in each of the hours
of the night were recorded throughout the year at intervals of ten days in
a series of special tables. Sets of these were provided on the ceilings of
certain royal tombs of the New Kingdom in order to enable the deceased
ruler to determine with their assistance both the hours in the sky and the
solstitial point in the year. Other sky charts pointed out to him the way
in the sky and served him as a calendar. One of the earliest and best of

the decan tables, dating from the middle of the Eighteenth Dynasty, was recently discovered on the ceiling of the tomb of Senenmut at Deir el-Bahri. The constellation of the Great Bear, shaped like the head of a bull, and the circumpolar stars are shown in the northern half of the sky, while Orion and the female figure of Sothis (Sirius) are conspicuous in the southern half. In addition, there is a list of the decans, the twelve ancient monthly festivals, each as a circle with its round of twenty-four hours, a procession of the celestial bodies of the northern sky, and, finally, a picture of the "Field of Reeds," the heavenly region in which the deceased was obliged to carry on his work.

Among the various astronomical observations of the Egyptians, one attained an especially practical significance. It had long ago been discovered that the day with which the Egyptian peasant started his new year and the beginning of the annual inundation of the Nile approximately coincided with the day on which the brightest of the fixed stars, Sirius, known as Sothis (Sopdet) to the Egyptians, first reappeared on the eastern horizon at dawn after two and a half months of invisibility. The interval between two such heliacal risings of Sothis was three hundred and sixty-five and one-fourth days. By adopting this event as New Year's Day, a fixed astronomical year was obtained which virtually coincided with the solar year. Of course, this year had not been in use in ancient times in civil life; the agricultural population had adopted a year of twelve months of thirty days each, with an additional period of five intercalary days to avoid too great variation from the true solar year. Since, however, this year was a quarter of a day shorter than the astronomical Sothic year, the New Year's Day of the civil (or popular) calendar fell after each interval of four years one day earlier than the Sothic New Year's Day, which occurred on July 19 in antiquity. It was only after the passage of 1,460 civil years that the two New Year's Days could be celebrated again at the same time. Yet, in spite of this awkward situation, it was only in the time of the Roman Empire, after the introduction of Christianity, that the Sothic year replaced the civil year in Egypt. It had been introduced into Rome by Julius Caesar in 45 B.C.—for that reason it is known as the Julian year—and it became the basis for the calendar which, somewhat more precisely corrected, we use to this day.

The annual inundation of the Nile, which with repeated regularity altered or obliterated the boundaries between plots of land, forced the

Egyptians at an early age to concern themselves with surveying and to acquire an exact knowledge of reckoning. Their methods of calculation were somewhat cumbersome, to be sure, and if we take a mere glance at the two mathematical treatises which have survived from the end of the Middle Kingdom and the Hyksos period, we cannot help wondering at the awkward manner in which the simplest exercises in arithmetic and geometry were solved. Nevertheless, the Egyptians mastered at a very early time some exceedingly difficult geometrical calculations the discovery of which is attributed to the Greeks, and Herodotus was not in error when he looked upon Egypt as the home of geometry. It must be admitted, in this connection, that the Egyptian handbooks on the subject are devoted exclusively to the treatment of practical problems and that they never made any attempt to treat mathematics as a science.

The situation was somewhat more favorable in the case of medical science, of which Herodotus says: "Egypt swarms with physicians, every single one a specialist." There developed a rather extensive medical literature, a considerable part of which was preserved in papyrus manuscripts. All in all, we possess eight more or less complete medical works. They were written down during the first half of the New Kingdom, about the middle of the second millennium B.C. The textual material, however, is of a considerably greater age, some of it reaching as far back as the beginning of the Old Kingdom.

One of these old treatises deals not with human diseases but with veterinary medicine. Of the remaining seven, four are of a diverse nature, containing a mixture of purely medical material and a number of prescriptions or recipes for home use, that is, cosmetic suggestions such as methods for dyeing gray hair, and formulas of a magical character. Three of the papyri, however, are thoroughly homogeneous. One is a treatise on gynecological disorders; another, of which fragments only are preserved, deals with conception, sterility, and the sex of the unborn child; the third is concerned with surgery.

All these works pursue a strictly practical purpose. They are intended to transmit medical experience empirically obtained to the physicians of the future, and each book is intended to be used as a practical vade mecum. Almost no attention is given to scientific systemization. Each is but a dull collection of prescriptions only rarely illuminated by a spark of reflective thought, as, for instance, in the instructions pertaining to the

Fig. 30.—Portion of a Page of the Edwin Smith Surgical Papyrus (Brooklyn Museum)

human heart and blood vessels. The physician generally contented himself with making as nearly correct a diagnosis as possible, with recognizing the nature and location of the disease, and with prescribing the proper remedy in accordance with his findings. These remedies were often enough not only quite rationally contrived but also not altogether ineffective; all too frequently, however, they depended on superstition for their healing power, and, wherever human knowledge failed, resort was made to magic and sorcery.

A fundamentally different and, it may be said, much more truly scientific impression is conveyed by a fourth handbook from ancient Egypt, the Edwin Smith surgical papyrus, one of the greatest treasures of the New York Historical Society, which has been superbly published by the late James Henry Breasted (Fig. 30). The oldest surgical treatise in the world discusses forty-eight cases in seven different sections arranged according to the parts of the body from the head downward, beginning with the skull and presumably ending with the feet.

Each of the cases discussed in this treatise is arranged according to a definitely fixed scheme. At the beginning stands the title with statement of the ailment; next follows the examination of the patient, introduced by the words, "If you examine the man," together with a statement of the symptoms; to these is added the diagnosis beginning with the phrases, "you shall say of him, 'he is suffering from' " this or that ailment, the name of which is appended. Next comes the doctor's professional decision, which may take any one of three different forms: (1) "an ailment which I will treat," a favorable prognosis; (2) "an ailment with which I will contend," a doubtful prognosis; or (3) "an ailment not to be treated," an unfavorable prognosis.

This remarkable ancient Egyptian textbook is not merely an accidental collection of arbitrary cases, like the other Egyptian medical books, but rather a treatise which its author, perhaps a court or army surgeon, compiled in a strictly systematic manner in order to present experience gained in practice by methodical examination and objective consideration. For this reason the Edwin Smith papyrus is not only a valuable monument for the history of medicine but also an eloquent witness of the scientific spirit which four thousand years ago or more guided at least a few choice men of ancient Egypt in their researches. It is a fascinating revelation of the human mind struggling with the first stages of the development of science.

The Egyptian language as represented by its latest form, the Coptic, was written with the Greek alphabet plus seven characters adapted from the Egyptian script. It came into use after Christianity had spread into Egypt to replace the ancient religion of the land. In fact, as the old religion gave way to the new, the knowledge of the hieroglyphic writing, which during the Greco-Roman period had been largely confined to the native priesthood, was gradually forgotten. The Coptic, with its simple and convenient script, became the language of the Christian church in Egypt. The Scriptures were translated into Coptic, and this language was widely used throughout the churches and monasteries of the Nile Valley. It continued in use until the Middle Ages, but after the Arab conquest (A.D. 641) it slowly expired as Christianity in its turn was replaced by the religion of Islam. Thus the ancient language of the Egyptians perished from its native soil, and in its stead prevailed the Arabic speech of the conquerors, which survives in one of its dialects as the language of the modern Egyptians.

XII

THE EGYPTIAN RELIGION

H E WHO desires to know the religious notions which prevailed during the golden age of Egypt must follow a backward course and attempt to fathom the cults of that dark primeval age in which the "Two Lands," Upper and Lower Egypt, still existed independently side by side, before there was a unified Egyptian nation. Each city, town, and village possessed its own protective divinity and its sanctuary to which the inhabitants turned for assistance in days of need and danger as they constantly sought the favor of the god by means of prayers and offerings. In his hand lay the weal and woe of the community; he was the lord of the region, the "god of the city," who, like an earthly prince or count, controlled the destiny of his vassals and defended them from their enemies. How closely the god was bound up with his district is very well indicated by the fact that he frequently possessed no name of his own but was simply designated by the name of the site of the cult which belonged to him and in which he was worshiped. Thus the local divinity of the Upper Egyptian city of Ombos was "the Ombite," and the god of Edfu was referred to as "He of Edfu." Of course, each local god usually bore a distinctive name the original meaning of which we are now seldom able to determine. Thus the god of Memphis was called Ptah (Fig. 31, a); the lord of Thebes was named Montu; the ancient tutelary divinity of Herwer was Khnum (Fig. 31, b); in Coptos it was Min, and in Heliopolis it was Atum, who was worshiped. Familiar names among the female divinities are Hathor, the "Lady of Dendera" (Fig. 31, c); Neith, the goddess of Sais (Fig. 31, d); and Sekhmet, the protective goddess of Memphis (Fig. 33).

The function of these local patron deities was usually limited to their concern for their city, and they possessed no power beyond its limit. There were a few of them, however, who attained a more extensive sphere of influence along with the increase in importance of their native cities. In this manner some of them developed into district or even national gods and acquired dominating positions in the Egyptian pantheon.

132

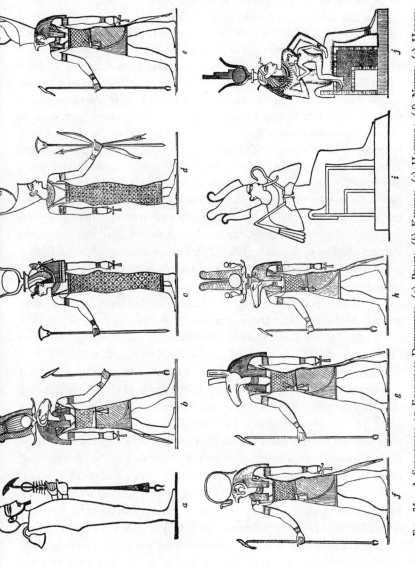

Fig. 31.—A Selection of Egyptian Divinities: (a) Ptah; (b) Khnum; (c) Hathor; (d) Neith; (e) Horus; (f) Re-Harakhti; (g) Seth; (h) Sobek; (i) Osiris; (j) Isis Suckling Her Son Horus

133

Thus, when Egypt still consisted of two separate kingdoms, the local gods of the religious capitals—Seth of Ombos and Horus of Behdet—came to be the protective gods of the two states; legend has preserved some memory of the wars which took place between the north and the south. As a pair of divine kings the two gods were supposed to have struggled with each other for a long time in order to determine which one should have the sovereignty over the Two Lands; but in the end a peaceful settlement was brought about between them under which each of them took as his share a half of the kingdom. When Egypt was later united into a single state, with Upper Egypt victorious over Lower Egypt, Horus became the national god, a position which he maintained through all successive ages (Fig. 31, *e*). The king was considered to be the incarnation of his patron lord Horus. Somewhat later, but still in the prehistoric era, when Egypt for the second time split into two independent kingdoms and established new capitals, the local divinities of these two cities—the vulture-goddess of Nekheb (Elkab) and the serpent-goddess of Buto—were elevated to the positions of national divinities, and their worship extended far beyond their original sphere of influence. In a similar manner the cosmic god Amun (Fig. 13) was transferred from Hermopolis to Karnak in the Eleventh Dynasty so that he eventually became the local god of Thebes and later, through identification with Re (Fig. 31, *f*), as "king of the gods," the national god of the New Kingdom.

It happened not uncommonly that the inhabitants of a city emigrated and founded a new home elsewhere. In such an event it is not surprising that they carried with them their patron deity and provided a new cult place for him in the new location. In other cases the people of one district became so impressed by the effectiveness with which some foreign divinity protected his community or the abundance of the blessings and miracles which he showered upon it that they began to make pilgrimages to his shrine or even to supply him with new temples in which, by the presentation of offerings, they also might win the benefits of his powerful favor. In this manner a god was occasionally transferred to a city where he had not originally resided. Sometimes he attracted a circle of worshipers away from the actual patron god of the town or even usurped the native god's position as the tutelary divinity of the city. It was perhaps in some such manner as this that the goddess Neith of Sais acquired her shrine at Esna, or the god Khnum, who was really at home in Hypselis, near Assiut, was accorded worship in Herwer, Esna, and Elephantine.

Already at an early date the concepts of some of the local divinities were extended through emphasis on certain aspects of their character. Some of them in consequence came to preside over certain of the crafts and professions. The falcon-shaped Montu thus became a war-god; Min of Coptos came to be the patron of desert travelers as well as the god of fertility and the harvest. Ptah of Memphis, in whose province the distinctive art of Egypt originated in historic times, was the patron of all artists, metal-workers, and smiths. The powerful Sekhmet of Memphis became a terrible fire-goddess who annihilated her enemies, while Hathor of Dendera was converted into a goddess of love and joy. Horus the falcon became the sun-god who illuminated the world and who as a youthful hero engages in perpetual battle with his adversary Seth the storm-god (Fig. 31, g). Thoth of Hermopolis (Fig. 32) was a moon-god who had created the divisions of time and the order of the cosmos; he was also counted the inventor of hieroglyphic writing, the "lord of divine words," and the god of learning. The crocodile-god Sobek (Fig. 31, h) was naturally considered a water-god; he received worship as a patron divinity in towns the special weal and woe of which were peculiarly dependent on water, as was the situation on the islands of Gebelein and Kom Ombo, in the oasis of the Fayyum, or at the town of Kheny at the Nile rapids near modern Silsila. Thus local gods very frequently developed into patron deities of certain professions or into nature gods worshiped throughout the length and breadth of the land.

In addition to these "city gods," there was also a very considerable number of lesser gods, spirits, and demons, who were considered able at times to be of benefit or injury to men and whose favor it was necessary to court, as well as an important class of fairies who rendered assistance to women in travail and who could either hinder or accelerate childbirth. Various protective household gods of grotesque stature were worshiped under the name of Bes. Musicians, dancers, killers of snakes, they also presided over the toilette, the bedchamber, and the pleasures of love. Among the great host of other divinities it is possible to mention here but a few: gods and goddesses of the harvest, spirits who provided healing in times of illness, gods and goddesses of war.

If the inhabitants of a locality lived in peace and carried on friendly

Fig. 32.—Anubis and Thoth Weighing the Heart at the Judgment (British Museum)

136

intercourse with its neighbors, it was natural that their patron gods should share their friendship. Like the men who worshiped them, they were accustomed to visit one another on certain days, and outside gods were frequently presented with special chapels and their own cults in the temple of a "city god." While the latter thus remained the chief god of his district, he was by no means the only divinity in it to receive the homage of its inhabitants. Instead, an entire circle of other gods and demigods stood beside him as his guests to share the praises and offerings of his worshipers. At a very early time, indeed, the priests undertook to bring various of these gods into some relationship with one another. As a result, it not infrequently happened that a goddess was assigned to the principal god of the city as his wife and a third divinity to the two of them as their son. At Karnak in Thebes, for example, the chief god Amun (Fig. 13) shared his worship with his wife, the goddess Mut, and their son, the moon-god Khonsu; in Memphis the tutelary god Ptah (Fig. 31, *a*) was given Sekhmet (Fig. 33) as a consort and Nefertem as their son; at Abydos, Osiris (Fig. 31, *i*), his sister-wife Isis (Fig. 31, *j*), and Horus "the son of Isis" constituted the "triad" or holy family.

Manifold though the Egyptian gods were in name, not less so were the outward manifestations which were attributed to them by their devotees. Most of them were somewhat crude and reminiscent of the fetishism which still holds in its clutches a large proportion of the uncivilized Negro tribes of Africa. The god of Busiris in the Delta was conceived as a pillar with the head and arms of an Egyptian king; the goddess Neith of Sais was a shield to which a pair of crossed arrows had been nailed. The god Ptah of Memphis and the harvest-god Min of Coptos, under whose protection stood the desert road which connected his native city with the Red Sea, were both worshiped as fetishes in semihuman form. However, the divinities were most frequently conceived in purely animal form: Sobek as a crocodile, the god of Mendes as a ram, Thoth of Hermopolis as an ibis, Khnum in the form of a ram; Horus in that of a falcon or sparrow hawk, while his adversary Seth was given the form of some kind of fabulous beast. The protective goddess of Buto was a serpent; that of Nekheb, like the goddess Mut of Thebes, was regarded as a vulture; while Hathor of Dendera was given the form of a cow.

These are all conceptions of the gods which at first thought appear to us not only inherently strange but even as utterly unworthy of a cultured

Fig. 33.—The Goddess Sekhmet (Metropolitan Museum of Art)

race. The Greeks and Romans reacted in the same manner when they became acquainted with Egypt, and they were free to express their contempt and scorn at finding such primitive religious ideas in a race so admirable for many of its achievements. Nevertheless, similar concepts were widely held by other civilized peoples, including certain of the Semitic tribes and even the earliest Greeks. The Semites found divinity in trees, stones, and animals; from the Greeks likewise we have any number of familiar myths which relate, for example, how Hermes, god of meadow and highway, manifested himself as a heap of stones, Apollo as a wolf, Zeus as a cloud, Artemis as a bear, Hera as a cow, while every student of classical mythology knows that the "sacred animal" of Athena was the owl and that of Zeus was the eagle.

It was customary to house the wooden statue of the divinity in the local temple in its own naos or shrine. On feast days the statue, still in its shrine, was carried in procession on the shoulders of the priests or transported on the river in a sacred bark. In addition, from the very earliest times a specimen of whatever species of animal happened to be sacred to a given temple—the animal in which the local god was accustomed to manifest himself—was kept and carefully tended in the sanctuary. The Greek traveler Strabo, who toured Egypt in the reign of the Roman emperor Augustus, has left a description of the crocodile sacred to the water-god Sobek which was cherished at Arsinoë, the capital of the Fayyum.

It is fed with the bread, meat, and wine brought by the strangers who come to see it. Our host went with us to the lake, taking along a small meal-cake, some meat, and a small flask of wine. We found the animal lying on the bank; the priests approached and, while some of them opened his jaws, another thrust first the cake into his mouth, then the meat, and finally poured the wine after them. Thereupon the crocodile plunged into the lake and swam to the opposite shore.

In the later period, after the religion had lost more and more of its inner vitality, and the people clung increasingly to outward forms, they carried the animal cults to such extremes that they came to regard each individual of the species in whose form the divinity was believed to reveal himself as sacred and divine. These animals were considered inviolable; to kill one of them in a place dedicated to its species was punishable by the death penalty. In fact, so extreme was the religious zeal of this epoch that it became the custom to embalm each one of the sacred animals at death and to bury it ceremoniously in special cemeteries dedicated to the purpose.

A forward step from crude fetishism was taken already in the prehistoric age when the Egyptian began to represent the divinity in human form. At that time the god appeared with a human face and figure and wore the same type of clothing as the Egyptians themselves. His head, like that of a prince or king, was adorned with a helmet or crown, while the simple skirt was decorated with the tail of an animal attached to the back the girdle as had been the custom of the rulers of the primeval time. His insignia of authority consisted of baton and scepter, while a goddess regularly carried a papyrus blossom with a long stem. This new interpretation of divinity was bound to react on the more primitive fetishistic beliefs. The crude anthropoid fetish of Ptah developed into a youthful figure "beautiful of face," with shaven head, enveloped in a tightly fitting garment, and standing on a stair or terrace with a scepter grasped in both hands. Those divinities which had formerly been conceived as animals became transformed into human figures surmounted by the heads of the sacred animals from which they were derived. Sobek became a man with the head of a crocodile, Khnum a man with a ram's head (Fig. 31, *b*); Thoth was represented in human form with the head of an ibis (Fig. 32), Horus with that of a falcon (Fig. 31, *e*), while Sekhmet became a woman with the head of a lioness (Fig. 33).

In addition to the local divinities which were conceived in animal form, still other sacred animals were made peculiar objects of worship. The best known of these is the Mnevis bull, which was honored in Heliopolis, the Buchis bull of Hermonthis (Armant), the "phoenix" (heron) of Heliopolis, and especially the Apis bull of Memphis. According to the late Greek account, the last named was begotten by a ray of sunlight which descended from heaven and impregnated a cow, which would thereafter never be able to give birth a second time. The Apis bull was black with white spots, including a white triangle on the forehead and the figure of a crescent moon on the right side. He usually wore a red cloth on his back. As far back as the Old Kingdom we know that priests were assigned to him, but more extensive information concerning his nature or his cult has not survived. In later times, however, theological speculations sought to create a relationship between this highly esteemed bull and Ptah, the ancient god of Memphis. These eventually resulted in the concept that Apis was the son of Ptah or, by a still more complex dogma, the actual image, "the living reincarnation of Ptah." In the New Kingdom, Amenhotep III caused the deceased bulls to be sumptuously interred in the necropolis of Memphis at Saqqara in mausoleums in the usual style of burial place. In the Nineteenth Dynasty, however, under Ramesses II, a magnificent mortuary gallery was laid out in which the sacred bulls were buried in splendid stone sarcophagi. This subterranean cemetery—a gallery nearly three hundred and fifty feet in length carved out of the solid rock, with a row of niches for the burials of the individual bulls—the so-called Serapeum, was highly venerated as late as the Ptolemaic period, when it attracted great hosts of pious pilgrims.

In general, our knowledge of the most popularly honored divinities is exceedingly limited; we are acquainted with their names and representations, but their nature and character are withheld from our understanding in spite of the multitude of poetic epithets which are applied to them in the hymns and liturgies. It is evident, however, that their gods were not merely the empty, shadowy figures to the Egyptians which they appear to us with our scanty information concerning them. Their ancient worshipers told many a tale of their exploits and marvelous adventures, and these myths will certainly have been elaborated, expanded, and reduced to writing in the bosom of the priesthood where they were principally cherished.

In addition to the local divinities whose activities were confined to a limited sphere on earth, there were other great powers who emerged in nature and embraced the entire world: heaven and earth, sun, moon, and stars, and the Nile. The sky was the "great god"; he was thought of as a falcon which spread his protective wings over the earth or over Egypt. His divine eyes are the sun and moon; when he opens them it is day, when they are closed it is night. The stars are attached to his body, the wind is the breath of his mouth, and the water is his perspiration According to another widely circulated myth, the sky is a goddess, sometimes known by the name of Nut. In primordial times she was closely embraced in the arms of the earth-god Geb, until the god of the atmosphere, Shu, separated them from each other by elevating Nut high above the earth on his uplifted arms and placing himself beneath her. From the union of Geb and Nut sprang a son, Re, the sun-god, and the most popular of the cosmic gods. He travels by day in his bark across the celestial ocean as on the Nile, until at eventide he transfers to another boat in order to descend to the netherworld and there continue his voyage. He was also conceived as a falcon who soared through the sky with bright plumage or as a young hero who carried on a constant struggle with the hostile powers of darkness. As the god of the Upper Egyptian city of Edfu he is depicted as the sun disk with extended wings, a form in which he regularly appeared as a symbol of protection over the doors and elsewhere in the decoration of Egyptian temples.

The nature gods in general never developed a special cult of their own. Gradually, however, an exception was made in the case of Re, and it became customary to present offerings to him under the open sky. The kings of the Fifth Dynasty, who were popularly regarded as children of Re, dedicated to him near the capital of Memphis a unique temple inclosure the chief feature of which was a peculiar type of obelisk erected on a huge stone substructure.

The evolution of religious ideas tended in general toward some connection between the local divinities and the celestial powers; the priesthoods of the former obviously sought every opportunity to enhance the reputation of their gods. Thus the falcon-shaped Horus, who by this time had developed into the national god, became identified with the sky-god who, as we have seen, was regarded as a falcon also; he became in consequence the "great god" or "lord of heaven" and received the name Harakhti ("Horus of the Horizon"). In addition, he was identified with Re and henceforth regarded as the sun-god Re-Harakhti. It was but a natural result that Re also should receive the form of Horus, and he is accordingly depicted as a king in human form with the head of a falcon surmounted by the sun disk with pendent uraeus serpent.

In a similar manner other local gods who originally had no connection whatever with the sun and who had never manifested themselves as falcons, as, for example, the crocodile-shaped water-god Sobek, the ram-shaped gods Khnum and Amun of Karnak, were identified with Re and assigned in consequence the sun disk and the sacred uraeus serpent as designations of rank. The local divinities retained through this development all their old attributes, and the myths which had centered about them were perpetuated by tradition; the inevitable result was a bewildering confusion of tangled and often self-contradictory ideas in the Egyptian religion. Efforts were made in the theology to distinguish at least the various sun-gods from one another; a distinct function was assigned to each one, according to which Khepri—the sun conceived as a scarab— became the morning sun and Atum was worshiped as the evening sun. Nevertheless, it does not appear that the learned priesthood ever succeeded in drawing up a comprehensive system of Egyptian theology.

A similar transformation may be followed among the local female divinities, who tended to become identified with the goddess Nut. So the cow-goddess Hathor developed into a sky-goddess, a fact which led to the logical if rather astonishing conclusion that Nut herself was a cow

FIG. 34.—THE SKY-GODDESS NUT AS A COW (BIBAN EL-MULUK, TOMB OF SETHI I)

which was held fast by numerous gods and supported in position by Shu, the god of the atmosphere, while the stars were all attached to her belly, and the sun-god traveled in his bark along her body (Fig. 34).

Numerous other local gods whose character or appearance was not very sharply differentiated became identified at an early date. Hathor and Isis were thus considered as the same person, while Amun of Karnak, Min of Coptos, and later even Khnum of Elephantine were combined into a single divinity. The tutelary cat-goddess of Bubastis was equated with the goddesses Sekhmet and Pekhet, both of whom were lionesses, and all of them, in turn, were identified with Mut, the mother of the gods and the consort of Amun.

It certainly should not have been too much for a clever brain to have constituted some sort of order out of this mixture of diverse mythological ideas. With some effort to combine the local gods and to conceive them as sun or sky divinities, the Egyptian might well have been drawn naturally to the conclusion that the adoration of ancient patron gods was an obsolete idea and that the worship of a small group of gods or even of one alone was the most reasonable point of view. But who would have possessed the courage to put such a theory into practice and to shelve the ancient cults in order to substitute a new one in their place? Would not the united priesthoods of the entire land have risen up against such an effort in order to defend the rights and individual prerogatives of their gods? Above all, how would the great mass of the people, who clung with deep veneration to the old gods of their homes without the slightest interest in a theological system, have received an announcement that the dominion of their divine protector was at an end and that he had been superseded by another to whom it was now ordered that they must address their prayers and present their offerings? And yet the day was not so far away when just such an attempt was to be ventured—an attempt to overthrow the gods of old and to replace them with a single god in heaven and on earth (see chap. xiv).

The Egyptians failed no less completely to achieve a consistent set of ideas regarding man's destiny in the life after death. Rooted deeply in the hearts of the people was at least the belief that death was really not the end of everything but rather that a man would continue to live on exactly as on earth, provided that the conditions necessary for continued existence were fulfilled. First of all, he must be supplied with food and drink; hence the anxious and constantly reiterated desire of the Egyptians to receive "thousands of loaves, geese, oxen, beer, and all the good things by which a god lives" in the life hereafter. To avoid suffering from hunger and thirst after death, each Egyptian provided his tomb with great jars filled with food and drink or, if he had the means, established endowments the income of which would secure for all time the necessities of life in the netherworld. If he had surviving children or other close relatives, piety demanded that they go forth on the great feast days to the cemetery in order to deposit food and drink offerings at the tomb. Nevertheless, all of these provisions were still insufficient. From the time of the Old Kingdom the walls of the tomb or at least of the coffin were covered with representations of all sorts of objects which by magic could be transformed into the actual products depicted, when they would become available to serve all the physical needs of the dead. The same magical power was believed to be inherent in the relief sculptures or wall paintings in the tombs of the wealthy, where the deceased is shown seated at a richly decked offering-table (Fig. 35), or where he witnesses the butchering and dressing of the offering-cattle or the rows of peasant girls bringing up products from the mortuary estate.

Beyond all these efforts to provide for the deceased, still another device was employed to achieve the desired end. Again and again one encounters inscriptions in the tombs appealing to each and every visitor or chance passer-by to repeat certain prayers which would conjure up by magic everything required for the enjoyment and nourishment of the deceased. In addition to the articles of food and drink, these objects include various oils, ointments, and cosmetics for the eyes—all of which were frequently provided for funerary use in exquisitely beautiful vases— jewelry, clothing, and even weapons for the protection of the dead against

Fig. 35.—The Daily Meal within the Tomb (Thebes, Tomb of Djehuti)

his enemies, as well as numerous other things. In the course of centuries the number and variety of such funerary objects greatly increased; how manifold the tomb equipment of the dead became in the golden age of the pharaonic empire is best illustrated by the treasure from the tomb of Tutankhamun (pp. 228 f.), which contains several thousand objects.

Another important popular belief was combined with these notions of the life after death and the requirements for its support. Each man was believed to possess not only a body but also a soul which survived in the hereafter. This was believed to take the form of a bird or, at a later time, the form of a falcon with the head of the deceased. After death it was thought to depart from the dead body and to fly about freely in the world, though it could at will, especially at night when evil spirits walked abroad, return to the safety of the tomb. However, this could occur only if the body of the deceased was properly preserved and prevented from decomposition. In order thus to enable the soul to recognize the body to which it belonged, the Egyptians from a very early time devoted the most careful attention to the preservation of the body.

Still another of the favorite Egyptian beliefs concerning the dead was the idea that the departed could assume different shapes and by means of magical formulas transform himself into all sorts of beings, such as a serpent, a falcon, a lily, a ram, or even a crocodile, and in such a form to move about the earth by day. These beliefs later became known to the Greek historians and philosophers, but they were misunderstood and led to the erroneous conclusion that the ancient Egyptians, like the Hindus, had believed in the doctrine of the transmigration of the soul.

The so-called "ka" played an important role in the Egyptian mortuary beliefs. This was a kind of protective spirit or genius which was born simultaneously with the individual and was closely united to him throughout life. In fact, the ka did not share the experience of death but survived the deceased in order to quicken him with its own life-strength and to protect him from his enemies in the hereafter.

The dead, like the living, continued under the protection of their domestic gods, who concerned themselves with the burial and especially with the safety of the departed ones in the grave. There were, however, in many cities special mortuary gods, such as Khenty-Imentiu, "the First of the Westerners" (the dead), who was regularly represented in the form of a jackal. At a very remote time all these divinities receded into the background in favor of Osiris. He was probably a deified king who had once ruled in the Delta city of Busiris and who had met a tragic and untimely death by drowning in the Nile. In the course of time his reputation and then his worship spread throughout Egypt, but the city of Abydos eventually became the chief place in which his cult was celebrated. The saga telling of his life and death became one of the most loved, as it was humanly the most universally comprehensible and appealing of all the stories of the Egyptian gods. Unfortunately, it does not exist in a homogeneous tradition in any native Egyptian text but only in an account recorded by the Greek writer Plutarch. According to his account, Osiris had once ruled as king of Egypt and had showered blessings upon his happy subjects. But he had a wicked brother named Seth, who had designs on his life and the throne. He concocted a conspiracy whereby he contrived by trickery in the course of a banquet to have his brother lay himself in an artistically wrought chest. Scarcely had Osiris taken his place in the casket when Seth and his seventy-two confederates sprang upon it, clapped down the lid, and cast it into the Nile, which bore it down to the sea. The waves eventually carried the chest and its contents to the beach near the Phoenician city of Byblos. Meanwhile Isis, the sister and wife of Osiris, wandered throughout the world seeking the body of her husband. After she had located and with some difficulty obtained possession of it, she carried it back to Egypt and mourned the departed Osiris in private. Then she concealed the coffin and departed into the Delta marshes to Buto, where her son Horus was brought up. During her absence Seth, while on a wild-boar hunt, came upon the corpse of his hated brother and, after having in fury divided it into fourteen pieces, scattered the remains throughout the land. The faithful Isis, nevertheless, sought out all the dismembered pieces and buried them wherever she found them, erecting a monument over each one of them. That is the reason why so many different tombs of Osiris were known in Egypt. But after Horus had grown to maturity in the Delta swamps, he came forth to avenge the murder of his father, and a terrible battle ensued in which Horus won the victory. In the end Osiris, through the application of all sorts of magical devices by his pious son, was reawakened to life and henceforth ruled in the west as king of the blessed dead.

The death which according to the legend was suffered by Osiris at the hands of his false brother Seth became the portion of every human being;

but, just as Osiris had risen again, so could each man also begin life anew if only the same formulas were spoken and the same ceremonies performed by a faithful son which Osiris' son Horus had once spoken and performed for his father. In this manner the deceased would not only come to Osiris; he was believed actually to become Osiris himself. The entrance to the empire of Osiris depended on magical formulas and spells which must be recited or the knowledge of which must be intrusted to the deceased, in addition to which, however, a virtuous life on earth was likewise regarded as essential to the attainment of eternal life. To that end it was necessary for each individual to appear after death at a judgment in the presence of Osiris and before a court of forty-two judges to declare himself innocent of wrongdoing. Only after this had been accomplished and after the heart of the deceased had been weighed in the balance of righteousness before the god Thoth and found true, was he permitted to enter the world of the hereafter (Fig. 32).

While the concept of a final judgment reveals at least that the Egyptian possessed lofty ideals of conduct in his daily life, we have but little information about the religious thought and practice of the average man. Nevertheless, the meaning of such personal names as Ny-wy-netjer ("I belong to God"), Mery-Re ("Beloved of Re"), Hor-hotpu ("Horus is merciful"), or Ptah-em-saf ("Ptah is his protection") would indicate that from an early time the Egyptian entertained a sense of intimate contact with his god and believed that the god was not only near to him but interested in his welfare and to some degree like himself. The ancient books of "Teachings for Life" (p. 126) definitely connect the good life as conforming to the will of the god. While the numerous religious hymns are mainly concerned with praise of the god as the lord of heaven and earth, they likewise recognize him as a hearer of prayers who loves and approves of his people. Shortly after 1300 B.C., however, a striking development of personal piety is manifest, and for the first time in Egypt we find the conviction expressed that, even though man is disposed to evil, God is inclined to forgive; while God is bound to punish wrongdoing, his wrath is momentary and his mercy abundant.

Various ideas prevailed concerning the dwelling-place of the blessed dead. For the most part it was thought to be somewhere in the west, in the region of the sunset. It was also believed that the departed were transformed into the shining stars of the sky. Or they lived on in the celestial fields of rushes, where, as formerly on earth, they cultivated the soil, plowed, sowed, and reaped, but where the grain grew to a height of seven cubits (twelve feet). This was truly a wonderful paradise for the Egyptian peasant. But since times changed for the ancient Egyptian also,

FIG. 36.—USHABTIU (ORIENTAL INSTITUTE MUSEUM)

so that field labor came to be regarded as beneath his dignity, after the Middle Kingdom he caused to be placed in his tomb a series of mummiform figures provided with farm implements or sacred symbols in order that they might perform his duties for him (Fig. 36). Upon these ushabtiu was written the name of the deceased together with a magical formula through which they were bought to life and enabled to perform their prescribed duties.

Another doctrine, which originally applied to the king alone, involved an attempt to unify the different conceptions of the hereafter. It was put into writing in the book entitled the "Book of What Is in the Netherworld" and in similar works. According to these texts, there is another earth beneath the familiar earth of men; it is covered by a sky, and through its entire length flows a stream (see p. 65). This netherworld is divided into twelve parts which correspond to the twelve hours of the night and which are separated from one another by great gates. The bark of the sun travels on the stream; in it stands the ram-headed sun-god surrounded like a king by his retinue, as he brings for a brief time light and life to the dark regions through which he fares. This nightly voyage is shared by the deceased, either as the companion of the sun-god or as that god himself, with whom he is thus sometimes identified and with whom he departs from the subterranean world at dawn to continue the journey across the celestial ocean in the bright light of day.

In the earliest times the dead were interred in the natural position of sleep, lying on the left side with knees drawn up against the body and hands before the face. In the Old Kingdom, at first probably in connection with the kings, it became the custom to lay the body in the tomb stretched out at full length. At the same time attempts began to be made to prevent the deterioration of the body by the art of mummification. So successfully was this accomplished that many mummies have preserved in an easily recognizable aspect the features of the deceased (Fig. 37). In the beginning mummification was, of course, exceedingly simple. The viscera were removed from the body, and the resulting cavity was filled with wads of linen cloth. The corpse was then saturated with natron and bound with linen wrappings. At a later period injections of cedar oil were also applied. In the course of time the technique of embalming underwent considerable development. It became the practice to remove the brain from the skull by the use of an iron hook, while resinous pastes were applied to preserve as fully as possible all the contours of the body. As far back as the Old Kingdom the viscera were interred in four vases; these were under the protection of four divinities who were responsible for guarding the deceased against hunger and thirst. In richer burials these vases were placed in chests constructed in the form of a chapel

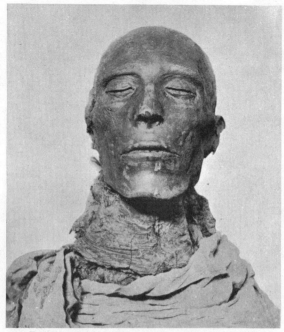

FIG. 37.—HEAD OF THE MUMMY OF SETHI I (CAIRO)

and adorned with appropriate representations of gods and with religious inscriptions (Fig. 38). The process of mummification lasted no less than seventy days, after which, all the proper burial ceremonies having been completed, it was laid in the coffin and removed to the tomb (Fig. 39).

The form of the coffin was altered during the course of the ages. In the Old Kingdom it consisted of a simple rectangular chest of stone or wood. It was a favorite practice to give to it the form of a house with doors in order to symbolize the concept that the coffin was the house of the dead. During the Eighteenth Dynasty it was considered very desirable to construct the coffin in the form of a man or woman arrayed in the costume of the time or in mummiform (Fig. 40) and to decorate it with all sorts of religious pictures and inscriptions. A single coffin, however, was quite insufficient for wealthy people; they insisted on being buried within the innermost of a nest of three mummiform coffins, all of which were in turn placed within an outermost houselike construction, so that the mummy was incased in no less than four different coverings.

Fig. 38.—Canopic Chest of Tutankhamun (Cairo Museum)

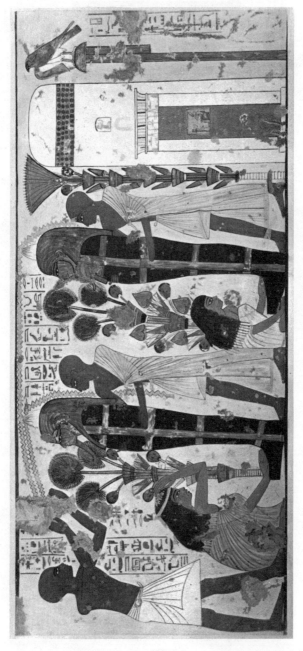

Fig. 39.—Final Rites before the Tomb Door (Thebes, Tomb of Nebamun and Ipuky)

153

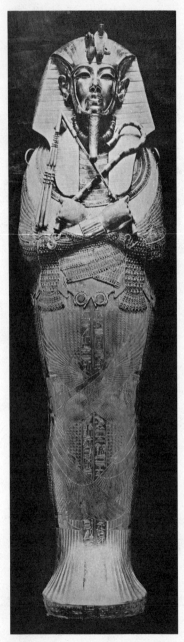

Fig. 40.—Gold Coffin of Tutankhamun (Cairo Museum)

Even for the nobles and the most wealthy people the grave in which the body was laid to rest was originally a simple trench excavated into the desert floor at sufficient height to be inaccessible to the water of the Nile inundation. A low mound of earth was heaped over it, before which a small court was laid out to serve as a cult place where offerings might be deposited for the benefit of the dead. It was from this type of grave that the mastaba, as the type of grave employed by the Old Kingdom officials is known to science, was developed. The mastaba consists of a rectangular superstructure built of sun-dried brick or limestone blocks; in addition, there is a vertical shaft or a stairway leading down to the underground burial chamber in which the body is deposited. The cult place lies on the east side of the superstructure; it is a court with a shallow niche, usually in the form of a door, marking the place which was believed to be at the same time the entrance to the tomb and that into the netherworld. A chapel was frequently erected in front of the niche; otherwise a proper cult chamber was constructed in the masonry of the mastaba in such a manner that the "false door" mentioned above was situated in its west wall. As time passed, the inner rooms increased in number as subsidiary chambers were added to the original one. The resulting development was a regular dwelling for the deceased, the walls of which were adorned with inscriptions and richly painted bas-reliefs. The deceased and the members of his family who were buried with him were represented by numerous statues placed in one or more rooms specially provided for the purpose, while figures of male and female servants made of stone or wood were included to care for the recurring needs of their master.

The tomb of the king was in the early period simply an especially large mud-brick mastaba of the type described, but a series of chambers was provided beneath it in order to accommodate his body and those of his retainers, together with all the necessary funerary supplies and equipment. This mastaba eventually developed into the step pyramid and thence into the true pyramid (Fig. 4), which from the beginning of the Old Kingdom to the end of the Second Intermediate Period remained the characteristic form of royal tomb.

XIII

THE ART OF THE EGYPTIANS

IN EGYPT more than in any other land of antiquity the periods of political and economic expansion coincide with the flowering of artistic achievement. Egyptian art had reached a pinnacle for the first time under the mighty kings of the Old Kingdom during the pyramid age. After several centuries of stagnation a second peak was attained under the Amenemhets and Senwosrets of the Twelfth Dynasty. Finally, after the domination of the Hyksos, the period of the Thutmosids and Amenhoteps of the Eighteenth Dynasty witnessed an upswing in original artistic effort which produced works of art rarely inferior to those of the earlier epochs and frequently greatly superior to them.

Under Thutmose I, as we have already seen (p. 37), a new type of royal tomb was created by the Eighteenth Dynasty architects. It is true that these tombs, hewn as they were deeply into the virgin rock, depended for their successful execution less upon the artistic genius of the designer than upon the technical skill of the stonemasons. But how vast and beautiful were the creations of artist and craftsman in that great age of temple and palace construction! It was a time of wonderful opportunities for them. Ruined sanctuaries of past ages had to be rebuilt, and new temples in honor of the gods were constantly being ordered; the pharaohs sought splendid new palaces which would be worthy of their great achievements. Material considerations were also favorable to the new age. Countless prisoners of war and captured slaves placed unlimited quantities of laborers at Egyptian disposal, while the booty taken on the field of battle, the plunder of conquered cities, and the tribute of vanquished nations provided every possible requirement for the conduct of extensive building operations and every encouragement for the architect to undertake magnificent tasks. A great treasury of architectural forms from the past lay ready to his use in case he desired to draw upon them, but where they appeared insufficient or inadequate for the demands of a new age he possessed ample creative genius and resourcefulness to meet any situation. And thus the temples from the time of Thutmose III and his successors far surpass anything which has been preserved to us among the surviving remains of sacred buildings in the Nile Valley; they reveal that period of Egyptian history to our eyes unconditionally as the flowering of architectural achievement.

The creations of this great era appear in no part of Egypt in such profusion and in such an excellent state of preservation as in the capital at Thebes, which benefited more than any other site from the piety of the pharaohs of the New Kingdom. Let us therefore attempt to gain some conception of the magnificent ruins of a capital whose architectural history embraces a period of more than two thousand years.

Thebes itself stood on the right bank of the Nile in a broad and fruitful plain, with the shapely peaks of the Arabian Desert bounding the eastern sky. A collection of smaller villages had gradually consolidated by natural growth into the mighty Thebes, that stately residence of the pharaohs whose fame had penetrated into far-distant Ionia, where the poet sang of her:

> Treasure-house of countless wealth,
> Who boasts her hundred gates, through each of which
> With horse and car two hundred warriors march.

First we shall visit the southern quarter, which is occupied today by the modern town of Luxor and which in antiquity bore the name of the "Southern Opet." Here stands the great temple which Amenhotep III erected, perhaps on the site of a still earlier sanctuary, and dedicated to Amun, the chief god of Thebes, Mut, his consort, and their son, the moon-god Khonsu (Figs. 41 and 42). Like the majority of Egyptian temples, which were arranged in imitation of human dwellings, it embraces a great open court surrounded by an ambulatory, a hypostyle hall, chapels in which the statues of the divinities were kept, and a number of small halls and subsidiary chambers. The columns which support the architraves of the ambulatory and the roof of the great hall are imitations of tied bundles of papyrus stalks with closed umbels, a favorite column form among Egyptian architects. The walls of the rooms are covered with bas-reliefs representing in noble proportions the king's relations with the gods and various religious ceremonies which occurred in the temple. A minor chapel contains scenes representing the divine generation, birth, and nurture of the pharaoh, while in another room the accession of the ruler to the throne is depicted in a series of reliefs.

FIG. 41 —COURT OF AMENHOTEP III (LUXOR TEMPLE)

Fig. 42.—Great Colonnade of Amenhotep III with Pylon of Ramesses II
in Background (Luxor Temple)

159

The passage from the entrance portal to the innermost sanctuary consists of a gigantic hall the roof of which, though never completed, was to
have been supported by fourteen enormous columns (Fig. 42) with open
umbels. The king was accustomed to approach the court in ceremonial
procession along this avenue and thence into the halls and chambers of
the "god's house" which were accessible to him and to the priests alone.

A causeway slightly over a mile in length originally connected the
Luxor temple with the great imperial temple of Amun at Karnak. On
either side of this imposing highway was a row of enormous stone rams,
the sacred animal of the god Amun, arranged at short intervals. They
were set on massive stone foundations, and, between the forelegs of each
one, standing against the breast of the ram, was a sculptured figure of
Amenhotep III, the builder of the causeway. At a considerable distance
from the main Karnak temple a branch road, flanked also by statues of
rams, leads off to the right. If we follow this for approximately an eighth
of a mile, we reach the entrance of an expansive temple precinct surrounded by a massive wall of mud brick, in the midst of which stand the
ruins of a temple dedicated by Amenhotep III to the goddess Mut, Mistress of (the lake) Ishru. This consists of a pair of open courts, one behind
the other, behind which are situated the inner halls and rooms of the
sanctuary. The most remarkable aspect of the building consists of the
numerous figures of the war-goddess Sekhmet (Fig. 34)—by this time
identified with Mut—which at one time surrounded the courts in long,
closely arranged rows, sometimes even double rows, to the almost incredible number of approximately six hundred. The goddess is conceived
as a woman with the head of a lioness—her sacred animal—holding a
papyrus stem with open flower in one hand as a scepter and in the other
the Egyptian symbol ♀ of "life" which she is understood always to be
ready to present to the king. Adjacent to this temple of Mut, as was customary in connection with all temples in ancient Egypt, there was an
artificial lake. While the usual temple lake was rectangular in form (cf.
Fig. 43), this one was shaped somewhat like a crescent moon, and it was
laid out in such a manner that it partially embraced the sanctuary of the
goddess. The relationship of this and other temple lakes to the cult is not
precisely known.

The "precinct of Mut" contains another much destroyed temple of
Amenhotep III and a third, on the west bank of the sacred lake, built by

Ramesses III. Proceeding to the north and leaving the precinct by the Ptolemaic portal, we enter another long avenue of stone rams. To the right is a ruined temple of Kamutef and opposite, on the left, the remains of a "station" (a small shrine for the visit of the sacred bark of the god), both jointly constructed by Hatshepsut and Thutmose III. In the distance are conspicuous remains of the massive mud-brick inclosure wall of the precinct of Amun, which we now enter by a lofty stone portal (Pylon X—Karnak pylons are numbered from west to east on the main, and from north to south on the transverse, axis of the temple) of Harmhab, probably the replacement of an earlier brick pylon built by Amenhotep II or III, since bases of their colossal statues still flank the entrance. At this point in any visit to Karnak it becomes evident that structures of different periods occur in close proximity, so that it is not easy to visualize the great complex as it appeared at any specific time. The imposing temple pylon is one of the most striking creations of the Egyptian architect. It consists of two gigantic towers built of massive blocks of stone on a rectangular base, with walls sloping inward toward the top in such a manner as to convey the impression, when viewed from the front, of a truncated pyramid with steeply sloping sides. The walls are framed at each corner in a torus molding and crowned at the summit by a cavetto cornice, the entire structure offering a vast expanse of wall surface for the conspicuous presentation of reliefs and hieroglyphic inscriptions (cf. Fig. 101). The actual portal is a stately construction between the two pylon towers; it, too, is adorned at the top with a hollow cornice, on which was regularly carved in relief a representation of the winged sun, the image of the sun-god of Edfu. Stairways inside the towers mount to small chambers within the pylons, lighted by slits in the masonry, and farther upward to the roof.

Having passed Pylon X, we are in a great court surrounded by a stone wall, on the east and west, probably the work of Harmhab and Ramesses II, and by Pylon IX, on the north. The east wall is interrupted by a small temple erected by Amenhotep II on the jubilee anniversary of his coronation. Largely destroyed by Akhnaton, we see it as rebuilt in the Nineteenth Dynasty by Sethi I. Pylon IX was probably completed by Harmhab, though much of its decoration dates from Ramesses II and later kings. Its portal opens to the north on an irregular court embraced, like the preceding one, by lateral walls and by a pylon (No. VIII) on the north. The south face of the latter was partially obscured by six colossal seated statues of Amenhotep I, Thutmose II, and Thutmose III. While the pylon is usually attributed to Hatshepsut, its original decoration was entirely cut away to make room for the reliefs and inscriptions which it now bears (with some usurpations); it may actually have been constructed by Amenhotep I or Thutmose I.

Between Pylons VIII and VII is a nearly square court which belonged to Thutmose III, for he not only erected Pylon VII, which contains

Fig. 43.—View across the Sacred Lake (Karnak)

records of his northern and southern conquests, including the names of more than six hundred captured cities, but also, between the east wall and the sacred lake of Amun (Fig. 43), an alabaster jubilee hall. This little temple, accessible from the court, was erected on the occasion of his first jubilee and enlarged when he celebrated the second. Pylon VII is connected with the principal structure of the entire temple complex by a final extensive court inclosed by stone walls. This is the famous "Cour de la Cachette" under the pavement of which, in the years 1903–5, more than six hundred statues and other monuments of stone and sixteen thousand copper or bronze objects were unearthed, where they may have been buried to save them from destruction when the Egyptian priests foresaw the decline of their religion.

The buildings along the "transverse axis" of Karnak, which we have just visited, join the main temple at the level of Pylons III and IV. The narrow court between these was once occupied by four mighty obelisks of red granite, two erected by Thutmose I and the other pair by Thutmose III. At present only the southern shaft of Thutmose I still stands, but this wonderful monument and the yet greater survivor of a similar pair placed by Hatshepsut east of Pylon IV (Fig. 11) are today the principal glories of Karnak. As we face eastward to pass through the portal of Thutmose I's Pylon IV, we have reached the sacred structure known to the ancients as Ipet-esowet. Most of the stone walls in this area of the temple were erected in the first half of the Eighteenth Dynasty. What lies behind us, to the west, Pylon III, the great hypostyle hall (cf. p. 257 and Fig. 100), Pylons II and I with their appendages, were the achievements of later kings, from Amenhotep III to the Ptolemaic period. While Pylons IV and V were both built by Thutmose I, the court which lies between them is in its present form largely the work of Thutmose III. It was originally a closed court with a single row of wooden columns supporting a wooden roof. These columns were later renewed in stone, but, during the reign of Thutmose I's daughter Hatshepsut, the north wall and colonnade were removed to provide facilities for the erection of her two obelisks in the court. Subsequently, the row of columns was replaced with a double colonnade and with a roof of stone by Thutmose III, while this king likewise tightly manteled his hated predecessor's two obelisks with solid masonry. Henceforth, the glistening granite shafts were visible only at a distance, from the exterior of Karnak, but were completely concealed from visitors in the very hall in which they were the principal feature. Thutmose III in like manner clothed all four walls of this court with an additional layer of stone, which was interrupted at close intervals by thirty-six engaged Osirid statues of Thutmose I.

Behind Thutmose I's Pylon V is a columned hall containing two important doorways. The principal one leads straight on toward the sanctuary, while the other, at the south end, provides a passage through the inner stone wall of Thutmose I to a small peripteral shrine believed to have been the place of enthronement for the king as he prepared himself

Fig. 44.—Heraldic Plants of Upper (*right*) and Lower (*left*) Egypt (Karnak)

for participation in the temple ritual and other religious exercises. It is probable that this sadly ruined chapel of Thutmose III stands on the site and in line with others built by Amenhotep I and other predecessors of Thutmose III, which were demolished and later used by Amenhotep III as building material for his pylon (No. III). The easternmost and smallest of the Karnak pylons is Pylon VI; it was probably built by Thutmose I, as its prolongation to north and south is the front wall of his temple of Ipet-esowet. The portal of the pylon gives access to the "hall of the annals" in front of the innermost holy of holies of Karnak. The most conspicuous feature of the hall is a pair of stately pillars of red granite, the southernmost of which is decorated in high relief with the "lily"—the plant device of Upper Egypt—while the northernmost bears the corresponding papyrus emblem of Lower Egypt (Fig. 44). The sacred sanctuary, in which the bark containing the statue of Amun was at home, is surrounded by an ambulatory whose walls are adorned with pictures of the "tribute" brought by Thutmose III from all the vanquished countries (pp. 56, 60) and with the beginning of the record of his military exploits which is continued in the hall before the sanctuary. On either side of the holy of holies is a group of rooms built and decorated by Queen Hatshepsut. The surviving granite sanctuary on this holy spot is the work of Philip Arrhidaeus; it replaces a vanished structure identical in plan of Thutmose III which that king had erected only after demolishing an exquisite sanctuary in quartzite and black granite of Hatshepsut. Fortunately for us, the dismantled shrine of the queen was employed by Amenhotep III in the core and foundation of his pylon, and three-fourths of the entire building has been salvaged in nearly perfect condition.

To the rear of the holy of holies lies a great open court entirely bare of ruins. This space was almost certainly occupied in the Twelfth Dynasty by the original buildings of the temple of Karnak, though it is impossible to locate in the area the exact site of the elegant chapel of Senwosret I, which has in its totality been rescued from the core of Pylon III and re-erected in the Karnak "museum" (cf. pp. 20–21).

A doorway near the southeast corner of Thutmose I's inclosure wall opens into the unique festival temple of Thutmose III. Its enormous columned hall was laid out as a five-aisled basilica lighted from above— the original example in history of an architectural form often imitated

later in Egypt and widely exported to other lands as well. While the
ceilings of the lateral halls were supported by rectangular pillars, that
of the loftier central "nave" rests on columns formed like tent poles,
with shafts larger at the top than at the base and with bell-shaped capitals (Fig. 45). Among the remarkable series of chambers accessible from
this basilica is one of unusual appeal: on its walls Thutmose III has left a
bas-relief depicting the plants and animals which he had collected in
Syria and brought home in the twenty-fifth year of his reign (Fig. 46).

East of the festival hall and backing the outer stone inclosure wall of
the main temple precinct is a somewhat mysterious sanctuary which
appears to have been begun by Hatshepsut and completed by Thutmose
III. It faces toward the east; its chief features were a chapel containing
the seated figures of the royal couple, the whole carved from a single
gigantic block of alabaster, a row of six Osirid or jubilee statues of the
king, and, flanking the north and south ends of the structure, a pair of
red granite obelisks (now fallen) of the queen. Somewhat farther to the
east, on the axis of this chapel and of the main temple, stood the single
obelisk of Thutmose III, largest of all these wonderful monoliths, now the

Fig. 45.—Festival Hall of Thutmose III (Karnak)

pride of the Piazza di San Giovanni in Laterno in Rome. Outside the eastern brick girdle wall of Karnak is the site of the enormous temple of the heretic king Akhnaton, which he built there before abandoning Thebes for his new capital at Amarna (cf. pp. 205–6). A number of colossal statues of the king in the hideous style of his earliest sculpture have been excavated in its ruins, but the temple was demolished by Harmhab, and tens of thousands of small blocks of stone, many of them covered with the unique reliefs of the Amarna period, were banished under the earth to serve as the foundations of Pylon II and other constructions of Harmhab in Karnak.

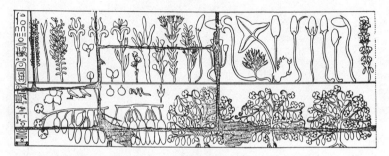

FIG. 46.—"BOTANICAL GARDEN" OF THUTMOSE III (KARNAK)

The principal other additions to Karnak in the Eighteenth Dynasty lie to the north. One of these, the temple of Ptah, is an elaborate and impressive structure begun by Thutmose III and repeatedly enlarged by subsequent rulers as late as the Ptolemaic period. Still farther north, within its own inclosure wall, and approached from the north by an avenue of rams, is the precinct of Montu, with an elaborate complex of temples and smaller chapels in honor of the Theban war-god Montu, the goddess Maat, and Harpre. Though begun early in the dynasty, the greatest *floruit* of the Montu temple occurred in the reign of Amenhotep III, when it was considerably enlarged and the court in front embellished with a pair of obelisks. It continued to flourish for a thousand years, but its subsequent destruction was so complete that its pristine grandeur was largely unsuspected before the recent excavations of the Institut Français d'Archéologie Orientale.

A street led from Pylon I of the Karnak temple down to the river quay from which it was possible to cross to the left side. There on the "west of

FIG. 47.—VIEW OF THE TYPICAL NECROPOLIS

FIG. 48.—TEMPLE OF QUEEN HATSHEPSUT (DEIR EL-BAHRI)

Thebes" was the necropolis (Fig. 47) with countless tomb caverns in the cliffs and on the desert floor as well as the host of memorial temples dedicated by the kings to Amun but primarily intended by their royal builders as chapels for the presentation of offerings for their own benefit in the years to come. In the necropolis were likewise the dwellings of the embalmers, rest houses for visitors to the cemeteries, shops where the countless objects to be presented to the departed could be purchased, workshops of stonecutters, guardhouses, stables, and granaries.

"Opposite Her Lord [Amun]" was the name of the oldest section of the city of the dead which spread itself out on the west bank of the Nile within sight of the precinct of Amun. In it were located the brick pyramids of the Theban monarchs and of the kings of the Eleventh and Seventeenth dynasties up to the time of Amenhotep I. Adjacent to them were the tombs of the nobles of that early period, as well as the unpretentious pits in which the dead of the lower classes had found their last resting-places. Somewhat farther to the west the declivities of the Libyan Desert hills rise precipitously from the plain and form a semicircular basin in the foothills. In this beautiful place, where one of the Mentuhoteps had already in the First Intermediate Period erected a wonderful mortuary temple, Queen Hatshepsut in turn built for herself a temple which she named "Splendid Are the Splendors of Amun," now known as Deir el-Bahri—"the northern monastery" (Fig. 48). It was dedicated to Amun of Thebes, to Hathor, and to the jackal-headed mortuary god Anubis, who, like Hathor, was honored by the possession of a special chapel. The temple rises from the plain in a series of terraces, and the rearmost rooms are hewn deeply into the cliffs behind. After traversing the avenue of sphinxes which forms the approach to the temple from the Nile and passing through the portal, we step into a great rectangular court. This is bounded at the rear by colonnades to the top of which a central ramp forms the sole means of access. The second terrace, like the first, consists of a spacious court and colonnades at the rear. The roof of the latter is supported by rectangular pillars, and the walls, like those of the lower hall, are adorned with reliefs. Some of these depict the trading expedition to the land of Punt (p. 101; Fig. 26) which was undertaken under the reign of Hatshepsut; others, like certain scenes in the Luxor temple (p. 157), represent the miraculous conception and birth of the queen. Adjacent to the left hall is the small chapel of the goddess Hathor; it consists of two successive halls the roofs of which are borne by columns and pillars surmounted by attractive Hathor heads and of numerous rooms hewn into the cliffs behind. The somewhat similar chapel of the jackal-headed Anubis, god of the dead (Fig. 32), is located in a corresponding position at the north end of the right hall. There is first a vestibule with twelve sixteen-sided ("proto-Doric") columns which gives access to three rock-hewn chambers with vaulted roofs and walls covered with splendidly carved bas-reliefs of religious scenes.

Ascending another ramp, we come to the third terrace and enter by a granite portal into the actual temple court, which lies at an elevation of approximately a hundred and sixty feet above the floor of the valley. There is a long row of niches in the rear wall of this court, while a door-way in the center constitutes the entrance to the holy of holies. Right and left of the court is a number of halls and chambers, chiefly devoted to the cult of the queen and her parents; there is also a small court containing an altar—one of the few still surviving in Egypt—dedicated by the queen to the sun-god Re-Harakhti.

A marvelous view is obtainable from the heights of the temple of Deir el-Bahri: the broad fertile plain whose soft expanse of green extends for miles on either side of the Nile, with here and there a noble grove of palms or a group of ancient temple ruins; beyond the silver Nile the buildings of Karnak and Luxor; on this side the cemeteries with their long row of memorial temples; beneath our feet the basin of the valley bounded to left and right by the jutting spurs of the western mountains. Our attention is especially attracted to the hill on the right, for countless tomb passages penetrating into its rugged walls have transformed it into the appearance of a colossal honeycomb (Fig. 47). Within its catacombs are the tombs of the high dignitaries of the Eighteenth Dynasty: the military commander Amenemhab, who accompanied his master Thut-mose III on his Syrian campaigns and once saved the king's life (p. 59); the vizier Rekhmire, perhaps the outstanding minister of his age; Harm-hab, the general of Thutmose IV; besides a host of others, the greatest men of that great era. The arrangement of all these tombs was nearly identical. A track mounted to a forecourt inclosed in a wall of mud brick; offerings were brought to this open place by the survivors of the deceased. Behind it was a broad hall hewn into the rocky hillside, its ceiling sup-ported by columns or rectangular pillars left during the excavation of the

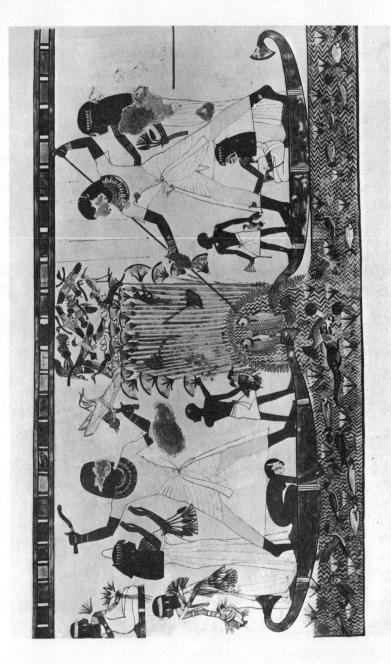

Fig. 49.—Hunting and Fishing in the Marshes (Thebes, Tomb of Menna)

hall. Farther, on the axis of the entrance and at right angles to the transverse hall, was a long corridor ending at the rear in a niche where stood a statue of the deceased and the most dearly loved members of his family. A shaft led downward to a small chamber which contained the sarcophagus with the body of the departed. The walls of the inner rooms of such a tomb were covered with representations, not as a rule carved in relief in this portion of the necropolis, owing to the friable character of the limestone, but for the most part painted in bright colors on mud-plaster wall surfaces coated with a type of whitewash. These paintings offer to our eyes a feast of beauty in the fascinating pictures showing the deceased carrying on the activities of his earthly routine: inspecting the field work on his estates, going on the hunt, enjoying himself in the company of his friends and relatives at the banquet (Fig. 50), presenting tribute to the king, reviewing his troops, or reporting to the ruler the state of the harvest (Fig. 51), the choice of scenes depending on the position or office which he had occupied during his career on earth (Fig. 52). The broad hall frequently contained a large stela carved or painted with a laudatory biography of the deceased, couched in a long series of bombastic phrases; these inscriptions, nevertheless, are often our chief source of information about the life and activities of their owner and the contemporary pharaoh. The walls of the corridor, on the other hand, were customarily devoted to pictures and texts concerned with man's destiny in the hereafter, including both the funeral ceremonies and the wanderings through the netherworld.

Fig. 50.—Singers and Dancers at a Banquet (British Museum)

Fig. 51.—In the Fields at Harvest Time (Thebes, Tomb of Menna)

FIG. 52.—HORSES AND MULES IN THE HARVEST FIELD (BRITISH MUSEUM)

If now we turn away from the hill of Sheikh Abd el-Qurna—as this part of the ancient necropolis is known to the Arabs—and proceed toward the cultivation below, we shall see to the south, stretching out for a long distance along the edge of the desert, an imposing row of memorial temples erected by the various kings of the Eighteenth, Nineteenth, and Twentieth dynasties. The first of these is the temple of Thutmose III; then we come to those of Amenhotep II and Thutmose IV—all dating from the Eighteenth Dynasty. The row is here interrupted by the gigantic mortuary temple of Ramesses II of the Nineteenth Dynasty, after which the preceding era is represented again by the small chapel devoted to the memory of Prince Wadjmose, a son of Thutmose I who died in youth. With the exception of the Ramesseum, all of these buildings have long been reduced to ruin as the result of earthquakes and the still more destructive hand of man (Fig. 53). We should likewise probably pass without noticing the enormous temple of Amenhotep III, which lay somewhat farther to the south, in the midst of the present cultivation, were it not for the fact that the two mighty statues of its builder, which were once stationed athwart its entrance, still stand to announce its vanished glory (Fig. 19; see p. 77).

The more northerly of these colossi was believed in Roman times to be a statue of Memnon, the son of Eos (Aurora), goddess of the dawn, and of Tithonos. During the Trojan War, Memnon had slain Antilochus, the valiant son of Nestor, and fell in turn at the hand of Achilles. And now— the legend goes on to relate—the departed Memnon is seated as a stone image on the Plain of Thebes and greets his mother Eos in wonderful sounds of lamentation each morning as she appears at dawn. Hearing the wailing of her son, the goddess lets fall her tears, the morning dew, on his beloved figure. Many Roman visitors testified in inscriptions scratched on the base of the great statue that they, too, had heard the sound of Memnon's mourning. The musical statue had for a long time stood in a damaged state as the result of an earthquake. When at length it was repaired in the reign of the Roman emperor Septimius Severus, Memnon's voice was silenced, to be heard no more.

We have now passed the southern boundary of western Thebes and arrived at Djeme, a suburb of the royal residence, known today as Medinet Habu. At this site Queen Hatshepsut and Thutmose III built a graceful temple which is famous as one of the best examples of the smaller sanctuaries of this era (Fig. 54). The foundation supports a platform on which rises the cella with an ambulatory whose roof rests on rectangular pillars connected to one another by a screen wall. Behind the cella are six small chambers devoted to purposes of the cult, all of which were decorated with bas-reliefs depicting the royal donors in their intercourse

FIG. 53.—THE RAMESSEUM (WESTERN THEBES)

with the gods. These reliefs, like so many of Hatshepsut's representations elsewhere, have been drastically altered in order that her figure and name might be replaced with those of Thutmose I, II, or III.

Any consideration of the plastic art of the period of the Thutmosids and the Amenhoteps must emphasize the fact that no fundamental change has occurred either in relief or in sculpture in the round since the dawn of Egyptian history. The creations of Egyptian art are based upon the very same laws which dominated the art of drawing among every other people who existed before the period of classical Greek art or who remained uninfluenced by the Greeks. When an Egyptian artist set out to reproduce on a flat surface a phenomenon of the natural world such as, for example, a pool containing fish and waterfowl and surrounded by vegetation (Fig. 55), he did not take the entire picture of the pool which

Fig. 54.—Temple of the Eighteenth Dynasty (Medinet Habu)

lay before his eyes as the pattern for his drawing; he sought to express solely the characteristic aspects which impressed themselves upon his memory. It naturally follows that his concept was that of a front view, since the appearance of an object is most clearly and distinctly rendered in that manner; the surfaces of the object, therefore, whether in part or as a whole, are sketched as if the draughtsman viewed them at right angles and not obliquely. Thus it is the surface of the pool which is rendered, while the flowers sprouting from its bottom, its fish and ducks, and the trees and blossoms on its banks are all shown in side view. Correspondingly, both a wooden jar stand and the vessel sitting upon it are drawn in side view (Fig. 56), since that is the principal surface that operates on the perception of the observer. Conversely, bunches of vegetables inside a shallow clay vessel are arranged above the vessel spread out to the greatest extent in order to make them as clearly visible as possible (Fig. 56); in a similar manner, the flowers which are really in the bowl as decoration are depicted above the vessel with coiled stems in a broad top view, while even the rectangular reed mat under the jar stands is represented on a top view though considerably contracted in its vertical dimensions by Egyptian convention. But the clusters of grapes, again, which lie on the mats are drawn in broad profile to emphasize their most characteristic impression. While some of the different objects assembled in this group are drawn in top view and others in profile, so that the artist was able without much trouble to transfer to a two-dimensional plane the impres-

FIG. 55.—A GARDEN POOL (BRITISH MUSEUM)

FIG. 56.—FEMALE MUSICIANS WITH THEIR INSTRUMENTS (THEBES, TOMB OF NAKHT)

FIG. 57.—WOODEN RELIEF SCULPTURE OF HESIRE (CAIRO MUSEUM)

sion of filled vases adorned with bouquets of flowers set on four-legged jar stands with grapes lying between them, his task was appreciably more complex when he undertook to sketch a human being such as, for example, a man standing in a relaxed position. Here he found it unavoidable to alternate in one and the same drawing between front and side views in order that the resulting picture would register as distinctly as possible the principal parts of the body (Fig. 57). Accordingly, he renders the head in profile, though the eye with its lids and brow are drawn as they appear in a full front view. Then the shoulders, like the eye, are sketched in a front view, but the remainder of the trunk, including the breast and abdomen, is outlined in profile. The navel, however, which would not appear distinctly enough in a profile view, is displaced slightly to avoid its coinciding with the outline of the body. The skirt with its peculiar arrangement of plaits is rendered in front view, with the belt-fastener displaced slightly, like the navel, in order to reproduce its characteristic form with proper distinctness. Finally, the arms, legs, and feet are drawn in profile, but the inner details of both feet are depicted within the outlines, so that the great toes alone are shown (see also Figs. 50 and 56).

While the artistic creations of the beginning of the Eighteenth Dynasty adhere very closely to the forms of an earlier era, especially to those of the Middle Kingdom, and reflect in consequence a certain restraint, from the end of the reign of Thutmose III they grow somewhat freer and tend more and more to cast off the shackles of tradition, especially in their treatment of space and bodily position. The man of quality, to be sure, was still rendered in the same dignified posture which the earlier period had established as the fixed standard (Fig. 58). However, when occasion arose to represent people of lower degree, such as servants and workmen or dancers and singers, freedom of composition was permitted which would never have been tolerated at an earlier time (see Figs. 49 and 50). From the beginning of the pyramid age (Third Dynasty), the human figure was on rare occasions sketched in pure profile; in the Eighteenth Dynasty front views or even three-quarter views are encountered, though they are exceedingly rare (Fig. 50). Thus, in its confidence of draughtsmanship and in the boldness with which the artist ventured to reproduce the most diverse phenomena of nature, the two-dimensional art of the Eighteenth Dynasty attained the utmost peak of success and left even the best creations of the old masters far behind it. The most beautiful examples of this art are indubitably to be found in the above-mentioned rock tombs of Sheikh Abd el-Qurna on the west bank of Thebes; they include such exquisite wall reliefs as this one from the tomb of the vizier Ramose showing two of his relatives seated at a family banquet, which dates from the end of the reign of Amenhotep III (Fig. 58), as well as a host of pictures painted on whitewashed plaster in tombs with limestone walls too friable or faulty for successful relief sculpture.

A study of these reliefs and paintings soon reveals how extensive has been the increase in the number of subjects depicted as the result of the expanding new imperialism. A large amount of space, for example, is now reserved for pictures of African and Asiatic tribute-bearers, such as the Syrian princes, enveloped in their characteristic robes, who either kiss the earth before the king, raise their hands in petition, or present their elaborate vases (Fig. 12); the slaves who labor in the construction of public buildings; and the numerous villas and gardens of the capital (Fig. 59). A favorite subject of the paintings is the banquet with dancing and music in the house of a noble, which is frequently set forth in all possible detail. There is infinite charm in the two dancing girls entertaining

FIG. 58.—BAS-RELIEF IN THE TOMB OF RAMOSE (THEBES)

Fig. 59.—Villa with Garden and Shadoof (Thebes, Tomb of Ipy)

Fig. 60.—Musicians at a Banquet (Thebes, Tomb of Djeserkare-seneb)

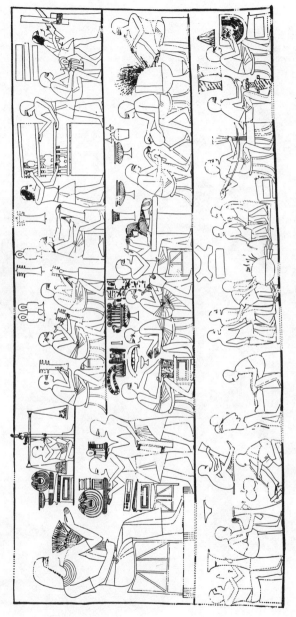

FIG. 61.—CABINET-MAKERS AND GOLDSMITHS (THEBES, TOMB OF NEBAMUN AND IPUKY)

a company of ladies, one of whom is playing a type of flute while two of the others beat the time with their hands in accompaniment to the music (Fig. 50); in the female quartette—harp, lute, flute, and lyre—with little dancing girl (Fig. 60), which constitutes a slightly less informal scene; and, above all, in the lovely trio depicted in the tomb of Nakht (Fig. 56). This beautiful painting of the nude lute player, dancing as she plays, and the graceful flutist and harpist who accompany her retains all its original colors and is without question one of the masterpieces of Egyptian artistry.

Many new scenes are introduced into old compositions so that even they create a different impression. Such variations on old themes are interestingly reflected in new representations of a cabinet-maker's workshop and a goldsmith's shop (Fig. 61), scenes of the grape harvest and wine press, the netting of geese in the papyrus thickets and the plucking of the catch (Fig. 62), boating and fishing in the marshes (Fig. 49), and the scenes of agricultural activities (Figs. 51 and 52). While in previous ages the king was only depicted in temple scenes in intercourse with the gods, participating in religious festivals, or in the conventional representations so familiar at Karnak, where he is shown smiting his enemies with his mace, now he is accustomed to appear even in the wall paintings and reliefs of private tombs, as he performs such functions of his office as receiving the gifts of conquered peoples or the reports of his officials. Strangely enough, battle scenes are lacking on the surviving temple walls of this militaristic age; such a warrior as Thutmose III is, so far as we know, never depicted on the field of battle. The oldest known battle scene occurs on the war chariot of Thutmose IV (Fig. 6), where the king appears together with the hawk-headed war-god Montu in his chariot; he drives headlong against the Asiatics, while the enemy fall in confused ranks under the feet of his horses and the wheels of the chariot or flee for their lives.

The passion of the Egyptian artist for symmetry—the desire to arrange the two halves of a scene in the utmost possible balance—which is a characteristic mark of the very earliest art, was maintained along with the freer compositions of the Eighteenth Dynasty. One scene of this type depicts a highly formal hunting and fishing expedition in the papyrus marshes (Fig. 49; contrast Fig. 94). The perfectly balanced composition is built up about a central clump of papyrus plants growing in the swamp, while on either side, with the principle of symmetry carried out almost to the last detail, the Egyptian noble is represented standing on his light reed skiff. On the right he is accompanied by his wife and two children as he spears fish in the water beside him. At the left, facing again toward the central papyrus thicket, he stands again in his boat, this time accompanied by three children, in addition to his wife, as he skilfully hurls his boomerang to bring down the ducks and other waterfowl rising from the thicket. It is to be assumed that we view in this charming picture not two different expeditions but rather two episodes on the same one. There is, of course, much in the representation which is only conventionalized. No effort is made to depict the various parts of the scene in the natural scale, and the skiff with its occupants is much larger than the clump of papyrus in which the events are taking place. The crocodile in the water beneath holds in its jaws a fish nearly as large as itself. And, while the various figures in the two skiffs stand or sit in the same relative positions, each one of them has a different posture, and the nude maiden at the left who leans over the side of the boat to pluck a lotus blossom is as unconventional a figure as was ever painted by an Egyptian artist. Finally, as if to break the excessive symmetry of his picture, the artist has caused the slender girl at the extreme left to turn her face toward the rear, as if her attention had been diverted by something quite outside the scene, perhaps by the sixth member of the family, the little girl whom the painter has introduced in the upper-left corner of his composition. It is evident that she must be sitting on the bank near by; perhaps she is chatting with her sister who stands at the stern of the skiff. Then, while the balance of the picture is achieved by having the principal figures face toward the center, a certain continuity and counterbalance have been produced by facing all the fish and fowl in the water toward the right.

New Kingdom sculpture was still subject to the same law which dominated the works of the early period—the "law of frontality." Like the two-dimensional art, it strove in the representation of men and animals to bring the essential features of the body into animated expression, and this was accomplished by rendering the human form in a quiet upright position viewed strictly from the front in such a manner that all its parts were given proper consideration. Like a soldier at attention in the presence of his superior officer, the statue directly faces the observer (Figs. 9, 10, 13–14, 63–65, 84, 85, 95, 98). The turns and half-turns employed by the later artist to enliven his subject are nonexistent.

In contrast to the past, a great many new positions are given to the human figure by the newer artists. Commonest of all, however, are the representations of the standing figure with left foot advanced and those of the figure seated on a chair. Even the scribe seated with crossed legs on the ground is still occasionally encountered. A new type is the figure of a kneeling man in the attitude of prayer, holding before him sometimes the image of a god and at others an inscribed tablet containing the text of his hymn of praise. More frequent than in previous ages are the sculptured groups of seated figures representing the deceased beside his wife and other members of the family, or those in which a royal couple or a pair of divinities are depicted side by side (Fig. 15). The artist has not made the slightest attempt to bring the different figures of a group into any significant relationship with one another and as a result to create a truly artistic composition. On the contrary, the adult figures sit stiffly on a seat, touching or embracing each other with the hands and arms, while the children are rendered not less rigidly standing beside their elders.

Sculpture in the round from the early years of the Eighteenth Dynasty no longer compares with the high standard of such works which was attained in the Middle Kingdom. The pieces to a large extent lack the earnest greatness which characterized the masterpieces of that period; they are feeble and dull, with no individual character.

The domination of the Hyksos had, of course, witnessed the extinction of the studios and workshops which had flourished in the court of the Amenemhets and Senwosrets and with it the death of the artistic tradition. Nevertheless, a renewed upward surge of the creative artistic spirit manifested itself as the Eighteenth Dynasty unfolded, and statues were produced at Thebes under Hatshepsut and Thutmose III which fully hold their own by comparison with any of the works of the previous age. To this new line of masterpieces belong such figures as the fine seated statue of Queen Hatshepsut (Fig. 9) and the wonderful figure of the youthful Thutmose III (Fig. 1), which is one of the best sculptures of all time. The proud and noble expression of the face with its firm nose and keen eyes reflect with magnificent success the heroic spirit of a man who is without question every inch a king.

The culminating plastic achievements of this period were attained in the reign of Amenhotep III. Among the greatest works surviving is the remarkable portrait figure of the sage Amenhotep from the temple of Karnak (Fig. 18). Another truly great piece is the beautiful statue of an

FIG. 63.—STATUE OF AN ELDERLY LADY (ARCHAEOLOGICAL MUSEUM AT FLORENCE)

elderly lady, now at the museum at Florence (Fig. 63), whose placid, aristocratic face is framed in one of those heavy wigs with countless braided locks which were the fashion of the time. Her dignity and poise are perhaps even enhanced by the somewhat conventional pose with the lotus flower in her hand. Probably the outstanding triumph of the period is the marvelous yew-wood head usually identified with Queen Tiy, the consort of Amenhotep III (Fig. 16).

Alongside these grave and earnest likenesses there stands a not less numerous group of portrait figures of individuals plainly filled with the very joy of existence—figures reflecting the prosperity, happiness, and fulness of life which prevailed in the Egypt of the successors of the great Thutmose III. It must be admitted that one may detect in their smiling faces a faint air of languid melancholy, as if in their happy days of festivity they already sensed the coming of other times. One of the most attractive works of this group is an ebony statuette of an elegant officer (Fig. 64); two others, figures of a man and a woman (Fig. 65), while they both have rather exaggeratedly pleasant faces, yet reflect a considerable amount of realism.

FIG. 64.—EBONY STATUETTE OF TJAI (CAIRO MUSEUM)

FIG. 65.—WOODEN STATUETTES OF MAN AND WOMAN (CAIRO MUSEUM)

Animal drawing was a favorite sphere of the Egyptian artist's activity from the very earliest times; the Old Kingdom tomb reliefs of cattle, donkeys, and the different creatures which inhabited in countless numbers the rank marsh thickets of the Delta bear ample witness to the remarkable understanding of every detail of animal life with which those ancient artists applied themselves to their work. Of animal sculpture in the round, the creations of the time of Amenhotep III are perhaps the most noteworthy, especially the unsurpassable images of rams and lions with which the king adorned his Nubian temple at Soleb, where even the limits of the supposedly irrevocable laws of form dating from the past have been exceeded. If the name of the artist who chiseled this granite lion (which bears an inscription claiming that Tutankhamun made it for "his father" Amenhotep III), with its overwhelming majesty and power, were known, it would be honored today as one of the outstanding names in the art of the entire world (Fig. 25).

In fact, the achievements in the realm of large decorative statuary during the Eighteenth Dynasty must be counted among the highest accomplishments ever made in this field. Even the technical capacity displayed by the sculptors and stonecutters in removing from the quarries blocks of stone such as those hewn for the colossi of Amenhotep III (Fig. 19)—each one was originally nearly seventy feet in height and weighed over seven hundred tons—in shaping them to their proper proportions with comparatively simple tools, transporting them to Thebes, and erecting them on their foundations is bound to call forth our astonishment and admiration. Many of the statues depict a strongly idealized countenance which represents the accepted standard of feminine beauty or manly dignity of the age. Others, like the gigantic group of Amenhotep III and Queen Tiy in the Cairo Museum (Fig. 15), demonstrate with what powerful effect the ancient artist could achieve a portrait on a huge scale, especially when the sculpture was viewed from the distance intended by its creator.

It would be improper to leave a discussion of Egyptian art without devoting a few words of consideration to the more significant branches of the applied arts. The Egyptian was not content unless not only his jewelry and decorative vases but even the most commonplace objects of daily use were manufactured in forms both appropriate to their use and pleasing to their user's love of beauty. The patterns for most of these works of art were drawn from the realm of nature which everywhere surrounded the Egyptian: the Nile, the canals which traversed the land in every direction, the marshes with their thickets of every kind of water plant. In these watery haunts the grandees were accustomed to ply their skiffs while harpooning hippopotami or crocodiles or while throwing their boomerangs at the waterfowl started up from the thick rushes (Fig. 49); here maidens came to swim in the refreshing pools or to gather flowers to make garlands for the wine jars at the next banquet or bouquets for the temples of the gods and the tombs of the departed. A second treasury of material was the wild life of the desert (Fig. 66); a third was found in the marvelous medley of strange forms which had come to the Nile Valley as hostages and prisoners of war, whose strange appearance and curious costumes gave full play to the skill of every artist and not seldom opportunity for humorous expression as well (Figs. 12 and 24). Flowers, sacred symbols, and pictures drawn from the hieroglyphic script were employed

Fig. 66.—Lion Hunt of Tutankhamun (Cairo Museum)

Fig. 67.—Tutankhamun Slaying Syrian Foes (Cairo Museum)

as decorative elements and cleverly adapted to whatever purposes the objects made from them were intended to meet (Figs. 61, 88, 90).

The technical arts were perhaps pre-eminently occupied in Egypt with the manufacture of jewelry and similar ornaments. The technical skill and artistic taste displayed by the goldsmiths (Fig. 61) are well illustrated by objects surviving from the mortuary equipment of Tutankhamun (Fig. 88). Of the great works of art, including the gold bowls and drinking vessels, which were dedicated to the temples by the kings or presented

Fig. 68.—Gold and Silver Vases (Cairo Museum)

to their followers as marks of favor, of the gold and silver images of the gods (Fig. 13) which once adorned the temples, only a few examples have survived. Among the noblest creations of the goldsmith's art of all time is the group of vessels assembled in Figure 68. They belong to the period of the Nineteenth Dynasty, but there is no evidence in their perfection of the decline which had already set in by the middle of the thirteenth century B.C. Observe the wonderful wine pitcher of silver with its gold handle in the form of a marvelously modeled wild goat, the smaller jug with engraved flower ornamentation, the gold chalice in the shape of a lotus blossom, and the gold bracelet ornamented with a pair of ducks' heads.

Though the Egyptians were not acquainted with precious stones, their artists often achieved exquisite results in the cutting of semiprecious gems. Two of these are shown in Figure 69 as they appear in modern settings copied after the style of ancient goldsmiths' work. The first, cut from a large carnelian, depicts Amenhotep III and Queen Tiy seated on thrones, while two princesses with sistra in their hands present to their parents notched palm branches, the symbol of a long reign. The other gem bears a double representation of the same pharaoh seated in the "jubilee hall" bearing the symbols of sovereignty; goddesses present him with the signs for life and a long reign.

The handiwork of the gold- and silversmiths is scarcely superior in excellence to that of the workers in other metals, particularly in copper and bronze. As a general rule, of course, the latter had much less opportunity to exhibit their skill, since no small part of their activity was devoted to the manufacture of tools and implements for other artisans or to the preparation of ordinary weapons and other gear. Greater demands on their artistic ingenuity were made, however, when orders were submitted for the fabrication of ceremonial weapons, axes, and daggers and for utensils employed in the temple cults. Washbasins and pitchers and bowls and cups for household use were turned out with engraved decorations which vie with those of the most costly gold and silver objects of the same class.

Glass manufacture, formerly incorrectly attributed to Phoenician inventors, was known to the earliest Egyptians. For the most part, it is true, frit was employed for the glazing of stoneware and clayware and for the manufacture of Egyptian fayence, which was in every period one of

FIG. 69.—JEWELRY OF AMENHOTEP III (METROPOLITAN MUSEUM OF ART)

the chief branches of Egyptian industry. Beads and pendants for chains, as well as figurines of human and divine beings and animals, were made of this material, while the oval base plates of "scarabs" were provided, especially in the Middle Kingdom, with the most attractive patterns and covered with a fine thin glaze. The fayence industry reached a particularly high level of development in the Eighteenth Dynasty, when the colored glazes achieved a brightness and clarity never successfully imitated in later times. Fayence objects from this period now preserved in museums are always conspicuous for the astonishing beauty of their pure deep colors. In addition to beads, amulets, and pendants of all sorts, there was an extensive development of rings, which had to some extent replaced the old-fashioned scarabs, as well as the tiles, flowers, plants, and other glazed ornaments now widely inlaid after the manner of mosaics in the walls and columns of palaces. Larger objects are frequent also, including cosmetic boxes in tubular form or gracefully shaped like a palm column; shallow green and blue bowls with painted decorations in black, often consisting of growing flowers or animated representations of pools with darting fish and lovely lotus blossoms; cups shaped like lotus flowers—one particularly beautiful cup is adorned with a bas-relief depicting an entire papyrus thicket through which a skiff of reeds is being rowed, while a row of fish swim in the water beneath (Fig. 70). In this period, as far as we know, large objects of glass were being made for the first time, though the use of this material for beads and other small objects was much older. The charming blue and black glass vases intended for holding ointments and fine oils were often embellished by the fusion of undulating bands of white, light blue, or yellow into the wonderful rich color of the background in patterns similar to those of modern Venetian glass (Fig. 71).

A people which, like the Egyptians of the era of the Thutmosids and Amenhoteps, lived in the possession of great wealth and all the luxuries of life, while devoting themselves to pleasure and the "celebration of happy days," was naturally no longer content with the plain household furnishings of their ancestors. They demanded for their rich dwellings furniture in keeping with the surroundings, such as their forefathers had never dreamed of. Their requirements were satisfied with incomparable skill in the well-organized workshops and studios of the land, where traditional forms were adapted to modern needs or new ones were added at

FIG. 70.—FAYENCE VASE (METROPOLITAN MUSEUM OF ART)

FIG. 71.—GLASS VASES (METROPOLITAN MUSEUM OF ART)

Fig. 72.—Wooden Ointment Boxes (Berlin Museum; British Museum)

will. Unusual color effects were obtained by the employment of gilding and colored inlays of fayence, glass, and semiprecious stones. Costly pieces became available for royal palace and patrician dwelling alike of such beauty and elegance of form and technique that even our pampered modern taste delights in their magnificence.

The technical skill and lively fantasy of the Egyptian was no more actively exercised in the manufacture of large and elaborate pieces of furniture than in the production of smaller and more delicate objects involving the art of wood- and ivory-carving or in the fabrication of little boxes, cups, bowls, hairpins and combs, ointment spoons, and the like, which were such an essential part of the well-to-do household. Among the most charming of these are a wooden ointment spoon with a richly carved handle in a complex design of flowers with a nude female lute player seated on a mat in a thick rank of growing plants (Fig. 72, *a*). A humorous touch is attained in the form of a dog fleeing with a stolen fish, the latter having been hollowed out to contain the ointment (Fig. 72, *b*). In both these forms it is evident that the Egyptian artist was simply recording with his creative genius scenes in life or nature which were constantly a part of his experience.

It is curious how little the Egyptians accomplished in the development of pottery. It is true that they produced a great diversity of forms, ranging from simple round basins to large jars fitted with handles. But the type of painted ornamentation which lends such charm to the Greek vases is comparatively rare in Egypt. Widely employed though they were in the earliest period, such decorations were almost entirely abandoned for many centuries, until they were at length revived in the fifteenth century B.C., when we find a wide distribution of pottery painted in blue, black, or red with designs of wreaths, flowers, and animals, or even with simple lines alone. More pretentious ware was fabricated from fayence, while, as in the prehistoric and early dynastic periods, large use was made of stone for the manufacture of ointment boxes, oil jars, perfume bottles, and the like. For such purposes even the hardest varieties of stone were utilized, but the favorite material was the Egyptian calcite ("alabaster"), which was always carefully selected in order that the beautiful veins of color might be embodied to the fullest advantage in the complete vase.

XIV

AMENHOTEP IV–AKHNATON AND
THE REFORMATION

AMENHOTEP III was succeeded, after a coregency of scarcely less than a dozen years, by his son Amenhotep IV, who assumed the official praenomen Neferkheprure (written Napkhururiya in cuneiform), "Beautiful of Form Is Re," with the additional epithet Wanre, "the Unique One of Re," and who is certainly the most anomalous personality who ever sat on the throne of the pharaohs (Fig. 73). An extraordinarily single-minded character, when once he had embarked on a purpose he held to it with tenacity and carried it through unwaveringly with nothing short of fanaticism. Though a religious zealot, he was tender and devoted in his family relations. In personal appearance he was not unlike his father; his face exhibits the same type of sharp, protruding chin and prominent cheek bones; his neck was long and thin; his arms and calves, slightly developed even for an Egyptian, were in sharp contrast to his fleshy thighs and his flabby abdomen. There was something strangely soft and feminine in the entire constitution of his figure.

He was married to the beautiful Nofretete, whose world-famous bust, found at Amarna and now in the West Berlin Museum (Fig. 74), has preserved in its delicate colors a delightful portrait of the royal lady. Her race and lineage are unrecorded. Some believe her to have been one of the foreign princesses who had by this time for several generations been sent by the rulers of western Asia to grace the harems of the pharaohs. Others hold her to have been of Egyptian blood, perhaps a half-sister of Amenhotep IV himself, and that his marriage with her was consummated in order to establish his right to the throne, in accordance with the custom which we know to have prevailed from the very beginning of the Eighteenth Dynasty.

It appears quite possible that the education of Amenhotep IV was considerably influenced by the priesthood of Heliopolis, which from the remotest times had boasted of unusual wisdom. In any case, he was thoroughly imbued with the concept so long cherished at that place that the

FIG. 73.—STATUE OF AKHNATON (LOUVRE)

Fig. 74.—Bust of Queen Nofretete (Berlin Museum)

sun-god was the greatest of all the gods, the creator and preserver of the world, and that he, Re-Harakhti ("Re-Horus of the Horizon"), was without his equal and entitled not only to the universal but even to the sole worship of his adherents. The other gods were nothing but different forms or manifestations of the sun-god himself. The position which the Theban god Amun (Fig. 13) had won a century before, the fact that he, until recently but an obscure divinity, had been elevated as king of the gods to be the chief divinity of the Egyptian world-empire, the power which had fallen into the lap of his ambitious priests in consequence of the lavish gifts of the kings—all these things had incited the envy, wrath, and hatred of the ancient clergy of Heliopolis. Every acre of land which Amun acquired at the hands of pious worshipers represented a corresponding shrinkage of the influence of Re-Harakhti; every chapel built for Amun was that much loss to the wealth and power of the ancient sun-god. Even under the most favorable circumstances, as in Nubia, Re-Harakhti was accepted as merely the patron god of the northern, and Amun as that of the southern, half of the empire, whereas the Heliopolitan priesthood held to the view that their sun-god was the undisputed master of the whole world. However, a doctrine seems to have developed in the theological school at Heliopolis whereby the purest form of the sun-god was to be found not in the falcon-headed "Horus of the Horizon" but in the dazzling physical orb of the sun itself, which was designated by an old name, Aton. Thus, Re-Harakhti, Aton, and Shu—a third sun-god worshiped in Heliopolis—were held to be the same form of the sun. The speculative mind of Amenhotep IV formulated this identity in a concisely conceived dogma: "Re-Harakhti lives who rejoices in the horizon in his name Shu who is Aton." Further contemplation of the nature of this god led the zealous prince to assign to him the role of a heavenly king, and, as he was accustomed to inclose his two official names in two cartouches, he adopted this device for writing the long name of the god:

(Re-Harakhti lives rejoicing in the horizon)

(in his name (of) Shu who is (the) Aton)

Immediately after his coronation in Hermonthis, the "Upper Egyptian Heliopolis," the coregent proceeded, in obvious estrangement from Amun, the guardian divinity of his forefathers, to promote respect for the new god throughout the land and to make him the center of universal worship. He openly proclaimed himself in his royal protocol as the "First Priest" of Re-Harakhti and decreed the construction in Thebes, to the east of the precinct of Amun (cf. p. 167), of a splendid new temple. The earliest reliefs on the walls of this new edifice, which as coregent he apparently shared with his father Amenhotep III, depicted the new god in precisely the same form as the old Re-Harakhti of Heliopolis, that is, as a man with the head of a falcon crowned by a sun disk with encircling uraeus serpent. Temples were built to the Aton in Memphis and other cities also. There was, however, still one thing lacking to the new god which the majority of the old divinities had possessed from the remotest ages—a special precinct exclusively his own, in which he ruled as lord and whose inhabitants worshiped him as their special protector. And so the king resolved that, as Thoth possessed his precinct at Hermopolis, Ptah his in Memphis, and Seth one at Ombos, so should the Aton also be provided with his own sacred city. It was perhaps in his fourth regnal year—thus during the early stages of his coregency with his father Amenhotep III—that Amenhotep IV issued a proclamation decreeing the provision of a special place of worship for the Aton in the great level plain now known from a Beduin tribe as Amarna, nearly midway between Thebes and Memphis. The site extended over a territory on both banks of the Nile in the "Hare" nome the capital of which was located at Hermopolis. The new district was given the name Akhetaton, the "Horizon of Aton," and it became the personal property of the new god with all its towns and villages, its fields and canals, its herds and peasants. Aton himself, the king reported, had expressed the desire that a monument be erected for him on this particular site which had never belonged to any god or goddess nor to any prince or princess, but which should now be established as the "Horizon of Aton." The boundaries of the holy city were marked out by great inscribed rock-hewn stelae.

The king's satellites, his courtiers and officials, following the example of their lord, espoused the new faith even though their hearts may not always have been in it. Notwithstanding the fervor which he devoted to his god, Amenhotep did not at first assail the cults of Amun and the other gods, nor did he hesitate to appear in inscriptions and temple reliefs as a worshiper of Amun, Thoth, Seth, and other divinities. Despite that fact, it is self-evident that the religious activities of the young ruler met with the utmost resistance of the various priesthoods of the land, especially with that of the priests of Amun at Thebes, who were clearly aware of their implications. This opposition caused not the slightest discouragement to the king, however, in introducing the worship of his god in every part of the country. Indeed, it was rather a spur to his fanatic zeal. Not without significance had he included in his official protocol the words that he "lived on the truth": this was not a mere phrase, it constituted a creed. And the truth-seeker followed his teaching to its logical conclusion. If all the gods were but different manifestations of the same god, the sun's orb, then they must be merged in him—and one god alone, the "living Aton," should be the sole object of universal worship. It remained but to make the culminating decision.

In the sixth regnal year the worship of the Aton was established as the religion of the state. Henceforth not only the Egyptians but the subject Nubians and Asiatics as well were to serve this one god alone. The temples of the other divinities were everywhere closed and their property seized. The statues of the old gods were to be destroyed, their figures in temple reliefs erased, and their names blotted out. A particularly intense persecution of Amun and his family was inaugurated not only in the temples but even in the accessible rooms of private tombs. The name of Amun was especially banned, and it was never permitted to remain immune. Whoever bore a name compounded with that of Amun was obliged to change it, and the king himself was among the first to do so. He abandoned the name Amenhotep ("Amun Is Satisfied"), which had been given to him at birth, and henceforth called himself Akhnaton ("He Who Is Beneficial to Aton"). Even the name of his father and coregent Amenhotep III and that of his ancestor Amenhotep II were regularly chiseled out on monuments and replaced by their praenomina which lacked the hated name of Amun.

Akhnaton now decided to make Akhetaton his own future residence; the old capital of Thebes with its age-long association with Amun was not a suitable place in which he could carry on the worship of his new god with proper tranquillity and fervor. He was resolved to build a new seat of government which should be in no respect inferior in splendor and glory to the old one. It may be that the king himself was responsible for the plan of the new city, the sites for the temples and palaces, and even the layout of the streets. At least two temples were to be built for the

Aton, as well as a splendid palace for the king and his consort. Then, in the hills which in semicircular form bounded the Plain of Amarna on the east, burial places were laid out for the high officials and favorites of the king, while rock-hewn tombs for the royal family were excavated in a more remote desert valley in imitation of the plan of the tombs of the kings in Thebes. Every means was utilized to speed up building operations and thus to fulfil the king's wishes in the shortest possible time. After only two years he was able to make a ceremonial tour of inspection to his new residence. He drove about through the sacred precinct of Aton in his chariot of gold, halting at each of the great boundary stelae and taking oath in the presence of the sun-god "never to extend these boundaries forever."

During his sixth year Akhnaton removed to the new capital at Amarna and took up his residence in the magnificent new palace which he had begun not far from the Nile. As planned, it would have been the largest secular building known in the ancient world. The approach from the north lay through an enormous area flanked on the east by a long row of mud-brick workshops and residential (sometimes referred to as "harem") buildings and on the west by a symmetrical wing of brick now covered by the cultivated land along the Nile. At the south of this vast "parade ground" were the state apartments of the palace, which were built of stone. The entrance was a lofty pavilion supported on twelve columns; it led to a broad but comparatively shallow group of six large halls in two rows, two of which were adorned with colonnades of unusual arrangement. The east-west axis of the northernmost row of halls continued by a unique overpass across the main highway of the capital to the king's residence. Over the middle of this avenue, in the center of the bridge, was located the great "window of appearance" or audience balcony. Here the king and queen, accompanied by two or more of the six princesses, were accustomed to show themselves on special occasions to the populace assembled in the street below; from this balcony, likewise, the king distributed to his favorites before the eyes of the exulting multitudes the tokens of his grace—gold chains, rings, and decorative bowls (Fig. 75). The royal residence, east of the avenue, was a vast walled compound containing extensive storehouses and gardens, a nursery for the princesses, and the large apartment of the pharaoh. In one room of the latter was discovered the enchanting painting of the two little princesses seated on cushions beside their mother and father, one of the most delightful child pictures of all time (Fig. 78). All these rooms were furnished with the utmost splendor. Paintings and inlays of gaily colored

Fig. 75.—Akhnaton and Nofretete in the Window of Appearance (Amarna, Tomb of Eye)

stones, fayence, and vitreous pastes were employed to lend to the columns, walls, and pavements the most splendid color effects imaginable.

The principal temple of the Aton was closely connected with the royal palace. It is probable that the former was planned after the great sun temple at Heliopolis. We are well instructed from the tomb reliefs and

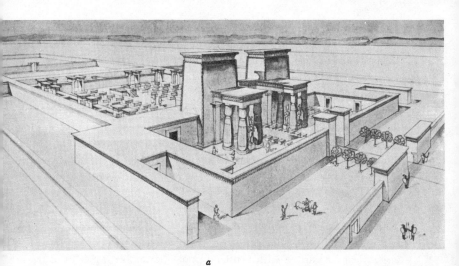

a

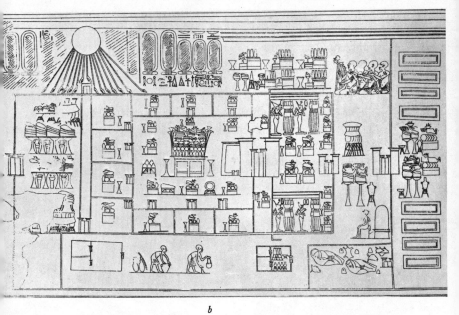

b

FIG. 76.—A TEMPLE OF ATON AT AMARNA: (*a*) ARCHITECTURAL RECONSTRUCTION; (*b*) AS
DEPICTED IN THE TOMB OF MERYRE

excavations concerning its arrangement and furnishings (Fig. 76). Since it was inappropriate that the worship of the orb of day should be celebrated in the narrow confines of obscurely lighted halls rather than under the brightness of heaven, the temple consisted of a series of open courts and halls connected by pylons in which the altars were set up to receive the offerings and which were flanked by the closed storerooms. In the center of a court much larger than the others stood the chief altar, on the steps of which the king, usually accompanied by his consort, was accustomed to pray to the Aton and to consecrate the rich offerings heaped before him on the altar.

In the southern region of the city, near the modern Hawata, the king laid out for himself, Nofretete, and their eldest daughter, Meritaton, a large pleasure garden with artificial pools, flower beds, groves of trees, and all sorts of buildings, including a summer pavilion, a small temple to the Aton, guardhouses, and the like. Their interior rooms were also adorned with gaily colored columns and pavements painted with the charming clumps of plants, flying birds, and capering animals characteristic of the Egyptian marsh landscape.

An important part of the new city, which was approximately half a mile wide and two miles long, was occupied by the streets along which were laid out the villas of the high officials of state. These were extensive establishments composed of a garden and a dwelling with administrative

Fig. 77.—Reconstruction of a Dwelling at Amarna (Oriental Institute Museum)

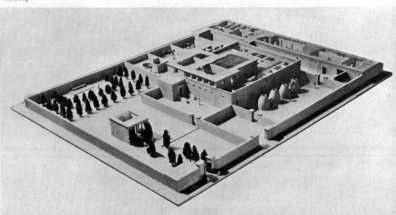

buildings, stables, and storehouses. All of them were designed according to virtually the same plan (Fig. 77). At one end of the well-kept garden an avenue of trees led to a pool behind which a kiosk with a columned hall was erected on a terrace. Near the kiosk but separated from it by a wall was the dwelling, which was accessible from the street by a doorway through the garden wall in front of the forecourt of the house. The principal rooms of the latter were the broad reception room and the long hall

FIG. 78.—TWO DAUGHTERS OF AKHNATON AND NOFRETETE (ASHMOLEAN MUSEUM)

adjacent to it that served as the dining-hall, the lofty ceiling of which was supported by two palm columns and the center of whose rear wall was adorned with a richly appointed architectural construction in the shape of a double false door or niche. The walls of this room were decorated with gaily colored representations depicting the royal family, usually worshiping the sun. About these two main rooms was grouped a number of subsidiary chambers, including a small living-room used by the family during the cold winter season, the workroom of the master of the house,

FIG. 79.—A DAUGHTER OF AKHNATON AND NOFRETETE (LOUVRE)

the bedchambers, the bathroom with closet, and various others of uncertain functions. The dwelling proper was surrounded by stables for the flocks and herds, beehive-shaped granaries, ovens, magazines, and servants' quarters.

In this section of the city was located the house of the sculptor Thutmose, who was active at the court of Akhnaton and whose works adorned the temples and palaces of the royal city. In his studio were created those masterpieces of Egyptian sculpture which ever since their discovery have engaged the admiration of the entire world and which so vividly portray before our eyes the chief actors in the great drama of Amarna. His works include the wonderful painted bust of Queen Nofretete (Fig. 74); the head of one of the little princesses (Fig. 79); the portrait heads of various

Fig. 82

Fig. 81

Fig. 80

Figs. 80–82.—Portrait Heads from Amarna (Berlin Museum)

213

courtiers whose names and stations cannot be determined but whose cheerful and candid (Fig. 80), or forbidding and sullen (Fig. 81), or affable and kindly (Fig. 82), dispositions are tellingly revealed in their features; and many others of equal charm or interest.

There was a special quarter of the city in the northern district which was separated from the rest by its own inclosure wall and characterized by narrow lanes and tiny houses. Here, isolated from the other inhabitants of Akhetaton, the workers who were engaged in the hewing of the rock tombs and in other capacities in the cemeteries maintained their miserable existence.

The teaching of the Aton spread its sanctifying power through all the life of Amarna, and its chief preacher was the king himself. What, then, was the nature of this new state religion, this "teaching," into which the pharaoh had plunged with such ardor and which he himself preached to his faithful followers as he sought to spread it by every possible means throughout the length and breadth of the land? The best answer to this question may be found in the great hymn of praise from the tomb of Eye (p. 240), which the king himself may well have composed and in which the Aton is invoked as the sole god, the creator of all life, the author and protector of the world.

> Thou appearest so beautifully in the horizon of heaven,
> O living Aton, thou who wert the first to live.
> As soon as thou hast risen in the eastern horizon, thou hast filled every land
>   with thy beauty.
> Thou art beautiful, great, dazzling, and exalted over every land;
> Thy rays embrace the lands to the outermost limits of all that thou hast made. . . . .
> When at dawn thou risest on the horizon and shinest as the orb of day,
> Thou dispellest the darkness and pourest forth thy rays:
> The Two Lands are in festival, men awake and stand on their feet, for thou hast
>   raised them up.
> They wash their limbs and put on their clothing;
> Their arms are lifted in praise, whenever thou risest.
> The whole earth goeth about its tasks:
> All the beasts rest then in the meadows;
> Trees and plants grow green;
> Birds flutter from their nests, and their wings do praise thee;
> Every wild creature springeth forth on its feet;
> All the birds aloft or alight,
> They live again when thou risest for them.
> Ships ply down the Nile and up again,
> And every road is open when thou appearest.

The fish in the river leap up before thy face,
For thy rays penetrate into the midst of the sea.
Thou who formest children in woman and createst the seed in man,
Who animatest the son in the body of his mother
And quietest him with that which endeth his tears, ...
When on the day of his birth he cometh forth from the womb of his mother,
Then openest thou his mouth completely and thou providest for all his wants.
The chick in the egg that peepeth in the shell,
Thou givest breath to him within it to maintain him;
Thou hast prepared for him his time to break his way from the egg,
And he cometh forth from the egg to peep at his time,
And so he walketh upon his feet after he hath come forth from it.
How manifold is that which thou hast made! . . . .
Thou hast made the earth according to thy will alone:
Mankind, cattle, and all other beasts, everything on earth that walketh on feet,
And everything lifted on their wings in flight;
The foreign lands of Syria and Kush, and the land of Egypt.
Thou settest each man in his own place and thou carest for his wants;
Each one hath his sustenance, and his time is reckoned.
[Men's] tongues and ears are divided by language,
Their character and their appearance are distinguished also—
So hast thou distinguished the nations.
Thou didst create the Nile in the netherworld
And broughtest it forth according to thy desire
To maintain the Egyptians, even as thou hast made them for thyself, their
    universal lord. . . . .
As for every distant land, thou hast provided their living [also]:
Thou hast placed a Nile in the sky to descend for them,
It maketh a flood on the mountains like the waves of the sea,
It watereth their fields and bringeth forth what they require. . . . .
Thou madest the faraway sky that thou mightest rise in it
And look upon all that which thou madest alone.
When thou risest in thy form as the living Aton,
Gleaming and dazzling, far away yet near at hand,
Thou makest millions of forms from thyself alone:
Cities, villages, fields, the road, and the river;
Everyone beholdeth thee before him, for thou art the orb of day above the
    earth.

Such are the chief doctrines of the new faith which sets forth the Aton as
creator, regulator, and governor not of Egypt alone but of the whole
world.   He was the king of the universe; it was for this reason that his
name was inclosed, in typical pharaonic style, in a pair of cartouches
with a series of appended epithets such as, for example, "the living
Aton, the lord of all that the sun encircles, he who illuminates Egypt, the
lord of sunbeams."   It is also quite evident that an effort had been made

to eliminate all polytheistic concepts from the "teaching" and to forge a pure if somewhat materialistic monotheism. However, what was cast off on one side was replaced on the other, for the king elevated himself to the position of a divinity and promulgated a doctrine of his actual identity with the Aton. Furthermore, the new faith passed through certain transformations even after becoming the official religion of the state, the most significant of which was an alteration in the didactic name of the Aton which was apparently made in order to eliminate from it the names of the old gods Horus and Shu. The resulting designation of the Aton in his two cartouches thus became:

> Re lives, ruler of the horizon rejoicing in the horizon

> in his name (of) father Re who has returned as Aton

The new "teaching" also broke with the old traditions in the outer forms of worship. While during the early years of Akhnaton the god was represented on monuments in human form with the head of a falcon, after the manner of the old Re-Harakhti, the new state religion permitted no representation of the divinity as a person and forbade any sort of image of the Aton. Worship must be directed toward the visible radiant orb of the sun alone. This was depicted in bas-reliefs as a disk from the circumference of which extended a series of long diverging rays ending in human hands which frequently held out to the noses of the king and the members of his family the hieroglyphic sign for "life" (Fig. 75). Offerings of food and drink were made and incense was burned to the god under the open sky, as already in the previous period to Re-Harakhti.

How far previous conceptions of the hereafter were altered in the new religion lies beyond our knowledge. It is certain, however, that the old mortuary god Osiris, "the Foremost of the Westerners," was suppressed and his place assigned to "the living Aton," who dispensed his rays to the blessed dead during the hours of the night. The mortuary practices in general appear to have remained without change. The body continued as of old to be embalmed and the mummy interred in the tomb; the viscera were buried as previously in four jars; a stone in the shape of the scarab beetle was placed over the heart on the mummy; small pyramids were erected at the tomb; and small magical figures continued to be provided to accompany the deceased and perform for him in the hereafter all the required field labor: irrigation of the land, breaking up the clods, sowing the seed, and harvesting the crops. Most of the old magical spells have disappeared in favor of prayers to the Aton. The covers of the four "Canopic" jars no longer depict the old divinities who were once believed to protect their contents but now carry instead the portrait head of the deceased (Fig. 38). The tombs of the nobles, which were hewn in the receding cliffs east of the new city, are indistinguishable in plan from those of the earlier period with which we have become acquainted at Sheikh Abd el-Qurna in the Theban necropolis.

But if the layout was the same as that of earlier tombs, yet how different were the pictures which adorn the walls of these tombs at Amarna! Here we no longer find long rows of scenes perpetuating the private life of the deceased, as he exercises the duties of his office, goes on the hunt, or sits with family and friends at the banquet. Gone are the pictures showing the funeral procession and the offerings provided by the family and retainers of the departed for his nourishment and pleasure in the hereafter. In the place of such scenes, all the reliefs of these tombs are devoted to the worship of the new god and the glorification of the king and his family; it is by way of exception that the owner of the tomb is occasionally depicted worshiping the Aton or shown in some aspect of his relations with the court of the king. Perhaps the royal couple with the little princesses and the assembled court leave the palace in their chariots, the king's bodyguard running ahead on foot, on their way to the temple of the Aton, before the doors of which priests and servants in humble attitude await the arrival of the rulers. Or the king with his family stands in a pavilion at the window of appearance of the palace, surrounded by a rich array of cushions, while they distribute, in the presence of the entire court, a great assortment of jewels and other gifts to the owner of the tomb (Fig. 75); an adjoining scene may show the delighted favorite, heavily decked with the honors so recently presented to him, as he leaves the palace and receives the congratulations and good wishes of his friends and relatives. We are even permitted a view of the inmost chambers of the royal palace: seated in a room with slender papyrus columns, Akhnaton and Nofretete caress and play with their daughters; the king is holding and kissing the eldest princess, the second sits prattling on her mother's lap, while a third on her arm plays with the crown (Fig. 83). Throughout the whole of Egyptian history the veil which so discretely and reverently concealed the private

life of the pharaoh had never been lifted as in these Amarna tomb reliefs.
In them we meet the "Son of Re" no longer as a god but as a man among
men; and, if we find this occurring in defiance of all previous custom and
tradition, we are not likely to go wrong in seeking the explanation in the
dogmas of the new cult, in "living on the truth."

In all these representations we are charmed by something else that is
quite strange, by the tones of a new language in artistic expression—tones
for which the king himself as founder and patron was alone responsible.
For it seems quite safe to assume that Akhnaton possessed a fine artistic
sensibility and that shortly after his accession he attracted to himself
and his court some particularly congenial artistic souls among the younger or less-appreciated artists of the time. In this manner prestige and opportunity for growth and self-expression were extended to an artistic
movement which had hitherto been obliged to carry on a shadowy existence in the background of accepted artistic tenets. Just as the new religion really exhibits little that is fundamentally new but grew rather out of
soil long cultivated, so also the relief sculpture of Amarna is directly con-

Fig. 83.—The Royal Family at Amarna (Berlin Museum)

nected with the fresh and vital designs characteristic of the time before Akhnaton in the Theban tombs; it is dominated by the same underlying principles as they were, and, like them, it has also not shaken off the fetters of the earlier laws operative in sculpture in the round. Nevertheless, a new spirit pervades the Amarna art, a striving after realism and truth and stark individualism. Completely vanished now are the barriers which confined the full freedom of earlier artistic expression to the portrayal of the world of animals and men of low degree. With the new religion of Amarna a new art made its entrance also. Completely liberated from every tradition, the nobles, the royal children, the queen, and the king himself could now be represented exactly as the artist saw them in life. No longer portrayed as an idealized, unreal demigod, as in the reliefs from the period anterior to the removal of the capital to Amarna, he now appears before us in a series of portrait figures which reveal his indolence of carriage, his haggard, unshapely body, his thick and flabby thighs, long neck, and grotesquely ugly facial features. It was not sufficient to represent the pharaoh alone in such an uncomely fashion; as might have been expected, his figure was accepted as the ideal Egyptian type. Thus, not only the queen, who may have been closely related to Akhnaton by blood, and the princesses, who may have inherited some real resemblance to their father, but other Egyptians as well were depicted as nearly like the king as possible. Accordingly, the already markedly prominent bodily peculiarities which nature had bestowed upon him became exaggerated yet more until they resulted in nothing less than veritable burlesque. It was therefore anything but beneficial to this fresh new art with its inspiring response to nature that it was adopted in Amarna, of all places, at a court whose outstanding feature was its inclination toward the unusual. The young Amarna art thus bore within itself the germ of its own destruction. It cannot be emphasized too much, however, that its works of sculpture in the round, especially those from the studio of the sculptor Thutmose, are among the best that Egyptian art ever produced, while even the relief sculpture was not infrequently held free of the tendency to exaggeration. Many of the representations on the walls and floors of the houses, palaces, tombs, and memorial stelae of Amarna stand very close to the top of all the works of Egyptian relief sculpture and painting.

It does not appear that particularly vigorous opposition to the introduction of the new religion was made. At least there is no surviving record of revolts against the king's authority. Most of the high officials obeyed the commands of the pharaoh; the exceptions will have been removed from office or disposed of otherwise. On the other hand, the masses probably paid but slight attention to the new cult and retained for the most part the familiar old gods of their fathers.

But however quietly the machine of state continued to operate in Egypt, the results of the religious reformation were tangible enough in Syria. While the tribute of the vassal princes may have continued to flow into the coffers of Egypt as regularly as ever, it is certain that their allegiance flagged when year after year no pharaoh appeared at the head of his army to put down with heavy hand even the feeblest hint of revolt. The internal feuds among the individual cities went on, and the weaker ones fell under the influence of the stronger, even though they still acknowledged their allegiance to Egypt. It was inevitable that they should ultimately ask themselves what profit they derived from their dependence on the empire on the Nile, if they were abandoned without notice or aid when threatened by their rivals so that they were obliged at length to surrender themselves to their treacherous neighbors.

Among the most powerful dynasts in northern Syria were Abdashirta and Aziru, princes of Amurru, who under Amenhotep III and Akhnaton had attempted to extend their domain and to overthrow the neighboring states, especially the wealthy cities of the Phoenician coast, Simyra, Byblos, Beirut, and various others. They found the most powerful support for the undertaking on two sides. From the north and the direction of Asia Minor the powerful Hittites had begun to press forward against the Egyptian empire. Many of the Egyptian towns had in fact already fallen into their hands. In alliance with them the warlike Habiru—a people whose name later became attached to the Hebrews of the Old Testament—invaded regions under Egyptian protection and robbed and plundered the villages. Against these powerful foes, who may well have benefited by the machinations of the kings of Hatti, Mitanni, and Assyria, the Egyptian military commandants were quite helpless; they may indeed have made common cause with them in order to eliminate the princes still loyal to Egypt.

Farther south in Palestine the situation was no better. In that region also there was no lack of princes who were eager to take advantage of

Egyptian weakness to gain their independence and to extend their private possessions. They found ready allies in the Habiru and the Suti Beduin. The faithful vassals, among others the prince of Jerusalem, turned in vain to the Egyptian court and begged the king "to care for his land. . . . . All the lands of the king have broken away. . . . . The Habiru are plundering all the lands of the king. If no troops come in this very year, then all the lands of the king are lost." The requested reinforcements were nevertheless withheld, the Habiru devastated all the dominions of the king without hindrance, and the day threatened when actually "the entire region of the pharaoh was lost."

With all his indifference to the affairs of state, Akhnaton could not fail to be disturbed at the uninterrupted flow of such disquieting messages into the administrative offices of the government at Amarna. We do not know whether he took effective action to meet the situation. But we do know that about the sixteenth year of his reign serious trouble developed in the new capital. Queen Nofretete fell into disgrace and retired to the north end of the city, where she built a new palace for herself. Objects found in its ruins point to the probability that she shared her new residence with the young Tutankhaton, at this time scarcely more than five or six years old, who later married her third daughter, Ankhesenpaton. With Nofretete banished from the palace, her place in Akhnaton's affections was taken by his eldest daughter, Meritaton, whose husband, Smenkhkare, the king had appointed as coregent. After a short residence in the palace of his father-in-law, Smenkhkare disappears from view, but he is recorded at Thebes in his third regnal year as the possessor of a temple of Amun, a fact completely inconsistent with a simultaneous alteration of his personal name to incorporate in it that of the Aton which it had not previously contained. If, as has been suggested, Smenkhkare had gone to Thebes to attempt a reconciliation with the adherents of Amun, his mission was probably not only a failure but it may well have cost him and Meritaton their lives. Meanwhile, affairs had taken a strange turn at Amarna. Akhnaton, perhaps in a last desperate effort to obtain a male heir to his shaky throne, took to wife his own twelve- or thirteen-year-old daughter, Ankhesenpaton. While he must have suffered dire disappointment at the result, for she presented him with another daughter, the name which he gave to the child, "Ankhesenpaton Junior," proves his unwavering loyalty to the god of Amarna.

XV

TUTANKHAMUN AND THE CLOSE OF
THE EIGHTEENTH DYNASTY

AKHNATON occupied the throne for a maximum of twenty-one years, nearly three-fourths of which he shared either with his father, at the beginning, or with his son-in-law Smenkhkare, at the end. In view of the political conditions abroad, the religious struggle with the various priesthoods of Egypt, and the domestic discord in the capital, the closing years of his life must have been sad and bitter. The accumulated evidence points to the probability that he suffered from a rare and progressively disfiguring ailment which may have affected his mind as well as his body. He will have succumbed to this malady when still under fifty years of age. The state of his much ruined mortuary equipment makes it exceedingly unlikely that he was ever laid to rest in the family tomb prepared for him in the valley east of Akhetaton, where his second daughter, Meketaton, had been buried.

While Akhnaton had undoubtedly expected his successor to be his young son-in-law Smenkhkare, whose right to pharaonic rank had been fortified by marriage with Meritaton, the immediate appearance on the throne of Tutankhaton, with Ankhesenpaton as his consort, seems ample proof that Smenkhkare and Meritaton had already perished before the death of the failing king. Perhaps one of his last acts had been to appoint a new successor, and *his* right to the throne would likewise depend on a proper marriage into the dynasty. Hence Akhnaton turned over to Tutankhaton the oldest princess of the house—his third daughter and at the same time his wife, Ankhesenpaton. Tutankhaton is believed by some to have been a younger brother of Smenkhkare. At his death the latter had been carelessly buried in an undecorated tomb in the Theban Valley of the Kings in a coffin made over for him but probably intended originally for one of Akhnaton's daughters, along with numerous funerary articles bearing the name of Akhnaton's mother, Queen Tiy. In spite, however, of his relatively crude burial, Smenkhkare had begun, during his brief Theban reign, to provide for himself a costly mortuary outfit. His sudden death before it had been completed left a number of important objects in the hands of his successor. Instead of making of these the pious and customary use for which they were intended, the partisans of Tutankhaton seized and held them in reserve until such time as they would be required for his or some other royal burial.

Thus a boy of eight or nine sat on the throne of the pharaohs, his legitimacy not too staunchly bolstered by his relationship to Akhnaton and Akhnaton's daughter but possibly strengthened a little through descent from Amenhotep III, who was probably his grandfather. Ankhesenpaton, probably four or five years older than Tutankhaton, was perhaps likewise his first cousin. (Before his death, nine years later, she was to bear him two stillborn children.)

Under the circumstances it was inevitable that the actual responsibility of ruling must fall upon the shoulders of officials of the court. The chief of these was the aged vizier Eye, who had been a sort of secretary and a favorite of Akhnaton and whose wife, Tiy, had been the childhood nurse of Nofretete. After a brief period as a sort of "elder statesman" and trusted adviser of Tutankhaton, Eye was actually elevated to the rank of coregent with the young king, and he not only carried on the rule of the Two Lands during Tutankhaton's lifetime but actually survived him, officiated at his funeral, and succeeded him as sole king.

In the death of Akhnaton the work of the religious reformation had suffered a fatal blow. The new king's party was not long in recognizing that it would be possible to remain in control of the government only by coming to terms with the supporters of the traditional faith. Tutankhaton was accordingly obliged to relinquish the "teaching" and together with his consort to acknowledge himself officially as an adherent of the previously persecuted Amun (Fig. 84). Just as Amenhotep IV had once changed his name because it contained the forbidden word "Amun," so now the royal couple altered their names, both of which were compounded with that of the now proscribed Aton. Henceforth the king was known officially as Tutankhamun ("Beautiful in Life Is Amun"), while the queen became Ankhesenamun ("She Lives for Amun"). Under the pressure of the counterreformation the king was forced to abandon the residence at Amarna, where he probably had been born, and to restore the court to the southern capital of Thebes. This act sealed the fate of Akhetaton. All the nobles, officials, mercenaries, artisans, and serfs who were in the service of the ruler naturally returned along with the royal court to the ancient capital. And so Akhetaton, the "Horizon of Aton," became a ghost city. Its temples and palaces, villas and office buildings, lay desolate; the highways and byways heard no longer the sound of human voices; and before many years had passed the city was reduced to a vast heap of rubbish. Recent excavations on the site have revealed that its destruction was accelerated by the fanatical persecution of everything pertaining to the religion of the Aton, which resulted in zealous and untiring efforts to blot out even in the abandoned city every memory of the religious movement which had created it and especially of the royal personality who had, after all, been its chief inspiration and most powerful adherent.

Thus the new "teaching" survived its founder but a few years at the most, and the hope of its loyal votaries that it would endure "until the swan grows black and the raven becomes white, until the mountains rise up to walk and the waters flow uphill" remained unfulfilled. The same fanaticism which Akhnaton had once directed against the old gods was now turned upon him. His name and figure were erased from the monuments; he was stricken from the official king lists; and he became known to posterity as "the criminal of Akhetaton." Such was the ultimate victory of Amun: "He who had attacked him was fallen; the house of him who had assailed him lay in darkness."

Disavowing some of the events of his past, Tutankhamun boasted how he "suppressed wrongdoing [perhaps a reference to the heretical cult of the Aton] throughout the Two Lands, so that justice was established, and falsehood made to be the abomination of the land, as in its first time." The young king (Fig. 85) is careful to refer to himself as one "beloved of Amen-Re, lord of the thrones of the Two Lands, the foremost of Karnak." He then proceeds to describe the sad condition of the country which prevailed at his accession:

Now when his majesty appeared as king, the temples of the gods and goddesses from Elephantine to the Delta marshes . . . . had fallen into neglect; their shrines had gone to ruin, having become tracts overgrown with thorns, their chapels were as if they had never been, and their temples had become trodden roads. The land was topsy-turvy, and as for the gods, they had turned their backs to this land. If troops were sent to Djahi to extend the boundaries of Egypt, their efforts came to naught. If one besought a god with a request for anything, he did not come at all; if one petitioned any goddess likewise, she

FIG. 84.—AMUN AND TUTANKHAMUN (LOUVRE)

would not come either—for their hearts were angry in their bodies, because they [the heretics of the Aton movement?] had destroyed what had been made.

But now when some days had passed after these things, his majesty appeared on the throne of his father and ruled the regions of Horus; Egypt and the foreign desert lands were under his control and every land bowed to his might.

Now when his majesty was in his palace which is in the estate of Okheperkare, then his majesty administered the affairs of this land and the daily needs of the Two Regions. . . . . His majesty took counsel with his heart, searching out every proper means and seeking what would be beneficial to his father Amun for fashioning his august image of genuine *djam*-gold. . . . . His majesty made monuments for all the gods, fashioning their statues of genuine *djam*-gold, restoring their sanctuaries as monuments enduring forever, providing them with perpetual endowments, investing them with divine offerings for the daily service, and supplying their provisions on earth.

The priesthoods were supplied with rich incomes, costly new barks for the Nile processions and other religious festivals were constructed, and male and female slaves were presented to the temples.

Beyond the facts just related, we actually have little knowledge of the reign of Tutankhamun. We do possess, however, one other major monument from his time, aside from the countless objects from his tomb, many of which are of little or no value for historical purposes. This is the tomb of Tutankhamun's viceroy of Nubia, Amenhotep, better known as Huy. We are informed in a series of painted scenes on its walls how he presented to his young lord the tribute of conquered Syria and Nubia (Fig. 24): horses, costly chariots, magnificent gold and silver vessels, wonderful engraved epergnes, Sudanese cattle, a live giraffe, and many other curiosities so fascinating to the Egyptian painters of the age.

Tutankhamun occupied the throne for nine years. When death cut short his youthful career, the throne was occupied alone by the surviving coregent, Eye, who presided over his funeral and caused him to be buried in the Valley of the Kings with a pomp that would have seemed incredible to us had the entire tomb treasure not been revealed to the world through its discovery by Howard Carter in 1922. Many of the objects in the funerary equipment, including the miniature Canopic coffins, one of the enormous gold shrines, and some of the adornments which covered the mummy itself, had originally been made for Smenkhkare and were usurped for Tutankhamun's burial.

The tomb is a relatively small one; it contains two large rooms, the anteroom and the sarcophagus chamber—the latter known to the Egyptians quite appropriately as the "house of gold"—as well as two smaller

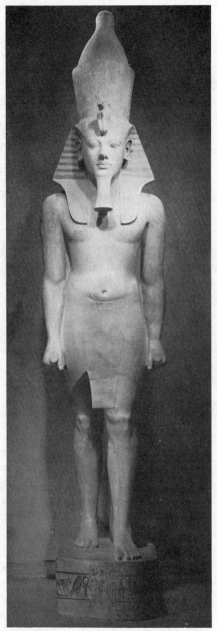

FIG. 85.—STATUE OF TUTANKHAMUN, USURPED BY EYE AND HARMHAB (ORIENTAL INSTITUTE MUSEUM)

227

subsidiary rooms, the storeroom and the "treasure chamber," as it was designated by the discoverer.

The sarcophagus chamber is the only one of the four with decorated walls; these contain a few scenes and inscriptions, principally of a religious character. One of them depicts the mummy of the king resting on a sledge under a canopy as it is being drawn to the tomb by the traditional nine courtiers. Another represents King Eye standing before the mummy of his predecessor and performing the ceremony of "opening the mouth," which was intended to awake the dead to renewed life.

This burial chamber was almost entirely filled by an enormous gilded wooden shrine whose sides of openwork consisted of the symbols of the mortuary god Osiris and of his divine consort repeated side by side in pairs. This great outer shrine or canopy inclosed, one within another, three other not less artistic ones, all covered with gold foil, the innermost of which in turn concealed the sarcophagus itself, which was hewn of a yellowish quartzite, covered with numerous religious inscriptions and pictures, and topped with a granite lid. At the four corners of the sarcophagus stand in bas-relief the four goddesses, Isis, Nephthys, Neith, and Selket, who protect with outstretched wings the sleeping king within (Fig. 86). Inside the sarcophagus, lying on a wooden bier carved in the form of a lion and covered with linen cloths, was a mummiform wooden coffin, finished in stucco and covered with gold foil. The youthful countenance with its thin cheeks and earnest mouth is an exceedingly successful attempt to render the noble likeness of the king, as is amply demonstrated by the long-known granite statue of Tutankhamun in the Cairo Museum. The arms are crossed on the breast, the hands holding the insignia of Osiris, the scepter and the so-called flail, both executed in the round and adorned with lapis lazuli. The whole creates an impression of astonishing freshness, as if the coffin had only yesterday been placed in its stone sarcophagus.

The outermost wooden coffin inclosed within it a second, likewise mummiform and of equal beauty with the first, while inside that was still a third and far more costly coffin of solid gold, which contained the remains of the young king (Fig. 40). The mummy was bound in the usual linen wrappings, with the head covered by an exquisite gold portrait mask of Tutankhamun (Fig. 87). The mummy was richly decked with jewels, and every sort of trinket which had delighted the boy king in life

Fig. 86.—Sarcophagus of Tutankhamun (Biban el-Muluk)

Fig. 87.—Gold Mask of Tutankhamun (Cairo Museum)

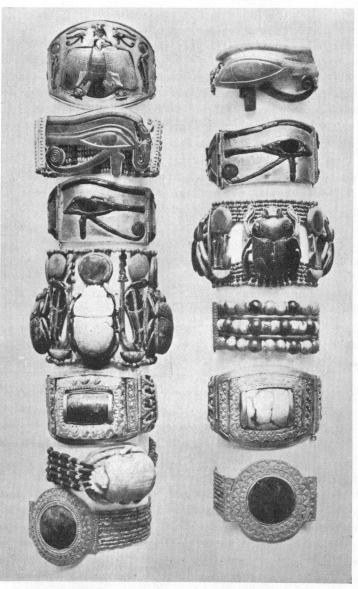

FIG. 88.—JEWELRY FROM THE MUMMY OF TUTANKHAMUN (CAIRO MUSEUM)

was permitted to accompany him in the tomb at death. Gold sandals clothed his feet, while each finger and toe was incased in its individual stall of gold. His fingers were resplendent with gold rings, many of which were adorned with scarabs engraved with the name of the king. Broad armlets graced his arms (Fig. 88), while his neck and breast were heavy with tastefully fashioned and arranged chains, collars, pectorals, amulets, and beads of gold, semiprecious stones, and fayence. Each and every one of these articles of royal adornment is an outstanding masterpiece of artistic workmanship and a magnificent credit to its creator.

Numerous mortuary gifts had been arranged in the spaces between the walls of the nest of shrines: great oil vases of purest alabaster, walking-sticks, scepters, bows and arrows, and many others. Among them were two ostrich-feather fans of the sort which was customarily borne at the right and left of the king by his attendants when he went out walking or riding. Their handles were covered with gold foil and decorated with embossed pictures. One shows the young ruler hunting ostriches in his chariot (Fig. 89); another depicts him returning from the hunt with an ostrich wing under his arm, while his attendants carry home the birds slain during the chase. The accompanying inscription identifies the object on which it is engraved as a "fan of ostrich feathers which his majesty took on a hunt in the eastern desert of Heliopolis."

It is possible to describe here but a small fraction of the hundreds of articles belonging to the treasure which was stacked high in the anteroom of the tomb. There were many fine pieces of furniture such as beds, chairs, stools, and tables, most of which had obviously been taken from the furnishings of the royal palaces in Amarna and Thebes. The most costly piece of furniture is the throne (Fig. 90), which is richly adorned with gold, colored glass, fayence, and stone inlays. Its legs are carved in the shape of lions' feet, and they are appropriately surmounted at the level of the seat by exquisitely wrought gold lions' heads. The two arm-rests of Tutankhamun's throne are shaped like winged serpents, each wearing on its head the double crown of an Egyptian ruler, while with its embracing wings it protects the king's name and thus, by Egyptian logic, the king himself. The back of the throne is likewise embellished by serpents with upraised heads, ready to strike death to possible enemies. The most magnificent part of the piece, however, is the forward surface of the back. The king is depicted on the left in high relief, seated comfortably on a throne decked with soft cushions. His left hand reclines lightly on his knee, while the right arm is bent at the elbow, with the hand resting languidly on the cushion over the back of the chair. He wears on his head a rich and elaborate crown consisting of a great complex of feathers, sun disks, and uraeus serpents. The delicately modeled face is unquestionably intended to be a portrait of the youthful Tutankhamun. Standing before him is the lovely girlish figure of the queen, who holds a small vase in her left hand, while with the other she daintily touches the

FIG. 89.—OSTRICH-FEATHER FAN OF TUTANKHAMUN (CAIRO MUSEUM)

broad collar of her husband with a drop of perfume from the vase. Ample transparent robes envelop her slender form, and she wears upon her head a high crown of the type customary for Egyptian queens and princesses. Above the royal couple, at the top of the chair back, shines the Aton each of whose diverging rays ends in a life-giving hand. The faces and other exposed parts of the bodies of the royal couple are executed of vitreous paste inlays of reddish brown, while the hair is rendered in blue fayence. The robes are of silver covered with a dull patina. Crowns, collars, and other details are wrought of inlays of colored glass, bright hues of fayence, red carnelian, and some kind of artificial material resembling millefiori glass. The background and the throne itself are covered with gold foil. Al-

though the colors have lost something of their pristine brilliance, the
entire piece has, nevertheless, retained a color harmony of extraordinary
elegance and charm. This lovely picture breathes forth an astonishing
vitality and the most delicate sentiment; it is one of those delightful
scenes from the private life of the pharaoh which was peculiar to the
Amarna style. In fact, the throne actually comes from the period when
the boy monarch still clung to the "teaching" of his father-in-law and
had Amarna as his residence. For he is still called Tutankh*aton* on the
throne, though in certain of its inscriptions the name reveals the alteration to Tutankh*amun*, which reflects his resumption of the traditional religion. It may be assumed that this throne was brought to
Thebes upon the removal of the court from Amarna and that it continued to be used in the palace in spite of the heretical scene on the back

Fig. 90—Panel on Back of Tutankhamun's Throne (Cairo Museum)

FIG. 91.—ALABASTER CENTERPIECE OF TUTANKHAMUN (CAIRO MUSEUM)

with its glorification of the Aton. Thus, in addition to its being a technical masterpiece of the highest order, this fine article of furniture must be
accepted as a not unimportant religious and historical document.

Of the numerous decorative vases and centerpieces of alabaster from
the tomb, some of which are decidedly baroque in style, it will suffice to
describe but one. This is in the form of a graceful boat, devised by the

FIG. 92.—ALABASTER LAMP OF TUTANKHAMUN (CAIRO MUSEUM)

ancient sculptor to appear as if it were floating in a pool, a favorite subject in Egyptian painting. The boat (Fig. 91) is adorned with ibex heads at prow and stern, while there is a delicately carved kiosk amidships, the roof of which is supported by four columns with composite capitals. Seated on the foredeck is the nude figure of a girl holding a flower to her breast; behind the kiosk, steering the skiff, is a nude female achondroplastic dwarf. The piece is exquisitely carved, with engraved details adorned with gold and colored pigments, while the headdress of the two sculptured figures is made of separate pieces of green stone. The hollow pedestal or pool in which the skiff is placed may have been intended as a vase for the arrangement of flowers and water plants such as would naturally occur in the papyrus marshes where the king and queen were accustomed to take their pleasure cruises and have their picnics.

Not less interesting of the alabaster pieces is a unique lamp (Fig. 92). It consists of a pedestal carved in a shape imitative of the wooden stands so frequent in ancient Egypt (Fig. 56), on which rests a chalice flanked with Egyptian hieroglyphic symbols conveying the wish for "millions of years of life" for King Tutankhamun. The chalice itself is most remarkable, for it consists of two exceedingly thin cups tightly cemented one inside the other. The outer surface of the inner one was painted with a brightly colored design showing the queen standing before her enthroned husband. This little scene was visible only when the lamp was partially filled with oil and the floating wick was lighted, so that the colors showed through the translucent alabaster.

A carved and painted ivory panel on the lid of one of Tutankhamun's chests is without question one of the greatest artistic masterpieces from the tomb (Fig. 93). The king and Queen Ankhesenamun stand facing each other in a pavilion richly decked with elaborately wrought bouquets of flowers and fruits. Tutankhamun stands in a relaxed posture, leaning lightly on a staff with one hand, while he extends the other to take a long bouquet which his wife holds out to him. She is slender and graceful, the lines of her girlish figure revealed through transparent drapery. At the base of the panel two kneeling Egyptian maidens are depicted as they gather flowers and the fruit of the mandrake for their royal master and mistress. The composition superbly illustrates the feeling for balance so dear to the Egyptian artist, yet so skilfully has it been achieved that none of the charm and freedom of the lovely little picture have been sacrificed to artistic convention.

That the youthful king and his pretty queen enjoyed many an excursion together is revealed by another charming scene of their intimate life together, in which the king is shown on a duck hunt in her company (Fig. 94). The composition is rendered in low relief on the gold-foil decoration of a small shrine. Tutankhamun sits rather indolently on a folding chair with cushioned seat, his pet lion beside him, while he draws his bow and aims an arrow at a flock of ducks rising from a clump of papyrus. The queen, seated before him on a cushion, hands him an arrow with her right hand while with her left she points toward the ducks. Both figures reflect the characteristic informality of the Amarna style, and the balance of the composition is retained without the repetition of a single decorative element.

Fig. 93.—Carved Ivory Panel of Tutankhamun (Cairo Museum)

238

The pictures which adorn the sides and lid of one of Tutankhamun's trunks must be considered among the highest achievements of Egyptian painting. The two sides are painted with vigorous scenes of battles in which the king engages the Negroes and the Asiatics, respectively (Fig. 67). In a chariot drawn by two spirited and richly caparisoned stallions, the king drives forward with drawn bow and speeding arrows, while the luckless foes rush about in headlong terror before the irresistible onslaught of the youthful pharaoh. The lid of the chest is decorated with a pair of hunting compositions similar in effect to the battle pictures. On one side Tutankhamun is shown hunting lions (Fig. 66); on the other his quarry is the smaller desert game. The king in his chariot occupies the center of the scenes; he is followed by his retinue, while the objects of his sport flee before his death-dealing weapons into the desert. The artist has succeeded in creating pictures of extraordinary vitality, pictures so packed with action that the observer seems to share the king's exciting experiences on the battlefield or in the chase. An almost overwhelming impression is created by the lions as they desperately but vainly attempt to escape the inevitable doom about to strike them down in the person of the terrible, invincible, oncoming king. Only once after this did oriental art succeed in bringing to expression so shatteringly this struggle and this agony of death; six hundred years later we find it once more in the lion

Fig. 94.—Tutankhamun and His Queen Ankhesenamun Shooting Wild Duck (Cairo Museum).

hunt of Ashurbanipal at Nineveh. But in these paintings on Tutankhamun's trunk the old Egyptian tradition flows through the feeling for
nature awakened at Amarna, draws a breath of Aegeo-Cretan genius,
and fuses into a finished unity.

If the tomb treasure of Tutankhamun is considered as a whole, it must
be admitted that its contents represent technically and artistically the
best that Egyptian applied art ever produced. With all their superiority
of technique, however, the multifarious stone vases and even the furniture
reflect a regrettable lack of the keen sense of the appropriate and the
feeling for form which distinguished the works of art from the middle of
the Eighteenth Dynasty. That is but one of the marks of the decline
which is already setting in and which in the next century or two will
advance with easily traceable acceleration.

Eye, who regularly called himself the "God's Father," possibly to indicate some relationship to the royal family now unknown to us, occupied
the throne scarcely more than four years. During the brief sojourn of the
court at Akhetaton, Akhnaton had caused to be excavated for his favorite
a splendid tomb in the hills near the city, and its walls were decorated
with reliefs showing the various honors which the king had in such rich
measure heaped upon him (Fig. 75). Since, however, he had himself become king and abandoned the now unprofitable "teaching," the most
remarkable document of which, in fact, he had carved in the doorway of
his Amarna tomb (see pp. 214 f.), he provided for himself at orthodox
Thebes a new tomb in the same branch of the valley to which Amenhotep
III had gone to prepare his last resting-place. Eye then decorated his
new Theban tomb in traditional if somewhat plebeian style with religious scenes and inscriptions, though he made no mention in it of the
name of Ankhesenamun, the widow of Tutankhamun, whom he is alleged
to have married in order to legalize his occupation of the throne. On the
contrary, Eye's queen as named in his tomb is the same Tiy who is known
to have been his wife from the records of his earlier life.

Indeed, it is extremely improbable that Eye was ever married to
Ankhesenamun. This young widow of Tutankhamun evidently possessed strong and original ideas regarding marriage and Egyptian politics
as well. Despite Eye's coregency with her young husband, she perhaps
never recognized the legitimacy of his rank. Moreover, she was determined to occupy the throne herself, with a husband of her own choosing.

Had she not been the queen of two successive pharaohs? Thus, rather than to marry one of her own servants, as she expressed it, Ankhesenamun (if she is really the Queen *Da-ḫa-mu-un-zu* of the letter, rather than a hitherto unknown second wife of Tutankhamun) addressed a cuneiform letter to the Hittite king Shuppiluliuma with the unprecedented request that he send as soon as possible a Hittite prince whom she might marry and elevate to the throne of Egypt. Copies of this remarkable document have survived on several clay tablets from the imperial archives of the Hittite capital found at modern Boğazköy. "My husband, Nib-khururia (the official name of Tutankhamun), has recently died, and I have no son. But thy sons, they say, are many. If thou wilt send me a son of thine, he shall become my husband." The king of the Hittites was not disposed to take this remarkable message without a grain of salt. He determined to send an envoy to Egypt to make a thorough investigation of the situation. "Go and bring back a reliable report to me. Perhaps they merely deride me; perhaps there really is a son of their lord." Disturbed by the skepticism of the Hittite king and the consequent delay, the queen of Egypt sent a second message to Shuppiluliuma, reproving him for his lack of faith: "Why didst thou say, 'They wish to deceive me?' If I had a son, would I of my own accord to the humiliation of my country write to another country? Dost thou not trust me now? . . . . Not to any other country did I send, but I sent to thee alone. Thy sons, they say, are many. Give thou one of thy sons to me, and he shall be my husband and, furthermore, he shall be king in the land of Egypt." The second communication apparently convinced the Hittite king of the queen's sincerity, and he decided to grant her request. A Hittite prince was accordingly sent off to the Nile Valley, but before he arrived at his destination he was waylaid and murdered, probably at the instigation of some other aspirant for the throne who may have learned of the queen's plans. In fact, it is not impossible that she shared the fate of her intended consort, for she passes at this point from the stage of history and is seen no more.

Neither Tutankhamun nor Eye had been in a position to mend the injured feelings of the various priesthoods, to reconcile the religious partisanship which had been stirred up, or to blot out the memory of the heresy of which they had both been avowed followers. A deep antipathy to these former persecutors of their god remained implanted in the hearts of the priests of Amun no matter how much these two rulers strove to win their good will. The entire land continued in a state of ferment. Unrest and uncertainty were everywhere dominant, and the fear that a new revolution might break and develop into open civil war held the people's minds in constant suspense.

At this critical juncture, however, when general anarchy threatened an explosion, a deliverer rose in the land who was sufficiently powerful and energetic to take over the ship of state and to steer it through stormy seas. Under the reigns of Akhnaton and Tutankhamun a man named Harmhab rose to high rank. He was commander-in-chief of the army, and he claims as deputy of the king to have attained the next place in the empire to the king himself. The patron god Horus of Hatnesut, his native city, was likewise the guardian of his destiny; he it was who had "elevated his son above the entire land" and guided his steps until "the day came when he should take over his office, the kingship." For the reigning king, Harmhab relates, took pleasure in him and appointed him to the chief place in the land in order that he might "administer the affairs of the Two Lands as prince of this entire land. . . . . When he was summoned by the king to the palace the people were astonished at his words, and when he answered the king he delighted him by his discourse." He was able to boast of himself that the virtues of the great gods Ptah and Thoth dwelt in him. He was ultimately appointed to the chief administrative position in the empire and given command of the entire Egyptian army, whereby supreme authority over both Nubia and the Syrian possessions automatically fell into his hands. "So he administered the Two Lands for many years. . . . . Reverence for him was great in the sight of the people," and, like the king himself, "people besought for him 'prosperity and health.'"

It had obviously not been the good will of the pharaoh alone which had elevated Harmhab to this powerful and influential position and made him the representative of the king in the land. His political sagacity and unswerving will-power had played no small part in bringing him to the fore. Harmhab was never converted to the Aton religion. In Memphis, where he had his residence, he remained loyal to the old gods, especially to the patron divinity of his native city and to Amun.

It is probable that Harmhab was chiefly responsible for preventing the peace of the land from being completely shattered during those troublous times. It may likewise have been Harmhab who frustrated the bold plan

Fig. 95.—Harmhab before His Accession as King (Metropolitan Museum of Art)

of Tutankhamun's young widow to win a Hittite prince for a husband and to turn over to him the throne; if that is the case, he may consequently have been responsible for the murder of the Hittite while he was en route to Egypt. Harmhab visited the court from time to time to report to the king; on such occasions he was received with all respect and favored according to the custom of the time with gold tokens of approbation. A mark of extraordinary royal grace was permission to place his statue in the temple of Ptah at Memphis (Fig. 95). It represents Harmhab as a royal scribe seated cross-legged on the floor and holding on his lap a papyrus roll containing a long hymn to Thoth, the patron god of scribes.

In his capacity of overseer of mines and quarries, he erected for himself in the necropolis of Memphis a tomb on whose walls, the reliefs of which are among the most wonderful surviving sculptures in the Amarna spirit, we see him presenting to the royal couple the hostages from foreign lands, together with their tribute, while he receives in turn the tokens of the sovereigns' appreciation of his services.

Despite the power and influence at court claimed by Harmhab in his biography, his ambitions for the throne were frustrated for four long years by the aged Eye. His death and the probable assassination of the "treasonous" Ankhesenamun at length provided the crucial moment for his assumption of the crown. Acting on his own authority and perhaps on that of the priesthood of Amun also, he marched at the head of the army to Thebes, enjoying an enthusiastic reception by the cheering population of every city through which he passed on the way. Greatest of all, of course, was the rejoicing in the capital, for the god Horus had accompanied him in person to Thebes "to introduce him into the presence of Amun and to confer upon him his kingly office." During a feast in Luxor, Amun beheld Horus and, in his retinue, his son Harmhab, who had been brought to receive "his office and his throne, and Amen-Re was filled with joy when he saw him." The coronation itself was consummated in a mysterious ceremony. Amun accompanied the king to the dwelling of "his august daughter," the lioness-headed Weret-hekau ("Great of Sorcery"), the personification of the royal diadem. Then, amid the plaudits of all the gods, Harmhab proceeded at once to promulgate his official titulary designations, since Amun had placed the crown upon his head and conferred upon him the sovereignty over "all that the sun encircles."

After the completion of the coronation ceremonies in Thebes the king returned to the north. And now the last memories of the religious revolution were swept away, and purged along with all possible reminders of Akhnaton were those of his immediate followers, Tutankhamun and Eye, as well; their names were all ruthlessly hacked from the monuments and replaced by those of Harmhab (Fig. 85). This persecution was carried to such lengths, indeed, that the reigns of the four heretics were treated as if they had never existed, and their reigns from the death of Amenhotep III were all reckoned to that of Harmhab. The temple of the Aton was completely destroyed and the site leveled to the ground, while its blocks of masonry were employed in the construction of new buildings which Harmhab erected in honor of Amun. The restoration of old temples which Tutankhamun had started was now resumed with increased energy. The sanctuaries of the gods in every part of Egypt, from the Delta marshes to the province of Nubia, were restored as they had been "in the primeval age, in the time of Re"; the scenes destroyed by Akhnaton were renewed and rendered "more beautiful than they had been," while the confiscated temple endowments were returned to the sanctuaries with additional donations. The customary offerings were re-established, and to them were added rich new gold and silver vessels.

If the king exerted himself so vigorously in the service of the gods and succeeded by the bestowal of costly gifts in winning the good will of the numerous priesthoods of the entire land, he was no less solicitous for the welfare of his subjects, especially for the oppressed peasant population, who had suffered sorely under the extortions of officials and the pillaging of soldiers. In order to protect them forever from similar abuses and at the same time to assure the proper delivery of income to the royal treasury, Harmhab issued a decree which he dictated in person to the scribe and caused to be chiseled on a great stela which he set up near one of the three pylons which he added to the temple precinct of Amun at Karnak (Fig. 96). It provided the severest penalties for all violations of the new laws. Any official who overstepped the bounds of his authority and deprived a soldier or any other Egyptian subject of a boat or robbed him of his property should have his nose cut off and be exiled to a border town in the eastern Delta. Officials were forbidden to impress for labor on their own private enterprises workmen who had been levied for public works. By these and a long list of other laws Harmhab strove "to recreate respect for law in Egypt, to prevent the practice of injustice, to eliminate crime, and to destroy falsehood."

In a similar manner the new king made every effort to restore the recognition of Egyptian authority in foreign lands. Trading expeditions to Punt, which had been interrupted during the ascendancy of the heretics, were resumed, and after a long absence representatives of that distant land appeared once more on the banks of the Nile to deliver their products and pay homage to the pharaoh.

During the dark period which had come to an end the Negro tribes of the Sudan had trespassed the southern frontier, invaded Egyptian territory, and laid waste the fields and settlements of that region. Harmhab led an army against them in person, put them to flight, and returned home in victory "with the booty which his sword had taken." Countless prisoners were carried off by his soldiers, and the obsequious cries of the captives, as they were led in triumph through the streets of Thebes, must have been pleasing to his ears: "Hail to thee, O King of Egypt, Sun of the

FIG. 96.—ONE OF THE PYLONS OF HARMHAB (KARNAK)

Nine Bows! Great is thy name in the land of Kush, and thy battle cry throughout their dwellings! Thy might, O good prince, hath converted the foreign lands into heaps of corpses. Life, prosperity, health, O Sun!"

The threat to Egyptian sovereignty was much more serious in Syria. While yet field marshal of the army under Tutankhamun, Harmhab had once led his forces to Palestine to quell a native revolt and hunt down the Beduin who were disturbing the peace. His expedition had met with success, and many prisoners had been brought back as hostages and presented to the king. On that campaign, however, it is not probable that he had encountered the Hittites, who by this time had become established in northern Syria and on the Lower Orontes. It is possible that Akhnaton, impotent to undertake operations against them, had already concluded a treaty of peace by which he yielded to them the former Egyptian sphere of influence in that country and acknowledged their king Shuppiluliuma as a friend with equal rights or even as a confederate. In like manner, the land of Amurru south of the Hittite country had succeeded after decades of warfare in casting off the Egyptian yoke and in forging, in alliance with the conquered coastal cities of northern Phoenicia, a vast independent state which was destined in the future to oppose the stiffest resistance to the pharaohs' lust for conquest. Thus, of all the proud domains which Thutmose III had once conquered in western Asia, Palestine alone remained under Egyptian control, and even she was in constant turmoil from repeated raids of the desert nomads.

When after a reign of about thirty-five years the aged Harmhab died and was buried in his unfinished tomb in the Valley of the Kings, he was succeeded on the throne by Ramesses I. He is identical with a certain Pramessu, son of an army officer named Sethi, who under Harmhab had risen to some of the highest offices in the country, such as "Commander of the Army of the Lord of the Two Lands, Chief Priest of All the Gods, Representative of His Majesty in Upper and Lower Egypt, Vizier, and Chief Justice." Chosen by the childless Harmhab to become his successor, Ramesses had received the supreme honor of being permitted to display his statue in the temple of Karnak beside that of the sage Amenhotep (pp. 75 f.) as a "reward from the king." Harmhab and Ramesses I share the honor of having founded the Nineteenth Dynasty, which once again brought more than a modicum of glory to the empire on the Nile.

XVI

THE AGE OF THE RAMESSIDS

IT IS certain that Ramesses I was already an old man when he came to the throne. After a reign of little more than a year he died and was succeeded by his son Sethi I (Fig. 37). Egypt now had once more as king a vigorous personality in the prime of life. The coronation ceremonies having been completed, Sethi lost no time in taking up the work of Harmhab. He immediately embarked on a program of conquest in an effort to re-establish in Asia the empire won by Thutmose III and lost by Akhnaton. First of all, the Beduin who were constantly threatening the Palestine frontier on the east were put to flight. Thence he advanced toward the north and vanquished the insubordinate princes of the Galilean cities. He subsequently erected a temple and a triumphal stela at the captured stronghold of Beth Shan, which controlled the eastern entrance to the Plain of Esdraelon (Fig. 97).

Sethi's next venture was a campaign against the Hittites, whose king Murshili II, the younger son of Shuppiluliuma, was forced to make peace with the Egyptian. A short respite at home enabled the king to restore certain of the temples which were still lying in ruins or in a damaged condition from the time of the heretic kings and to honor the gods with new ones.

While the Egyptian victory in the struggle with the Hittites for the sovereignty of Syria had resulted in a truce, no really final decision had been reached. Now, however, Muwatalli took advantage of the armistice which had been forced upon his father to consolidate his forces and win allies, with the intention of pushing such an overwhelming offensive against the Egyptians that they would be driven completely out of Syria and their hopes for world power brought to a permanent end. At first, it must be granted, he gave every indication of desiring to keep the peace. For when Ramesses II (Fig. 98) came to the throne, Muwatalli requested his friend the prince of the North Syrian land of Qode to hasten to Egypt and pay homage to the young pharaoh. Nevertheless, after a few years he appeared at the head of a great Syrian confederation as a dangerous and

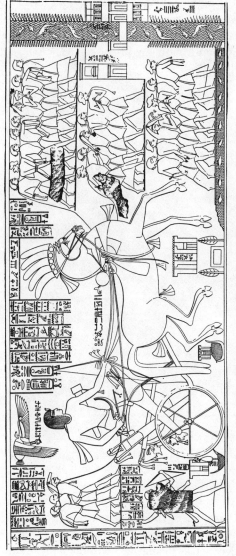

Fig. 97.—Return of Sethi I from a Syrian Campaign (Karnak)

249

aggressive rival to Egypt. He had "assembled all the foreign lands as far as the ends of the ocean" and organized an army of 25,000–30,000 men. "The entire Hittite land came and Nahrin likewise," as well as the powerful Syrian and Anatolian princes of Carchemish, Kizzuwatna,

Fig. 98.—Statue of Ramesses II (Turin Museum)

Ugarit, Qode, Nuhashshe, Kadesh, and various other towns, in addition to levies from Arzawa. In the spring of his fifth regnal year Ramesses left Egypt with an army of Egyptian infantry, chariotry, and foreign mercenaries not inferior in strength to the Hittite forces, with the purpose of meeting the aggressor at the earliest possible moment and coming to a decision. He marched along the coast of the Mediterranean and thence eastward over the Lebanon Mountains into the valley of the Orontes. The Hittite confederates, concealed and ready for battle, awaited the advancing Egyptians in ambush northeast of the fortified town of Kadesh. Ramesses had apparently been deluded by false reports into the belief that the enemy was stationed much farther away in northern Syria. He carelessly set up a fortified camp northwest of Kadesh with his own division of the army and prepared to rest from the strenuous march, when suddenly the Hittites burst forth from ambush and furiously attacked the astonished Egyptians, who fled in panic-stricken disorder from the field of battle.

The Egyptians would without the slightest doubt have suffered a crushing defeat had not Ramesses II by his personal intervention saved the situation and rescued his forces from utter annihilation. "He prayed to his father Amun, and the god helped him." Not one of the enemy dared fight on, for "their hearts were faint and their arms weak. They could not shoot and had not the courage to take their spears." Ramesses drove them before him to the Orontes and "cast them into the water like crocodiles; they fell on their faces, one on top of another, and he slew whomever he desired." It is obvious, however, that the king had not really gained the brilliant victory painted by the Egyptian eulogist. On the contrary, he was obliged to give up the struggle and lead his weakened army back to Egypt. In fact, Muwatalli boasts of having pursued the discomfited enemy as far as the region of Damascus.

The following year witnessed repeated battles in Palestine and Syria, but one after another they were without positive results for the Egyptians. This state of perennial warfare was at length brought to an end in the twenty-first year of Ramesses' reign by the conclusion of an Egyptian-Hittite treaty of friendship with Hattushili, the brother and second king after Muwatalli. The nonaggression pact, the sole surviving document of its kind between mutually independent powers of the ancient Orient, has fortunately been preserved in both the Egyptian hieroglyphic and the Hittite cuneiform version. According to its terms, both states should in the future stand on equal terms, while eternal peace was to prevail between the kings and all their descendants. The spheres of interest of the two empires were specifically defined. Northern Syria and especially the bitterly contested empire of Amurru were to be relinquished to the Hittites, while southern Syria together with the whole of Palestine was to remain in the possession of Egypt. Confirmation was later given to the treaty by Ramesses' marriage with a daughter of the Hittite king and her elevation to the position of "Great Royal Wife." This settlement of the Hittite question enabled Ramesses II to finish out his reign in peace.

When after a reign of sixty-seven years death came to Ramesses II about 1232 B.C., he was succeeded by his thirteenth son Merenptah, who was himself well advanced in years. There was a minor revolt in Palestine which he put down with little difficulty. It is commemorated by a song of victory in which the pharaoh's power is eulogized and the boast made that "Israel is laid waste and has no seed." This is the only mention of the name of Israel in any Egyptian inscription.

The most important event of the reign of Merenptah was a war with the Libyans which fell in his fifth year (1227 B.C.); it is the more significant in that it was the first hostile meeting of the Egyptians with the peoples of Europe. At this period a great migration of races had upset the eastern half of the Mediterranean world. The immediate cause of the movement appears to have been pressure by the peoples dwelling in the northern regions of the Balkans. We have already seen how, a century and a half before, the Achaeans had invaded Crete and brought the brilliant Minoan culture to disaster (p. 113). Now, under Merenptah, perhaps under pressure from the Phrygians and other tribes, a confederation consisting of the Akaiwash, Tursha-Tyrsenians, Shekelesh, Lycians, and various others began to move southward across the Mediterranean. The impact of these mighty waves eventually reached the African coast and caught in their vortex the native Berber tribes, the Hamitic Meshwesh (probably the Maxyes of Herodotus) and the light-skinned, blue-eyed Libyans of the Temeh tribes. Both of these races turned eastward toward Egypt and, having formed an alliance with the sea peoples, invaded the Delta under the leadership of a certain Mery. A battle was fought in the vicinity of the modern town of Bilbês in which the Egyptians were overwhelmingly victorious, Mery was put to flight, thousands of the invaders were slain, and many were taken prisoner. By this action the threat from Libya was temporarily allayed and the frontiers of Egypt secured for a time.

Sore calamities were, nevertheless, in store for Egypt in consequence of strife over the succession to the throne which broke out after the death of Merenptah. Usurpers succeeded in gaining temporary possession of the crown, only to be suppressed in favor of other claimants. "One united with another in order to pillage; gods were treated like men, and offerings were no longer brought to the temples." But the land was eventually rescued from this sorry state of affairs by a man of unknown origin named Sethnakht, who was the founder of the Twentieth Dynasty.

Sethnakht appointed his son Ramesses to be his successor, and it was not very long until he succeeded to the throne as Ramesses III. Looking upon the second Ramesses as the shining example of everything a pharaoh should be, he sought as a result to imitate Ramesses II to the minutest detail. He even adopted the same royal praenomen Usermare; he named his sons for the sons of the great Ramesses and conferred upon them the same offices which Ramesses II's sons had occupied two generations before. And fate appeared to confer upon him the same success in war which had attended his great predecessor. The Libyan Meshwesh had once more taken advantage of the political confusion and lack of unity in Egypt to make fresh incursions into the fertile meadows of the Delta. Along with the sea peoples and new allies which they found in the Peleste (the Philistines of Hebrew history) and the Tjeker, they had swarmed past the western frontier. Ramesses III went out to meet them in the fifth year of his reign and defeated them decisively. According to the Egyptian account of the battle, no fewer than 12,535 were slain, and more than a thousand were carried off as prisoners of war. In order to protect the frontier from a repetition of the invasion, Ramesses ordered the construction of a fortress which bore the proud name, "Ramesses III Is the Chastiser of the Temehu."

The western frontier having been secured, Ramesses was now able to assemble all his forces to oppose the dangerous migration which was surging on through Syria against the eastern boundary. The once-powerful empire of the Hittites had already been swept away by its momentum. "No land could stand before their arms, from Khatti [the Hittites], Qode, Carchemish, Arzawa, and Cyprus on, but they were cut off in one place. A camp was set up in one place in Amurru. They desolated its people, and its land was like that which has never come into being." In addition to the Peleste and the Tjeker, the invading hosts included yet other tribes which have not been identified with certainty. It is possible that the destruction of the citadel of Troy sung by Homer in the *Iliad* is a reflex of events connected with the invasion in the reign of Ramesses III. Some of the strangers advanced overland with their wives and children in cumbersome oxcarts, while another powerful contingent traveled by sea in a stately fleet. Ramesses proceeded toward the Palestinian border with his army and met the land forces of the enemy in a great battle which resulted in a crushing defeat for the foreigners. The fleet, which had sought to effect a landing in certain of the Nile mouths, was likewise engaged, and the ensuing naval battle ended in a signal triumph for Ramesses' forces (Fig. 99). The impact of the mighty attack was broken and the enemy held at bay in the north. However decisive their defeat, they had not been destroyed; the Peleste established themselves on the coastal plain of "Philistia," where they founded their own principalities in Gaza, Askalon, Ashdod, and other cities, while the related Tjeker settled in Dor.

Meanwhile the Meshwesh had recovered from their defeat and now sought by uniting with other Berber tribes once more to win past the western frontier of Egypt. A battle was fought in the very shadow of Ramesses' border fortress, and the Meshwesh with their confederates were defeated a second time, their chief was taken prisoner, and huge stores of booty as well as thousands of captives were taken. This decisive battle marked the end of Libyan offensive action for all time. Thereafter they trickled across the Egyptian frontier singly or in small groups in order to take up service as mercenaries in the pharaohs' armies. They were quartered in various Delta cities and ultimately came to constitute a special military caste in their new home which in time developed, like the Mamelukes of the Middle Ages, into both a strong support of and a serious threat to the sovereignty of the native dynasties.

The second half of the thirty-year reign of Ramesses III was less prosperous than the first. Repeated wars, extensive and costly temple-building projects, and the enormous gifts showered by the king upon the various temples of the land all combined to drain the treasury of the state. While the priesthoods continued to enrich themselves more and more, while the stables, granaries, and gold hoards of the temples increased to the bursting-point, the royal magazines and treasure-houses grew ever more nearly depleted. Means were actually lacking at the capital to deliver to the hungry workers their earnings of grain; revolts broke out in consequence, and strikes were resorted to in an effort to force on the government the payments of hard-earned dues.

This universal dissatisfaction at length spread to the royal house itself.

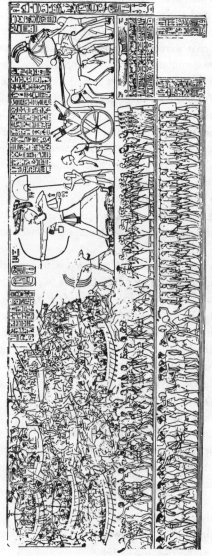

Fig. 99.—Naval Battle of Ramesses III (Medinet Habu)

A conspiracy was hatched which aimed at nothing less than the assassination of the king and the elevation to the throne of one of his sons borne to him by a woman of low degree. The focus of the plot was the royal harem; involved in it were not only high functionaries and officials of the state but even the commandant of the colonial army stationed in Nubia, who stood ready to participate with armed forces at the proper cue. According to the official but not necessarily truthful records, the plans of the conspirators were foiled. Ramesses III did actually succumb to the attempt on his life, but his "legitimate" successor, Ramesses IV, was able to overcome the "traitors." The leaders were captured and punished with severe penalties. The unlucky "pretender" was forced to kill himself, and, in the case of various others of the criminals, "no punishment was inflicted, for they took their own lives." Some of the harem ladies who had been parties to the plot were condemned to suffer the shearing-off of their ears and noses. Under such suspicious circumstances Ramesses IV mounted the throne.

The ambitious new pharaoh was received with acclaim throughout the land. It even appeared as if he might be able to put an end to the dismal situation which had developed in that decadent age. At his coronation a long proclamation in the form of a testament of the late king was published. The military victories of that king were recalled, and a vast, detailed list of all the benefactions conferred during his reign on each and every large and small temple of the land was promulgated. In this manner the new king contrived to confirm the clergy in their holdings of property and to gain their influential good will for his own reign.

One of the most significant political and social events of the early Nineteenth Dynasty was the transfer of the seat of the government from Thebes to the Delta city of Avaris-Tanis. This town had been forsaken since the expulsion of the Hyksos and had probably fallen into ruin, but it was re-established with great ceremony by Sethi I. The old local god Seth was presented with a splendid new temple which Ramesses II enlarged and greatly enriched during his reign. This king took up his residence in the vicinity at a place which he named "Ramessesburg," the modern Qantîr and the biblical town of Ramesses, to the building of which the children of Israel are related—perhaps anachronistically—to have contributed their forced labor. The court poets of the Ramessid era never grew weary of praising the beauty of their new residence city.

His majesty has built for himself a great castle called "Great of Victories." It lies between Palestine and Egypt and is filled with food and provisions. . . . . The sun rises in its horizon and sets within it. All the people forsake their cities and settle within its regions. Its western portion is a temple of Amun, its southern a temple of Seth; Astarte is in its Orient quarter, and Uto in its northern precinct. The castle which is in its midst resembles the horizon of heaven, and Ramesses, beloved of Amun, is in it as god.

It is obvious that the purpose of this new residence was to create a capital at the very hub of the empire, which still embraced Palestine and part of Syria in the north and Nubia with the Sudan in the south.

The old capital at Thebes was shorn of much of its significance through the construction of the new Delta residence of the Ramessids. Thebes, nevertheless, continued to hold its old position as the most highly esteemed city of the pharaonic empire on the Nile. After all, it was the site of the greatest temple of the land, the mighty sanctuary of Amen-Re, king of the gods and ruler of the universe, the enlargement and sumptuous decoration of which each successive king considered to be one of his chief duties and highest privileges.

Ramesses II completed the construction and decoration of the great hypostyle hall at Karnak, which had been started by his father Sethi I between the pylons of Amenhotep III and Harmhab. This gigantic hall was justly considered to be one of the wonders of the ancient world. With its area of more than six thousand square yards, its site is large enough to accommodate the entire Cathedral of Notre Dame in Paris. It is probably the largest basilica construction ever erected (Fig. 100). A short distance to the southwest of the second pylon and the entrance to the great hall, Ramesses III immortalized himself in a splendid little temple which is relatively well preserved to this day. The same king was also responsible for the temple of the moon-god Khonsu a hundred and fifty yards to the south—a temple which, by reason of its clear and simple plan, is regarded as a model of Egyptian architecture (Fig. 101).

At the temple of Luxor, Ramesses II constructed a large colonnaded court in front of the completed temple of his predecessors and erected a massive pylon at the north end to provide a monumental entrance portal to the entire temple complex (Fig. 42). Before the pylon he placed six colossal statues of himself and set up two beautiful obelisks of red granite, one of which still stands *in situ*, while the other has since 1836 been the central adornment of the Place de la Concorde in Paris.

Fig. 100.—The Great Hypostyle Hall (Karnak)

FIG. 101.—TEMPLE OF KHONSU (KARNAK)

259

FIG. 102.—AIRPLANE VIEW OF MEDINET HABU

260

The lonely Valley of the Tombs of the Kings and the necropolis on the west bank of Thebes continued as before to be an important burial place. The royal tombs of the Nineteenth and Twentieth dynasties are among the most imposing monuments produced by the hands of men in all the Nile Valley, and already in antiquity the technical perfection of their design aroused the astonished admiration of travelers.

Farther to the east, where the foothills of the western desert descend to meet the fertile land, the memorial temples built by Sethi I and Ramesses II (the so-called Ramesseum) surpassed in size, choice of material, and splendor the neighboring sanctuaries dating from the Eighteenth Dynasty (p. 176). This mighty row of temples on the west of Thebes was ultimately completed on the south by the magnificent temple complex of Ramesses III, known today as Medinet Habu (Fig. 102). As a result of its excellent state of preservation, including often the very colors with which its reliefs were painted, it offers the best available picture of an inclosed temple precinct of ancient Egypt. In addition to the principal temple structure itself, the enormous walled inclosure contained numerous dwellings for the priests, officials, and soldiers, administrative buildings, magazines, granaries, gardens, and pools. The main entrance to the vast precinct was a unique structure at the east end, the so-called "high gate," which was modeled after Syrian fortified strongholds (Fig. 103). Its lofty windows afforded a magnificent view across the Theban Plain, with its monumental buildings on both sides of the Nile. The temple proper stood at the very center of the great precinct.

Not Thebes alone (Fig. 104), but many other cities as well, were glorified by the building activities of the Ramessids. At Abydos, for example, the city sacred to Osiris, no fewer than three different sanctuaries were built during this period, all of them principally devoted to the cult of the dead appropriate to the city of Osiris. The first of these was a delicate little temple of Ramesses I which has wholly vanished from its original site, though most of its surviving remains have fortunately been rescued from destruction and are now preserved in the Metropolitan Museum of Art in New York. Then Sethi I built both a wonderful temple, still splendidly preserved, which contains some of the most exquisite bas-reliefs in the Nile Valley, and a unique cenotaph, while his son Ramesses II when yet a young prince erected a fine temple of his own not far from those of his father and grandfather.

It was, however, the southern province of Nubia which owed to the zeal of Ramesses II and his provincial governor the majority of his surviving temples and, above all, a new development in sacred architecture—the rock temple. Since the cultivable land along the Nile in Nubia was exceedingly narrow and far too valuable for building-sites (Fig. 23), the architects decided to locate at least a portion of the rooms within the very cliffs. To be sure, this bold plan to hew from the solid rock a complete temple, from entrance pylon to the holy of holies, was fully realized at Abu Simbel alone. However, in the larger of the two temples at that

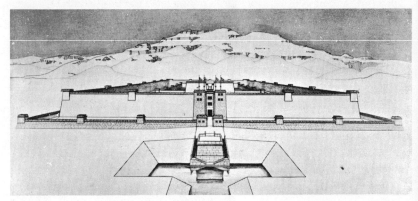

FIG. 103.—RECONSTRUCTION OF THE QUAY AND TEMPLE PRECINCT (MEDINET HABU)

place—the so-called king's temple, as it is dedicated to the cult of King Ramesses II himself, in addition to the chief Egyptian gods Re-Harakhti, Ptah, and Amun—this concept was brilliantly conceived and executed. Nature was here subdued with tremendous power, and the result is one of the most gigantic works of man on earth. The smoothly dressed face of the cliff constitutes the usual form of sloping temple pylon; before it, hewn in spite of their enormous size from the virgin rock in perfect proportion to every detail of the façade, are four seated colossi of the pharaoh (Fig. 105). The visitor passes through the great portal into a mighty hall corresponding to the first court of a normally constructed temple; the ceiling of this rock-hewn hall is "supported" by two rows of four pillars in front of each of which stands a portrait figure of Ramesses II more than thirty feet in height (Fig. 106). The usual subsidiary rooms of the Egyptian temple structure are provided beyond and at the sides of the great

Fig. 104.—Court of Ramesses II (Luxor Temple)

Fig. 105.—Façade of the Temple of Ramesses II (Abu Simbel)

Fig. 106.—Interior of the Temple of Ramesses II (Abu Simbel)

Fig. 107.—Queen Nofretari (Wife of Ramesses II) Worshiping (Valley of the Tombs of the Queens at Thebes)

Fig. 108.—Painting of Ramesses II (Thebes, Tomb of Nakhtamun)

hall, and at the west end, approximately two hundred feet from the entrance, is the inner sanctuary with its four rock-hewn cult statues of the three gods and the king seated side by side, still preserving much of the color with which they were originally painted. This wonderful rock temple and most other ancient Egyptian monuments between the first and third cataracts are now unfortunately doomed to certain destruction by the recent decision of the Egyptian government to build a new high dam south of Assuan.

The plastic art of the Nineteenth Dynasty is no longer on the level of that of the Eighteenth. A majority of the royal statues and those of private individuals is strictly conventional, though there are outstanding exceptions, such as the famous statue of Ramesses II in the Turin Museum (Fig. 98). One is conscious of a distinct decline in creative power, both in painting and in relief sculpture. There is an increasingly rank growth of the superficial, while the once-splendid scenes from the daily life in the tombs of the nobles gradually give way before the typical stilted representations of gods and mortuary subjects of the age. It would be unfair, however, to deny that the Ramessid period made not a few achievements of considerable importance, especially in the delicate bas-reliefs of the temple of Sethi I at Abydos, in the reliefs and paintings on the walls of the tombs of the kings and queens at Thebes (Fig. 107), and among the representations in the private tombs (Fig. 108). The Nineteenth Dynasty is, above all, worthy of the highest praise for one artistic attainment of vast significance. It transferred the figure of the victorious king from a mere type—the pattern for which had already been shaped out in the early period—to the world of reality. Sethi I's struggles against the Libyans and the Syrians are represented in an entire series of individual scenes (Fig. 97). Ramesses III in a similar manner caused to be recorded in enormous painted reliefs the records of his victorious battles with the Libyans and the sea peoples (Fig. 99), while his hunting expeditions after wild bulls, wild asses, and smaller quarry once more opened a broad field for artistic creative effort. Through these highly successful contributions, the art of the Ramessid age bore fruit of lasting worth, so that it would be quite untrue and unjust to designate the period as one of unqualified sterility.

XVII

THE DECLINE AND LOSS OF EGYPTIAN INDEPENDENCE

THERE is but little recorded and still less worth describing of the deeds of Ramesses IV and his seven successors who assumed as king the name of Ramesses in their efforts to be recognized as descendants and rivals of the great Ramesses II. Nubia continued under Egyptian rule and was governed for the pharaoh by the "King's Son of Kush." Palestine and Syria, on the other hand, were lost to the empire on the Nile. It was the time in which Tiglath-pileser I founded the Assyrian empire and gained a foothold in northern Syria, while farther south the Hebrew tribes of Israel and Judah pressed in from the desert and gradually took possession of the strong cities of the cultivated land. Instability was on the increase in Egypt, and the country was torn by political unrest and civil war. The Theban cemeteries suffered an unbroken series of robberies, which extended not only throughout the tombs of the ancient kings whose burial places lay at the north end of the necropolis, opposite Karnak, but even into the sacrosanct Valley of the Tombs of the Kings itself. The police were no longer strong enough to prevent these plunderings, and it finally became necessary to remove the mummies of the great pharaohs—most of which had already been violated by tomb-robbers—from their own splendid tombs and find for them a place of permanent security. They were successfully transferred to an unadorned shaft in the cliffs near the temples of Deir el-Bahri, where they rested undisturbed until their discovery by modern descendants of the ancient plunderers about seventy-five years ago.

As the authority of the state grew weaker and more ineffective under the last of the Ramessids, the power and prestige of Amun and his priesthood expanded proportionally. All important public and private affairs were regulated and decided either by the priesthood or by an oracle which operated in some mysterious manner in the imperial temple at Karnak or in the Khonsu temple near by (Fig. 101). The real power, however, rested with the army, the Upper Egyptian and Nubian contingents of which were commanded by the viceroy of Nubia. This official appeared in Thebes in times of crisis in order to restore order with his militia. It was one of these viceroys—a man named Panehsi—who in the reign of Ramesses XI appointed one of his junior officers, Hrihor by name, as high priest of Amun at Karnak. Not many years after this, Hrihor himself became viceroy of Nubia and commander-in-chief of the army; when, a little later, he took over the vizierate of Upper Egypt as well, he had united under his personal control all the highest spiritual, military, and civil functions of the state. It was but a single step more to put aside the impotent Ramesses XI and ascend the throne in his place. By this act of usurpation (1085 B.C.), the secular state of the pharaonic empire was ushered to its grave and an ecclesiastical state was erected in its place, in which the chief god of Thebes exercised the authority through the medium of his priesthood. His range of power, to be sure, did not extend much beyond the Thebaid nor was it destined to long survival.

At Tanis, where the last of the Ramessids had probably maintained their residence, a certain Smendes proclaimed himself "King of Upper and Lower Egypt." Thus the empire threatened once again to fall into the same two divisions which had existed before the dawn of history. The priest-king Hrihor was, however, equal to the occasion. He formed an alliance with Smendes whereby the two shared the rule over the entire state. Hrihor's grandson, Panedjem I, in his turn promoted unity by a marriage with the daughter of the second Tanite king, Psusennes, after whose death he became ruler of the entire land, while his sons were appointed to the high-priesthood of Amun.

The four hundred years which followed the establishment of the ecclesiastical state (1085–670 B.C.) were a period of political, economical, and cultural decline for Egypt. The center of authority of the empire was shifted to Lower Egypt. The dynasty of Smendes at Tanis was succeeded by two dynasties of Libyan leaders of mercenary troops who resided in Bubastis and by a dynasty of petty kings who maintained their capital at Sais.

Taking advantage of the weakness of the mother-land, Nubia had also gained her independence in the middle of the eighth century. A native princely house founded an independent kingdom with its capital at Napata. Amun, the Theban king of the gods, was adopted as the national god, while the state was to be considered as a model theocracy and

its king the true guardian of unadulterated Egyptian character and culture. As the petty rulers of the Delta dissipated their energy in internal
struggles, the Ethiopians pressed into the north until they occupied
Thebes and ultimately conquered virtually the entire country. In the
place of a native Egyptian pharaoh or of the usurping Libyans, the throne
of Egypt was occupied by a Negro king from Ethiopia! But his dominion
was not for long. In Asia the Assyrian empire had risen to new power
after a period of decline, and a great part of Syria had fallen once more
under its sway. The petty assistance which the Ethiopian rulers of Egypt
were now able to extend to the hard-pressed Syrian princes and other
leaders, including Hoshea in Israel (II Kings 17:1–6), was quite inadequate to halt the Assyrian advance.

And so the Assyrians finally marched into Egypt, overthrew the in-
significant kings of the Lower Egyptian cities, and expelled the Ethiopians. Nevertheless, when after a few decades they were obliged to retreat into Asia and withdraw their garrisons, a brief day of freedom
dawned once more for the land of the Nile. A prince of Sais united the
country again, and under his successors, the kings of the Twenty-sixth
Dynasty—Psamtik, Apries, and Amasis—Egypt shook off the mournful
memories of the last few centuries to enjoy a short new day of glory.

This newly attained freedom gave birth to a new sense of life. There
was, however, a distinct realization that the contemporary age was empty and exhausted. The inevitable result was a tendency to direct the view
to the days of yore, and it was concluded that the period of the pyramid-
builders had been the golden age in which all that was essentially Egyptian had come into existence. Nevertheless, in addition to this development of a national consciousness which wistfully yearned for the return of
the remote past, it must not be forgotten that the new age possessed its
own peculiar character. For Egypt now made herself more accessible to
foreigners than ever before. Commercial relations with Greece were extensively fostered, and the old intercourse with Phoenicia was resumed.
The result was a marked revival of economic prosperity.

Amasis' reign of forty-four years was one of the most prosperous and
peaceful which Egypt had experienced for five centuries. As it drew to a
close, however, a furious tempest broke once more which, in the next
reign, under Psamtik III, caused the destruction of the Egyptian kingdom
and the loss of political independence for the dwellers on the Nile. As

once before, the storm came from the east. In 525 B.C. a Persian army under the leadership of Cambyses crossed the eastern frontier, and Egypt was integrated as a Persian province into the effectively consolidated administration of the new world-power centered at Persepolis. While the foreign yoke was shaken off from time to time during the following two hundred years, each brief hour of freedom eventually had to be expiated with the most bitter penance. When finally Alexander the Great in 332 B.C. turned his triumphal course into the valley of the Nile, he was acclaimed by the Egyptians as the savior and liberator of their land. Little did they realize that he whom they received with open arms had come to take away their free native rule forever. He converted the ancient empire of the pharaohs into a province of the Greek world, and that it remained for three hundred years, when it fell victim to the rapacious empire of Rome. And with the tragic end of Antony and Cleopatra ended also the ancient glory of Egypt.

Fig. 109.—Thebes, Capital of the Egyptian Empire

There are five principal groups of monuments surviving in various stages of preservation in Thebes: (1) On the east bank of the Nile, the great temples at Karnak and Luxor; on the west side of the river, (2) the row of structures beginning with the temple of Sethi I at Qurna, running in a southwesterly line, and ending with the palace of Amenhotep III and the pleasure lake excavated by him for Queen Tiy; (3) hundreds of tombs of nobles and private citizens of the ancient capital, from Dra Abu en-Naga on the north to Qurnet Murai on the south; (4) the terraced temples of Mentuhotep and Hatshepsut at Deir el-Bahri; and (5) the royal tombs of the Eighteenth, Nineteenth, and Twentieth dynasties in the Valley of the Tombs of the Kings and the Valley of the Tombs of the Queens.

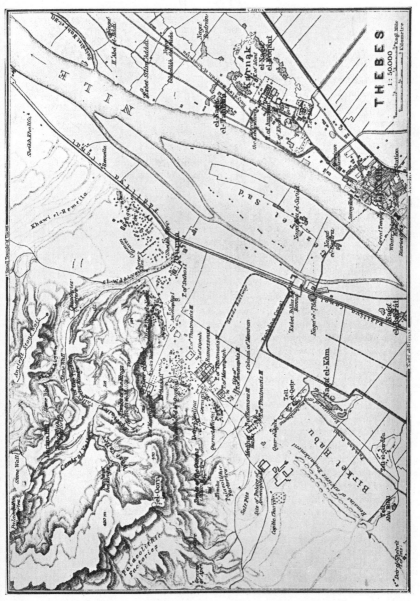

Fig. 109

273

OUTLINE OF EGYPTIAN HISTORY[1]

Prehistoric Period: Before 3200 B.C.

Protodynastic Period: 3200–2800 B.C.

First and Second dynasties: Menes traditionally the first king of united Egypt. Royal tombs at Abydos and Saqqara.

Old Kingdom: (Pyramid Age) 2800–2250 B.C.

Third Dynasty: Djoser builds great mortuary monument at Saqqara.

Fourth Dynasty: Khufu, Khafre, and Menkaure build the Great Pyramids of Giza.

Fifth Dynasty: Sahure, Neferirkare, and Niuserre build pyramids at Abusir. Unis inscribes his pyramid at Saqqara with the earliest religious texts. Flowering of Egyptian sculpture.

Sixth Dynasty: Teti, Pepi I, Merenre, and Pepi II build pyramids at Saqqara. Decline of the centralized state.

First Intermediate Period: 2250–2000 B.C.

Seventh to Tenth dynasties: Collapse of the Old Kingdom. The Herakleopolitan period. Development of classical literature.

Eleventh Dynasty: The Intefs and Mentuhoteps build a centralized state at Thebes.

Middle Kingdom: 2000–1780 B.C.

Twelfth Dynasty: Powerful centralized government with capitals in Memphis and in the Fayyum. Important building operations in Dahshur, Lisht, Illahun, Hawara, and Karnak. Empire extended to Nubia. Extensive intercourse with western Asia. Kings Amenemhet I–IV and Senwosret I–III.

Second Intermediate Period: 1780–1546 B.C.

Thirteenth and Fourteenth dynasties: Period of great obscurity. Numerous petty kings, some apparently ruling contemporaneously.

Fifteenth and Sixteenth dynasties: Invasion and conquest of Egypt by the Hyksos. Kings Salatis, Khyan, Apophis. Introduction of the horse and chariot into the Nile Valley.

Seventeenth Dynasty: Theban rivals of the Hyksos. War of liberation. King Sekenenre perhaps killed in battle. Kamose defeats the invaders. Ahmose completes expulsion of the Hyksos.

New Kingdom: 1546–1085 B.C. *When Egypt Ruled the East*

Eighteenth Dynasty: Amenhotep I (1546–1525 B.C.) makes war in the south and west. He and his mother Ahmose-Nofretari later become tutelary divinities of the Theban necropolis. Thutmose I (1525–1508). Thutmose II (1508–1504). Queen Hatshepsut (1504–1482) usurps the power from her nephew Thutmose III. Egypt is at peace under her rule and gathers strength for the conquests of Thutmose III (alone 1482–1450).

Amenhotep II (1452–1425), famous sportsman in his youth, carries on the conquests of his father. Thutmose IV (1425–1412) excavates the sphinx and marries a

[1] Most dates in Egyptian chronology are approximate. Fixed dates for the period covered by this book depend on synchronization with western Asia, but the Assyriologists are at present in sharp disagreement over matters of chronology.

Mitannian princess. Amenhotep III (1412–1375) "the Magnificent." Marries a commoner, Tiy. His reign a great building epoch. The Colossus of Memnon.

Amenhotep IV–Akhnaton (1387–1366), long coregent with his father Amenhotep III, starts religious reformation, wars against Amun, removes the capital to Amarna. His son-in-law Smenkhkare (*ca.* 1370–1366) apparently has no independent reign. Tutankhamun (1366–1357) restores worship of Amun and returns to Thebes. Eye (1357–1353) buries and succeeds his coregent Tutankhamun. Harmhab (1353–1319) counts himself the legitimate successor of Amenhotep III. He reorganizes the Egyptian state and re-establishes strong government. He ushers in the

Nineteenth Dynasty: Ramesses I (1319–1318). Sethi I (1318–1299) begins in earnest the reconquest of the Asiatic empire lost by Akhnaton. Capital removed to the eastern Delta. Ramesses II (1299–1232) wars against the Hittites and concludes treaty of peace with them. Greatest of Egyptian boasters. Builds many temples and usurps the monuments of his predecessors. His son Merenptah raids Israel and engages for the first time peoples from Europe. Merenptah, Amenmose, Siptah, Sethi II, and other ephemeral kinglets (together 1232–1200) are too weak to maintain a powerful state.

Twentieth Dynasty: Sethnakht (1200–1198) restores order. His son Ramesses III (1198–1167), a strong king, repels invaders from the west and north and saves his country. Dies at the hand of an assassin. Ramesses IV–XI (1167–1085) witness the steady decline of the state and growing influence of the priesthood of Amun. The dynasty is overthrown in 1085 B.C. by the high priest of Amun, Hrihor, who stands at the head of

The Decline: 1085–332 B.C.

Twenty-first Dynasty (1085–945): Kings from the families of the high priests of Amun at Karnak and the princes of Tanis. Nubia sets up an independent state under its own kings, with capital at Napata.

Twenty-second to Twenty-fourth dynasties (945–712): Egypt under the rule of Libyan kings. Sheshonk I sacks the temple at Jerusalem in the fifth year of King Rehoboam of Judah.

Twenty-fifth Dynasty (712–663): Ethiopian period. Egypt conquered by Nubian kings (Shabaka, Shabataka, Taharka). Resisting native princes, especially those of Sais, temporarily regain independence. Esarhaddon the Assyrian conquers Egypt (670) under Taharka.

Twenty-sixth Dynasty (663–525): Psamtik I (663–609) in 663 B.C. expels the Assyrians, overcomes rival Egyptian princes, and establishes a new dynasty in a united Egyptian state. A period of renaissance in Egypt, with imitation of the art and culture of the classical age. Kings Nekau (609–594), Psamtik II (594–588), Apries (588–569), Amasis (569–526); Psamtik III (525) witnesses the conquest of Egypt by the Persians under Cambyses.

Twenty-seventh to Thirtieth dynasties (525–332): Egypt under Persian rule, sometimes with local kings under Persian domination, including Nectanebo I (378–360) and Nectanebo II (359–341).

332 B.C.: Conquest of Egypt by Alexander the Great. The end of native rule. After Alexander's death (323 B.C.) Egypt under the rule of the Ptolemies until the death of Cleopatra (30 B.C.), when it becomes a Roman province under Augustus.

INDEX OF DIVINITIES, PERSONS, AND PEOPLES

Names of gods and goddesses are designated "(G)"; major Egyptian royalty, "(K)" or "(Q)."

276

INDEX OF PLACES

Egyptian places are designated "(E)."

GENERAL INDEX

Agriculture: beginnings of, in Neqada II culture, 13; aided in Nubia by irrigation, 98

Alphabet, known but not really made use of, 119

Amharic, 116

Animal husbandry, beginnings of, 13

Annals of Thutmose III, 66, 165

Architects: Imhotep, 14; Amenhotep (son of Hapu), 76

Architecture: earliest stone, 12; imitated from wooden construction, 14; development of, into pyramid, 14–18; "labyrinth" of Amenemhet III, 20; new type of tomb in Eighteenth Dynasty, 37, 156; temple architecture, 156–77; flowering of, 157; imitation of papyrus stalks, 157; basin ("sacred lake") in connection with temples, 160; temple pylons, 161; unique columns of Thutmose III, 165; palace of Amenhotep III, 177; palace of Akhnaton at Amarna, 207

Army, 76–77, 89–93; introduction of chariotry, 27; first employment of mercenaries, 27–28, 93; infantry, 31; wages, 91; land grants to soldiers, 93

Art: relief scenes of daily life, 16; finest relief sculpture, 20; blossomed with expansion of power, 23; best colossal statues, 72, 78, 193, 262–64; portraiture in reign of Amenhotep III, 74, 189–91; highest level of animal drawing, 100, 192; magical character of funerary art, 145; plastic art completely static, 178; "frontality," 178; combination of front and profile views, 182; expansion of subject matter, 183; few battle scenes in Eighteenth Dynasty, 187; symmetry, 187–88; pinnacle of sculpture and painting under Akhnaton, 218–19; Tutankhamun's treasure, 230–40; Aegeo-Cretan spirit of Tutankhamun's art, 240; decline of art, 268

Aryan, 24, 51

Astronomy, 8, 128

Beard, ceremonial, as badge of kingship, 41

Birth, divine, of king, 41

Blue crown, 84

Booty: captured at Megiddo, 55; in Amenhotep II's second campaign, 70

Brick: early use of, 13; manufactured under supervision of vizier, 86–87

Burial; see Tombs

Calendar, chronology, 6–8, 128

Canopic coffins, 226

Canopic jars, 217

Capitals: Behdet, 11; Ombos, 11; Pe and Dep, 12; Nekhen and Nekheb, Memphis, 12; Thebes, 20; It-tawy, 20; Tanis-Avaris, 256; Napata, 270; Sais, 271

Cataracts, Nile, 22, 35, 36, 60, 94, 96, 114

Census, cattle, 6

Chariots, chariotry, 27, 28, 55, 59, 66, 69, 70, 72, 91, 107, 226; description of Egyptian, 91; drawn by oxen, 98

Christian, Christianity, 128, 131

City-states, 11, 48, 52

Coffins, different forms of, 151

Colossi of Amenhotep III, 78, 193

Conspiracy, harem, to assassinate Ramesses III, 256

Contacts, earliest foreign, 13

Coptic, 131

Costume: Egyptian, 48; Asiatic, 48; of a Negro princess, 98; Cretan, 112; foreign influence on, 114

"Cour de la Cachette," 162–63

Crocodiles, 188, 193; sacred, 20

Culture, Egyptian, in Asia, 21

Cylinder seals, 13, 26

Dams, early construction of, 8

Death, life after death, the dead, etc., 5, 144–50

Double crown of Upper and Lower Egypt, 84

Dynasties: division of Egyptian history into, by Manetho, 7; First, 13, 14; Second, 14; Third, 7, 14, 182; Fourth, 14; Fifth, 16, 18, 86, 124, 142; Sixth, 7, 18, 20, 21, 124; Seventh, 7; Eleventh, 7, 19, 134, 170; Twelfth, 7, 19–23, 35, 89, 96, 156; Thirteenth, 7, 23, 26; Fourteenth, 23; Fifteenth, 26; Sixteenth, 26; Seventeenth, 7, 26–27, 28, 170; Eighteenth, 7, 21, 92, 98, 101, 128, 151, 156, 163, 167, 171, 176, 178, 182, 187, 189, 192, 197, 201, 240, 261, 268; Nineteenth, 123, 141, 176, 195, 247, 256, 261, 268; Twentieth, 7, 176, 253, 261; Twenty-sixth, 271

Egyptians: linguistic and racial affinities of, 9–10; physical characteristics of, 48

Elephants, 13, 107; elephant hunt of Thutmose III, 59